Quantification in
Cultural Anthropology

Quantification in Cultural Anthropology

An Introduction to Research Design

ALLEN W. JOHNSON

Stanford University Press, Stanford, California

1978

Stanford University Press
Stanford, California
© 1978 by the Board of Trustees of the
Leland Stanford Junior University
Printed in the United States of America
ISBN 0-8047-0941-6   LC 76-54091

Published in the U.K. in 1978 as
Research Methods in Social Anthropology
by Edward Arnold (Publishers) Limited
25 Hill Street, London W1

For My Parents

Preface

OVER THE PAST eight years I have taught courses in research methods to anthropologists—primarily to graduate students, but once in a while to undergraduates, too. Perhaps the outstanding lesson I have come away with has been that our training of anthropologists lays too much stress on the elaboration of typologies, arguments, and schools of thought, and too little on methods for collecting data. Yet when I teach the basics of scientific method to anthropologists, I notice that many, fed up with the ambiguities and complexities of cultural anthropology, turn fervently to "science" as though all previous anthropologists had overlooked a simple and obvious cure for our woes. The art of teaching research methods thus becomes one of balancing the appeal of straightforward techniques of testing hypotheses by using statistics and quantitative analysis against the necessarily complex business of developing cross-culturally valid methods and concepts for the study of human behavior.

At times in the development of a scientific discipline it becomes helpful to debate issues that cannot be resolved with data. Such debates identify priorities and problem areas, and may consequently stimulate new hypotheses and research efforts. They are, therefore, part of the cultural context within which science is done. To the degree that we are aware of the ideological character of these debates—that is, aware that personal feelings, political consider-ations, or cultural values may influence the outcome more than predictions tested with empirical data—they provide a wholesome antidote to a narrow preoccupation with scientific rigor and "facts."

In anthropology, however, it sometimes seems that we have the proportions wrong: there is too much ideology seasoning a some-what thin factual soup. At this point students are apt to say, "I thought it was the other way around, that anthropology was buried in facts." Even though this sometimes appears to be the case, this overabundance is largely illusory. Anthropological facts appear numerous because there are seldom well-established connections between them; they tumble all around us and seem less to confirm particular theories than to refute all of them. Indeed, one of the useful functions of anthropology (within limits) is to find exceptions to everyone else's rules.

The benefits of a scientific approach flow from continuous interac-tion between theories and data: theories predict specific sequences of observable events, and data confirm or deny the predictions, leading to acceptance or revision of the theory. Anthropology, which has not found the means to reduce its subject matter to a single, mathematically integrated theory with an associated mea-surement scheme, is especially susceptible to the ill-effects of separating the construction of theories from the collection of data.

In the last several years, a number of "overviews" of the subfields of cultural anthropology have appeared that have done a fine job of ordering the literature into patterns based on theoretical similarities and differences. It is clear that anthropologists have developed comprehensive, multifaceted theoretical approaches. But when one tries to see which specific hypotheses have been generated by those theories and tested with reliable data, the comprehensiveness evap-orates and large blank spaces appear. This posed a problem for me in deciding what to include in this book. My decision has been to concentrate on research designs that have firmly faced the difficul-ties of translating anthropological theories into operational, usually quantitative, data gathering. I have not included some important topics where little or no reliable quantified data have yet been collected—not because those topics are uninteresting, but because further discussion here in addition to the existing theoretical literature will not be especially helpful to students until more reliable research has been done.

Through the experience of teaching the materials in this book, I have learned to be less concerned about which theoretical approach students select than about how they use it after they have selected it. All of the theoretical orientations commonly used by anthropologists have been fruitful, and can be even more so when used in combination than when isolated. What matters most is to have the proper perspective about theories, to regard them as tools, as preliminary means of organizing knowledge that will be subject to continuous challenges and corrections as knowledge increases.

In this book I have adopted an ecological orientation. Within this framework, it is possible to relate many disparate concepts and findings from cultural anthropology. In some cases, I have no doubt pushed a bit hard to get an example to fit in the ecological frame, but my intention has been not to subject every anthropological pursuit to a single domineering viewpoint so much as to give the subject some kind of ordering, which it sorely needs. Those who agree with the framework will, I hope, be comfortable with the way I have made use of it; those who do not will at least have something to react to, and might be encouraged to formulate alternative ways of viewing the scientific enterprise in anthropology.

Students seeking to develop workable and productive research projects will find many examples in this book that will suggest elements of potential usefulness in designing a given project. However, because the examples are summarized, with only aspects of them receiving attention here, the student should expect to read very carefully the original publications referred to in the text before attempting to use these methods in new research.

This book was written over a period of several years, and many people have helped me in working the material into its present shape. Formative years at Stanford and Columbia universities certainly had most to do with it. Students in my research design courses have always taken very seriously their obligation to reeducate their teacher; their questions and arguments in class gave the book its specific form. Orna Johnson first had the idea that I should write the book, and was always near with support and advice when I needed it. Marvin Harris, Pertti Pelto, Roger Sanjek, and Benjamin White read the manuscript with great care and gave me energetic, but entirely constructive, criticisms. To all colleagues who have generously shared with me their time and ideas, and who have taught me that anthropology is not only a profession but a way of life entailing broad commitments and responsibilities, I wish to express my fond appreciation and gratitude.

A.W.J.

Contents

Illustration Credits

Fig. 1.1 is an adaptation of Table 1 from "Cultural Constructions of Reality" by Roy G. D'Andrade. Reproduced by permission of the American Anthropological Association from CULTURAL ILLNESS AND HEALTH, Anthropological Studies #9, 1973.

Fig. 3.1 is adapted from the chart on p. 74 of Hobhouse, Wheeler, and Ginsberg, eds., THE MATERIAL CULTURE AND SOCIAL INSTITUTIONS OF THE SIMPLER PEOPLES (1915), and appears by permission of the publisher, Routledge & Kegan Paul Ltd.

Fig. 6.1 is adapted with permission from B. Whiting and J. Whiting, *Children of Six Cultures*, line drawing facing p. 1 (Harvard University Press, 1975), © 1975 by the President and Fellows of Harvard College.

Fig. 6.2 is adapted from Erich Fromm and Michael Maccoby, *Social Character in a Mexican Village*, Fig. 5.6, p. 124 (Prentice-Hall, 1970), and appears by permission of the authors.

Fig. 7.1 is an adaptation of drawings on pp. 22–23 of G. William Skinner, "Marketing and Social Structure in Rural China," Part 1, Vol. 24, No. 1, 1964, in *The Journal of Asian Studies* and appears by permission of The Association for Asian Studies.

Fig. 8.1 is an adaptation of Tables 1–4 of "Some Procedures and Results in the Study of Native Categories" by Duane Metzger and Gerald Williams. Reproduced by permission of the American Anthropological Association from the AMERICAN ANTHROPOLOGIST, 68 (2), 1966.

Figs. 8.2 and 8.3 are adapted from a diagram on p. 147 and figs. 3 and 9 in "Cognitive Aspects of English Kin Terms" by A. Kimball Romney and Roy G. D'Andrade. Reproduced by permission of the American Anthropological Association from the AMERICAN ANTHROPOLOGIST, 66 (3, part 2), 1964.

Figs. 8.4 and 8.5 are adapted with permission from Figures 3–1 and 3–3 from Chapter 3, "Classification," in THE CULTURAL CONTEXT OF LEARNING AND THINKING: An Exploration in Experimental Anthropology, by Michael Cole et al., © 1971 by Basic Books, Inc., Publishers, New York.

Fig. 8.6 is adapted from drawings in Marvin Harris, "Referential Ambiguity in the Calculus of Brazilian Racial Identity," SOUTHWESTERN JOURNAL OF

ANTHROPOLOGY, Vol. 26, No. 1, 1970, p. 4, and appears by permission of the journal and the author.

Fig. 8.7 is an adaptation of tables 1, 2, 3, 4, and 6 from "Brazilian Racial Terms: Some Aspects of Meaning and Learning" by Roger Sanjek. Reproduced by permission of the American Anthropological Association from the AMERICAN ANTHROPOLOGIST, 73 (5), 1971.

Fig. 8.8 is adapted from the drawing on p. 58 of Francesca M. Cancian, *What Are Norms?* (Cambridge University Press, 1975), and appears with permission of the publisher.

Fig. 9.1 is an adaptation of fig. 4 from "The Colors of Emotion" by Roy G. D'Andrade and M. Egan. Reproduced by permission of the American Anthropological Association from the AMERICAN ETHNOLOGIST, 1 (1), 1974.

Fig. 9.2 is adapted with permission from the chart on p. 62 of B. Whiting and J. Whiting, *Children of Six Cultures* (Harvard University Press, 1975), © 1975 by the President and Fellows of Harvard College.

Quantification in
Cultural Anthropology

CHAPTER ONE

Introduction

RESEARCH DESIGN is a central problem of the sciences, and with few exceptions cultural anthropologists think of themselves as scientists—despite great differences between individuals in conceptions of what science is and what scientists do. Scientific reasoning and methods have developed to permit discovery of a particular variety of "truth." Two aspects are involved here. On the one hand, the analytic or theoretical aspect of science is concerned with making explicit—in logical or mathematical terms—arguments or explanations that relate particular statements (e.g., "solid objects fall toward the center of the earth") to general assumptions or laws (e.g., "the law of gravity"). On the other, the empirical aspect of science is concerned with testing whether the statements used in theoretical arguments, or derived logically from them, conform to events that can be directly observed and measured (in our example, "the center of the earth" must be located, and a range of "solid objects" observed while falling). Both of these aspects must be present in a scientific undertaking. For example, even a mathematical argument, no matter how elegant, does not achieve fully scientific status until it is tested against empirical observations, as mathematicians working on problems in "pure mathematics" freely acknowledge. Similarly, pragmatic knowledge of the sort acquired by everyday interaction with the environment—as in the experiences of craftsmen, farmers, or mechanics—is not usually called scientific because an explanatory scheme is either lacking or else implicit and informal. The purpose of research design is to use theoretical arguments to develop expectations about the world, and then to test them by collecting empirical data that either do or do not conform to the theoretical expectations, the ultimate goal being to add to our store of scientific truth about nature.

Some scientists fall into the habit of thinking of science as a pathway to absolute truth, free from anything so confining as a set of implicit cultural biases. Anthropologists, however, will argue that science in general, and anthropology in particular, is a cultural phenomenon, historically specific and embedded in extensive networks of values of which individual scientists may be unaware (see Nadel 1951:2–3, 48–55; compare also Holton 1973:57). We do not detract from the value of scientific endeavor in recognizing that individuals are motivated to pursue it by the existence of a reward structure including wealth, fame, authority, and special prizes. Indeed, it can be said that the scientific fields where the most honors and rewards are to be gained are those valued most within the cultural system bestowing the honors. It is a vexing ethnocentrism to assume that science is or ever can be completely culture-free. Science is infused with bias; bias gives it meaning and purpose. Recently, philosophers of science have been exploring the relation between culture and science (Kuhn 1970; Bohm 1965; Toulmin 1972; Holton 1973). Awareness that scientists' behavior finds its significance within a far broader context than the theoretical and empirical activities of particular disciplines has, not accidentally, accompanied a renewed popular insistence that scientific work, for which nonscientists are paying the bills, be relevant to the goals and policies of the larger society (see, e.g., Greenberg 1967; Stever 1975).

For social scientists, however, the matter is especially complicated. The relation between scientific activity and the cultural context may be seen in two quite different lights: first, science may fulfill cultural goals by providing the basis for technical change; second, science may offer an analysis and critique of the goals themselves. All science contributes to the former activity; the latter, however, draws more heavily on the social sciences, because cultural goals are themselves sociocultural phenomena and need to be investigated in a framework of social-science concepts (e.g., "norms," "class," "authority"). A major responsibility of cultural anthropology is to extend the frame of reference beyond our restricted cultural perspective to include the principles by which systems of values arise and are implemented in the full range of human societies. This is necessary if we wish to avoid becoming "culture bound" in the process of trying to find alternatives to received values and means for putting those alternatives into effect.

Indeterminacy in Sociocultural Research

The situation is in certain respects analogous to the "indeterminacy principle" in physical science, arising from the uncertainty introduced when the instrument of observation observes itself. The problem is that much of what we take for "reality," including what is regarded as so obvious we never discuss it, can be shown to be unconscious constructions learned in specific settings that may have nothing obvious about them at all. For example, the task of observing a small set of human interactions and shortly thereafter reporting what we observed may appear to be an obvious sort of task; we merely tell what we observed. But one study has shown important differences between those observations of interpersonal relations coded at the moment of observation and those based on recall after a period of time (D'Andrade 1973; 1974). The difference is between "short-term memory" (within a few seconds to a few minutes after the event) and "long-term memory" (10–15 minutes, or more, after the event).

Four kinds of data were gathered in that study:

1. Groups of American college students were given the task of discussing a "social-emotional problem" (fraternity pledging practices). An observer coded individual behavior just after it occurred, that is, using short-term memory. The coder was a professional psychologist trained to code behavior; examples of codes include "shows solidarity," "jokes," "disagrees," "shows tension," and "is antagonistic."

2. After the group discussion was over, the psychologist was asked

to recall (long-term memory) the proportions of each individual's behavior that fell into each of the different coding categories.

3. Also after the discussion was over, the students themselves were asked to recall (long-term memory) the proportions of each other's behavior that fell into the coding categories.

4. Finally, in a separate study, American college students were asked to judge the coding categories according to similarities and differences among them. For example, students felt that "shows solidarity" and "is antagonistic" were very different from each other, whereas they felt "is antagonistic" was very similar to "shows tension."

First, the study found a very large difference between the last data, which we might call a "cognitive map" of what kinds of behavior *ought* to go together, and the first data, based on direct short-term memory of which behavior actually occurred. In fact, the correlation coefficient relating the two sets of data was $-.05$, indicating no significant relation. This discrepancy between "cognition" and "behavior" is interesting in its own right, but even more interesting is that the long-term memories of both the psychologist and the students were far closer to the cognitive map than to the short-term memory codings of observed behavior.

Two aspects of the results are worth emphasis:

1. The short-term memory data reveal much less patterning than the long-term memory data. For example, the psychologist's long-term memory was that people who made frequent suggestions were also the ones who disagreed most often ($r = .54$); but according to his short-term memory coding, the relationship between these behaviors was non-existent or even negative ($r = -.11$). Students' long-term memories were likewise more orderly than observed behavior had been.

2. The patterning in the psychologist's long-term recall and the students' long-term recall are similar. Both are also similar to the cognitive map of semantic similarity judgments (see Figure 1.1).

In sum, there are at least two kinds of bias in the way we remember what we have experienced. First, there is a bias toward *orderliness*; behavior that was disorderly is selectively remembered

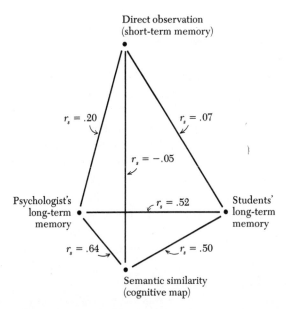

Fig. 1.1. Correlations between short-term memory, long-term memory, and cognitive maps of categories of interpersonal behavior (r_s is the Spearman rank correlation coefficient). Source: D'Andrade 1973:122.

as orderly. And second, there is a bias toward a *particular kind of order*, such that "contradictory" behavior is selectively remembered as conforming to the observer's prior expectations; this order is shared by many observers and can be investigated with cognitive psychological research procedures.

The above example relates to the general problem of ethnocentrism. Though there is considerable controversy among anthropologists about whether thought processes are the same in some fundamental sense for all humans (see Cole & Gay 1972:1066), there is widespread agreement that the categories of thought, and their conceptual organization, vary considerably across cultural settings. We can see the dilemma: if we set out to observe and discover the patterns in human behavior and thought, we will unconsciously look for certain aspects, and overlook others, in accordance with our own ethnocentric bias. In the example just cited, the psychologist's recall of interpersonal behavior was similar to the students', not because of underlying similarities in the observed behavior, but because both, as members of the same culture, had the same shared set of prior expectations about how behavior *should* pattern.

This example shows that informants, when asked to describe aspects of their own behavior or the behavior of others some time after the events have taken place, are not the "videotape-like creatures with near-perfect retrieval systems" that some research methods appear to assume (D'Andrade 1974:124). Social scientists, who rely very heavily on informant recall, or on their own recall at the end of an observed event (e.g., a "write-up" after a meeting, or at the end of a day's fieldwork), apparently need to depend much more on direct observations made immediately after the events are observed. This would do much to overcome the first source of bias, the tendency to find highly orderly domains where there is really much less order.

Cultural anthropology appears to be entering a phase of concern for behavioral descriptions, as opposed to a concern for sweeping global descriptions based on very long-term memory. The net effect of this is liable to be disconcerting, for as soon as one anthropologist states, in a constructive spirit, that a kind of order has been found, another is liable to present data suggesting that such an order is not there. For example, Siskind (1973) proposed, on the basis of intuitive conclusions reached after a long period of residence in an Amazon Indian community, that women use sexual favors to reward men who are good hunters; in the exchange of sexual intercourse for meat, the good hunters acquire more lovers while the poor hunters are cuckolded. But quantitative data on hunting returns and love affairs among another Amazon Indian group fail to show any such pattern (Vickers 1975).

This discrepancy in results, and the difference in methods used, might leave us wondering if any advantage has been gained by the exercise. The process of developing careful observational procedures in order to help overcome the erroneous "order-seeking" tendencies of memory has a destructive aspect that can be very discouraging. Anthropologists have to work very hard as a rule to come up with orderly descriptions, and there are always those who will seize the opportunity to say there is no order or sense to the world. But if we ask what is being destroyed, we see that it need not be the search for order itself, but only an ambitious and unrealistic concept of the kind of order we can expect to find in human behavior and thought. To a degree, we must lower our sights; instead of simple, mechanical descriptions, we must aim for descriptions of patterns in the behavioral and ideational aspects of community life that will be *statistical* (with many exceptions). The order that we ultimately find may not be the intuitively obvious one.

Still, the recognition that memory may play tricks on us, and that direct observations will help sort accurate from inaccurate memories, only brings us to a further difficulty. Behavioral observations based on short-term memory still employ *categories* that select from the stream of behavior only a limited number of events, which are then "described" (Harris 1964:8–18). In the case of the college students cited earlier, no observations were made on blood pressure, clothing styles, wallet contents, or myriad other possibilities. The selection of the basic categories of observation followed from explicit or implicit preconceptions on the part of the researchers.

In cultural anthropology, for example, we tend to favor descriptions of exotic, and especially primitive, peoples. When anthropologists study small societies in isolated areas, their interest is often not with the community life as it is now, but with life as it was before modern change. In many published reports, therefore, it is impossible to judge the degree of recent change; the text neglects to mention the prevalence of industrial technology, Western dress, evangelical activities, or wage labor, and photographs are selected to concentrate on "native" scenes such as rituals and dances. Yet research can be designed to maintain a clear distinction between ethnohistory and current practices. If we recognize that these two kinds of data are gathered by different, specifiable research procedures, both the inferred past and the observed present can be described with professional standards of reliability.

In a cross-cultural perspective, there are ample, carefully collected data from many different cultural settings to demonstrate that the categories by which people describe such diverse everyday phenomena as plants, diseases, colors, and other people vary remarkably from one setting to the next. The conclusion anthropologists draw from this, strengthened over decades of research, is that there are different "cultural constructions of reality" (D'Andrade 1974); more bluntly, there are different realities. Among the most valuable results of long-term study in another culture is that we learn to respect and even admire systems of beliefs and values different from our own. This experience, multiplied among many individual anthropologists, is the basis for the anthropological ideal of *cultural relativism*, which holds that no single cultural construction of reality is absolutely better than any other.

The perspective of cultural relativism requires that we eliminate ethnocentric values from anthropological research. This is easier said than done; even cultural relativism is itself a value, and one that the majority of mankind do not appear to share. The very fact that we go to another society in order to return and report on it has a certain inevitable element of ethnocentrism to it. Because the primary goal of most cultural anthropologists is to describe another culture with faithfulness to the culture itself and not ethnocentrically—in a sense to act as agents to the rest of the world on behalf of those among whom we have lived for a period of time—it is especially painful to accept that, with equal justification, we can be described as agents of our own society, representing it to the people whom we visit. This brings us too close for comfort to the category of missionaries and other agents of Western civilization. Interestingly, the people we study are usually not mystified on this subject; one of their first questions to the newly arrived anthropologist is "who paid you to come here and what do they expect in return?" The anthropologist who insists that this is not an important question, or that nothing is expected in return, runs the risk of appearing deceitful, or at best foolish, to people who take it for granted that behavior is self-serving.

In any practical sense it is impossible to enter a community to do fieldwork without bringing along a baggage of cultural preconceptions—some explicit, but many others implicit and even unconscious. Thus it is fair to say that anthropologists do not so much describe other cultures as "invent" them (Wagner 1975). It is better not to assume that "cultures" exist as discrete entities "out there," waiting to be described "as they are." Rather, a culture is invented by the anthropologist in the process of describing it. There is no automatic guarantee that another anthropologist, with a different background and different goals, would invent the same culture by working in the same community; and it can be taken for granted that the subjects of the study will not hold quite the same view of themselves as the anthropologist develops in the course of fieldwork. This is a serious epistemological problem for anthropology, inviting skepticism if not outright cynicism: we are supposed to eliminate ethnocentric bias, but the whole enterprise of cultural anthropology is inextricably caught up in a net of specific cultural values. The problem is real for any science that deals with cross-cultural concepts (e.g., "human nature," "culture change"), but it becomes a fundamental problem for anthropology because the cross-cultural framework is at the heart of the discipline.

The Anthropological Approach to Research

Out of the attempts of many separate researchers to come to grips with this problem has emerged a general anthropological approach to cross-cultural research. Cultural anthropologists may be defined as those social and behavioral scientists whose data are typically gathered through long-term *participant observation* in unfamiliar sociocultural settings, who employ a *holistic* frame of reference, and who aim at the development of theories of human thought and behavior that are *cross-cultural* in scope. Research in other fields sometimes fulfills one or more of these criteria, but only cultural anthropology as a discipline maintains all three as primary requisites of its research program.

Participant observation is the main anthropological means to counter ethnocentrism. Anthropological fieldwork calls for long periods spent in unfamiliar settings, and has three goals: the development of intuition; the gathering of dependable data; and the formation of a holistic viewpoint.

The first goal is intuitive understanding, which can only be acquired slowly through the researcher's integration of his experiences; it is thus distinguished from *impressionistic* understanding, which is based on casual, uninvolved, and usually short-term observations. Sometimes called "culture shock," the development of an intuitive understanding of another culture is by its very nature painful and disorienting, for basic assumptions are tested and found wanting, and habitual ways of behaving fail to bear accustomed fruit. Finding new explanations requires trying new lines of inquiry—a process that is scientific in form (though largely implicit and qualitative) since possibilities are formulated, tried, and retained, if successful, to be built into a new understanding over time. The researcher eventually develops strong notions about what is possible within the community and what is not—notions no outsider could ever develop. The result is still an "invention," and intuitions can be quite wrong; but intuition remains a powerful guide for generating new and more precise hypotheses and for criticizing facile theories, and its development through participant observation is apparently the only way we as individuals can become fully aware of the extent of our own ethnocentrism. The more directly involved the anthropologist is in the life of the community, the more dependable and far-reaching intuition becomes. Appreciation of the complexity of the activities we describe is heightened when we learn how to do them ourselves (Nelson 1969:394–95). In fact, much of anthropological fieldwork amounts to the researcher's overcoming barriers of diffidence or secret feelings of superiority.

The gathering of accurate and dependable data is the second goal of participant observation. The anthropologist is distinguished from other social scientists by working most commonly at the level of the small community, where interactions are predominantly face-to-face and where individuals have extensive personal knowledge of one another. Depending on the purposes of the research, the unit of social-science analysis may be as small as one individual plus family and friends, as often happens in clinical psychology, or as large as an entire nation, suitably sampled, as in voting studies. Anthropological research seeks a middle ground. Taking "culture" as something shared by many individuals, anthropologists prefer to study groups of more than a few persons. On the other hand, they have doubts about the quality of data gathered from very large samples, especially where the researchers spend small amounts of time administering questionnaires (or having them administered): informants are careful in what they say to strangers; their answers may vary with the seasons or with changing circumstances in the home or community; they may be very inaccurate at remembering certain kinds of information; and time may reveal substantial differences in behavior and opinion among community members who appear outwardly similar. Thus even when anthropologists have worked in large cities, their research has usually been focused on small neighborhoods where they can live and participate on a personal basis in the lives of the people they are studying.

The third goal of participant observation is the development of holistic descriptions. Holism means taking as relevant together perspectives that have become the separate provinces of such disciplines as biology, psychology, economics, political science, and history. This approach has both weaknesses and strengths. On the one hand, by spreading the fieldworker's training and time over a wide range of phenomena, holism dissipates energy and expertise, and is to a degree incompatible with methodological sophistication. Indeed, it has been argued that the growing importance of scientific standards of research in cultural anthropology is making holism obsolete (Cohen & Naroll 1973:3–4). On the other hand, though, holism draws attention to the systemic nature of human social life. After all, events are not readily analyzed into isolated categories labeled "political" or "economic"; the more we look for relations among separate events, the more we find them. As a goal holism is valid and historically central to anthropology (see Keesing 1974:73), but as we shall see below, methodological improvements are needed if holism is not to degenerate into the trivial form, "everything is related to everything else."

The results of successful fieldwork along the lines indicated above are the rich, complex descriptions of particular communities that have perhaps too often made anthropologists the "biographers of single societies" (Nadel 1951:4–6). Although descriptions of individual societies are of interest in themselves, they do not necessarily lead to the development of general theories capable of explaining cultural similarities and differences. For this we require some cross-cultural comparability in the descriptions. This in turn implies that anthropologists agree on what to describe and how to describe it, and that they arrive in the field already equipped with some set of cross-cultural categories with which to begin fieldwork. Such categories have been slow to develop in anthropology, because each new field situation is unique; in one view, "you do not come to the community with a set of queries prepared beforehand. You must formulate questions as they arise in the context of people's lives. It has been the experience of anthropologists that you cannot ask reasonable questions before you know something of the shape and texture of this strange and unfamiliar life; the ability to find such questions comes only after protracted contact with the people" (Wolf & Hansen 1972:76). True as this is in one sense, anthropologists nonetheless do arrive in the field with "questions," even if only in the form of those implicit cultural preconceptions we discussed earlier. And anthropologists continue to compare societies in terms that are presumed to apply in many societies, despite large cultural differences. Whether we will be able to develop general theories of human thought and behavior that will be valid across the whole range of known cultures depends on whether we can improve the comparability of the descriptions resulting from anthropological fieldwork.

Cultural Anthropology and the Domain of Science

As we have seen, science requires both an explanatory framework and empirical procedures for testing that framework. Integrating these two parts can be difficult in any science, but the difficulties in cultural anthropology are compounded by a lack of development in both parts. Figure 1.2 depicts the "domain of science" within a larger domain of what might be called "belief." We note first of all that both "faith" and "unobservable events" are left out of the "domain of science." Starting at the top, the distinction between faith and science is that difference between statements that cannot be

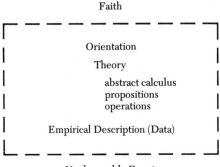

Faith

Fig. 1.2. The domain of science. The dotted lines enclose the "universe of potential observations" and mark the limits of scientific inquiry.

"falsified" and those that can be (at least in principle). A falsifiable statement is one that can be shown to be false by observation (e.g., "it will rain here tomorrow"); statements that cannot be refuted (e.g., "it will rain or not rain here tomorrow") do not fall in the domain of science (Popper 1968:41). Though we might want this distinction to be as clear and absolute as possible, the qualification that scientific statements are falsifiable *in principle* suggests that it is not; we will return to this point below.

Saying that unobservable events are also outside the domain of science is a necessary caution about what we can and cannot know. Reality as such, in the sense of everything that exists, is beyond the reach of human experience, for there are (we believe) events occurring in the universe that we cannot at present observe. Thus we narrow science's domain to the "universe of potential observations" (Coombs 1964:4).

In this book the concept of an "orientation" plays an important part. In Figure 1.2 an orientation falls somewhere between "faith" and "theory." Because of this liminal position between science and nonscience, it is very difficult to be precise about what an orientation is. It will help if we look first at how philosophers of science view the concept of a theory, and then see how an orientation differs from a theory.

Scientific theories. Formally, a scientific theory is made up of an "abstract calculus," on the one hand, and "rules of correspondence," or "operations," on the other (Nagel 1961:79–105). An abstract calculus is most commonly a set of mathematical statements cast in a deductive form, from which specific "propositions" can be derived by deductive logic from general assumptions and laws. The propositions in turn can be verified or falsified by comparison with empirical data by means of specific operations.

For example, in a classic syllogism, the specific proposition "Socrates is mortal" follows logically from the law "all men are mortal" in conjunction with the statement "Socrates is a man." Represented in abstract calculus, such arguments lose their everyday connotative meanings and reduce to purely symbolic form. For example, in set theory notation the syllogism reads:

$$\{(X \subset Y) \cap (Z \subset X)\} \subset (Z \subset Y)$$

Thus expressed, we can see that if we are interested in whether the abstract calculus can be used to make reliable statements about empirical situations, we need some way of relating the symbols to observable events. Operations, or rules of correspondence, offer rigorous means for relating theoretical abstractions to empirical data. In this case, rules need to state that X includes the class "men" (perhaps along with other classes), that Y includes mortality (again, other states might be permitted, such as "warm-bloodedness"), and that Z may be represented by an individual named Socrates. Furthermore, operational rules will specify the measurements needed to verify or falsify specific propositions of the theory. In this case, reference would be made to criteria for determining that Socrates was indeed mortal.

In everyday conversation we are apt to speak of "theoretical" as distinct from "empirical" statements, but in the above example we learn that a theory in the strict sense includes both analytical abstractions and operational methods. This description of scientific theory comes primarily from the physical sciences, and tends to place the social sciences in an unfavorable light. As Nagel put it (1961:447): "In no area of social inquiry has a body of general laws been established, comparable with oustanding theories in the natural sciences in scope of explanatory power or in capacity to yield precise and reliable predictions." It is tempting, especially when the difference is described in terms of "scope," "power," "capacity," and "reliability," to conclude that the social sciences are somehow weaker or less scientific than the physical sciences. But many social scientists object that the physical-science conception is too narrow, basing its capacity to predict on research designed to reduce complex phenomena to situations where two variables interact in controlled laboratory settings (this is discussed further in Chapter 2). Nonetheless this version of scientific theory can help us see how far short of scientific ideals the bulk of research and theory in cultural anthropology falls, and how much room there is for improvement in research design and fieldwork.

To consider first the problem of research operations, it has been observed that "the most pressing problems in improving anthropological research design lie in the structure of primary data gathering" (Pelto 1970: 19). Here the fundamental shortcoming is a failure of the discipline at large to agree on procedures for describing the main theoretical concepts. Most scientific disciplines regard training in professional standards of measurement to be an integral part of the educational experience. Students of chemistry, for example, are required from their first introductory course to measure weights and volumes following precisely formulated procedures: specimens must be properly dried, balances must be dust-free, and so on. Only if the "community of chemists" can assume that descriptions are based on measurements taken at an appropriate level of accuracy, according to procedures shared by different researchers, can results be compared and a reliable body of knowledge accumulated.

Among anthropologists, there is often little agreement on the research procedures necessary for providing many of the major terms employed in theory construction with empirical content. Such terms as "adaptation," "efficiency," "authority," "lineage," and "marriage" are poorly defined in most anthropological studies, and some of them may not even be definable at all for research purposes (see Goodenough 1970). How are we to know, for example, when we have encountered a lineage system in the course of fieldwork?

And how can we be satisfied that what others have found were also lineage systems? Many conclusions about other communities are reached only gradually, by mental processes that are liable to emphasize order—and certain kinds of preconceived order at that, as D'Andrade's memory study showed.

> Ethnography impels us to state that a society has lineages, whereas it may only have certain values for lineages and tendencies to approximate what we conceive to be a lineage organization. Nonetheless, analysis proceeds upon the assumption that lineages do exist in the society and are fairly uniform within it, and that their existence in the ideal form can then be analyzed relative to ritual, and so forth. The concept is further hardened when this society is compared to other societies that have somewhat different lineage ideologies, but with which they are lumped because of a further reduction of typological criteria and a growing amorphousness of definition (R. Murphy 1971:59).

Such "hardening of concepts" is a problem of the utmost seriousness for cultural anthropology, responsible for much of the failure of anthropological theory to predict cross-cultural variation. It is probable that "cross-cultural comparisons" compare dissimilar things as often as similar ones (more on this in Chapter 3).

Some observers have identified a sort of "factual bias" in cultural anthropology on the part of a previous generation, which believed, erroneously, that "descriptions" of cultural differences could be given without reference to theory. We recognize now that all descriptions reflect theory, or at least bias, whether we are conscious of it or not. The problem for our generation is the opposite one—that theoretical arguments are being developed without concern for their empirical usefulness (Levine 1973:69; McEwen 1963:155).

A good example is the concept of "adaptation," certainly one of the most frequently used in anthropology. The concept originates in biology, where its primary operational meaning is "differential reproduction." That is, better adaptation means successful transmission of genetic material, particularly relative to transmission by competing organisms. This meaning has sometimes been applied to cultural systems as well, but anthropologists are becoming increasingly skeptical of the value of population growth as an indicator of human adaptiveness—with good reason. So anthropologists loosen the term to apply to a much broader set of circumstances, such as "response to hazards" (Vayda & McCay 1975) or "goodness of fit with the environment" (Alland 1975:69). But once the close connection to biological research has been cut, the concept becomes free-floating with respect to data. Notions such as "internal coherence" or "individual well-being" come into play, which are sometimes so vague as to seem to include nearly all aspects of community life. Adaptiveness, instead of being a description of some situations as opposed to others, becomes tautologically true for every situation. A theorist who is genuinely concerned with comparing adaptive and nonadaptive situations, or in saying that certain alternatives are more or less adaptive than others, has to define the concept more carefully, and provide instructions for measuring it in various contexts.

Orientations. Theory, in the sense of closely linked abstract calculus and operational definitions (the sense in which philosophers of science use the term), does not exist in cultural anthropology. Our calculi are neither logically nor mathematically abstract, and our operations are not very precise. Anthropological theory is embedded in a number of distinct "orientations" whose operational structures are vague. An orientation is a coherent perspective or point of view from which cultural systems can be investigated. It provides criteria for separating the "important" from the "unimportant" questions, and for deciding when a particular description is "complete." Scholars working within the framework of a single orientation are fairly certain of talking about similar phenomena in a similar way, but it is characteristic of workers from different orientations that, even though they may feel themselves to be in opposition, their statements about reality never make contact. They are like trains that from a distance appear about to collide but at close range are seen to be moving on separate tracks.

An example of this has been the debate between substantive and formal economics in anthropology. The position of the adherents of formal economics comes from a "maximization" orientation that begins with human individuals and interprets behavior as the outcome of choices made from a set of alternatives in such a way that some index of satisfaction, or "utility," is maximized; this is the view of "economic man" allocating scarce means among competing ends. The adherents of substantive economics take the economy as an "instituted process"; here the focus is on the institutional structure within which economic productive processes are embedded. Individual choice does not enter in because the structure determines the outcomes.

Both viewpoints share a common interest in the description of actual processes of production ("input-output") and distribution ("exchange"); but adherents of each viewpoint, emphasizing the differences between them, have denied the validity of the other (Nash 1967:250; Sahlins 1972:ix–xiv). The issue sometimes appears to have fallen into the hands of "professional debaters" for whom nothing serves quite so well as an issue that cannot conceivably be resolved. Substantivists have accused formalists of ethnocentric "bourgeois" bias in assuming that everyone maximizes profit; formalists have countered by showing that maximization theory assumes no particular index of utility, which may be profit or one of countless other considerations (obedience to parents, security) in any particular instance. The substantive position is likewise invulnerable, since no case of human decision-making can be observed outside some institutional setting, be it family, lineage, church, or some other social structure. To argue either way, that choices are structure-free or that structures preclude choices, is specious.

This line of thought brings us to a very real dilemma in cultural anthropology—the dilemma of eclecticism. Since the differences between orientations cannot be resolved with reference to data, we seem to be presented with a range of statements of faith, with no clear means for choosing among them.

Orientations should be seen as neither competitive nor contradictory, but rather as complementary. One of the important developments in physical science in this century has been the acceptance of the idea that differing theoretical viewpoints may be complementary, especially in border regions where single frameworks are not adequate (Blackburn 1971). Yet the social sciences remain characterized by the coexistence of different "schools," or orientations, which Kuhn (1970: 16–17) takes as a sign of their immaturity among scientific disciplines:

> No natural history can be interpreted in the absence of at least some implicit body of intertwined theoretical and methodological belief that permits selection, evaluation, and criticism. If that body of belief is not already implicit in the collection of facts—in which case more than "mere facts" are at hand—it must be externally supplied, perhaps by a current metaphysic, by another science, or by personal and historical accident. No wonder, then, that in the early stages of the development of any science different men confronting the same range of phenomena, but not usually all the same particular phenomena, describe and interpret them in different ways.

This situation may have less to do with the maturity of a discipline than with the range of phenomena it subsumes. Only time will tell whether anthropology ever achieves the kind of agreement on basics that Kuhn finds in the "mature" sciences.

On one side of the dilemma of eclecticism we confront the problem of *relativism*, the view that one perspective is as good as another. Extreme relativistic eclecticism presents several dangers. First is simple confusion: eclectic analyses tend toward haphazard, opportunistic use of explanatory constructs that mix different orientations carelessly. Second, eclectic research tends to be ineffective, as concentration on the problems at hand is constantly broken by "new perspectives" and "other factors that have to be taken into account." Third, scientific research is often concerned with phenomena, such as the psychological roots of German fascism or the technical basis of modern atomic weaponry, whose relation to concepts of "good" and "evil" is so direct that a relativistic, unbiased perspective, though it may be desired, is realistically out of the question.

Scientific "objectivity" does not provide a fully satisfying resolution to the problem of relativism. Objectivity in social science is achieved only in a version of science that tries "to reduce a subject to its logical components, where emotions disappear, and the problem becomes amenable to analysis in the light of empirical evidence" (Ben-David 1973:34). The preference here for logic at the expense of emotions is an unexamined bias; it may be a useful one, but it is still a bias. Social science, or at least anthropology, does not reduce just to an objective side: "Our knowledge of ourselves and of the universe within which we live comes not from a single source but, instead, from two sources—from our capacity to explore human responses to events in which we and others participate through introspection and empathy, as well as from our capacity to make objective observations on physical and animate nature" (Mead 1976:905).

And this brings us to the other side of our dilemma. It seems that a substantial amount of anthropological research proceeds from a researcher's intuitive mix of preconceptions, feelings, and experiences; eclecticism is avoided by limiting research to "important problems" and "appropriate methods." But we are entitled to ask whether this "solution" is rooted in science or in faith. The distinction between faith and science, resting on the notion of falsifiability, is so important one would hope it was at least clear and unequivocal. Indeed, in the 1930's, the philosophical school of "logical empiricism" took the distinction to be nearly absolute, teaching that theorizing in the absence of clear rules of correspondence could not lead to scientific advances. But more recently even the strictest empiricists have recognized the existence of concepts, such as that of the "Deity" in Newton's physics (Holton 1973:52–53), that refer to nothing observed, yet are important at certain stages of scientific reasoning. Instead, the criterion has become "confirmability-in-principle" (Feigl 1956:13–19), which holds that nonoperational concepts must at least have a logical connection with concepts that are fully operational.

Since "orientations" in cultural anthropology generally have the capacity to avoid falsifiability, as we saw in the example of substantive and formal economics, it would seem that they fall outside the boundaries of science and in the camp of faith. The problem with such an abrupt distinction between science and faith is that it ignores the process by which scientific problems are generated. Popper, for example, excludes this process from the proper subject matter of the philosophy of science (Popper 1968:31). Nonetheless, since individual scientists are motivated, have feelings, and hold faiths, the practice of science includes these processes. A more useful distinction refers to the individual scientist rather than to the scientific enterprise in the abstract. The difference is in attitudes: if one proceeds from a position of faith, as a true believer, then one is uninterested in whether statements about observable reality are confirmed or not; failure to predict is not seen as a flaw in the belief system requiring repair, but as the result of faulty or "trivial" observation. By contrast, if one proceeds from a definite orientation, aware both of the presence of bias and of logical indeterminacy in the reasoning, but with the main goal of developing statements about observable reality that can be falsified in a way that will lead to corrections in the belief system, then the attitude is scientific and the results will approximate scientific ideals. Anthropology is a science not because its procedures mimic the strict forms of physical science, but because the attitude of the vast majority of anthropologists is scientific. In Homans's words (1967:4): "What makes a science are its aims, not its results. If it aims at establishing more or less general relationships between properties of nature, when the test of the truth of a relationship lies finally in the data themselves, and the data are not wholly manufactured—when nature, however stetched out on the rack, still has a chance to say 'No!'—then the subject is a science."

CHAPTER TWO

Cultural Systems and Ethnographic Research Design

W<small>E HAVE SEEN</small> that our scientific activities are constrained by goals and priorities we hold as individuals and often share as communities. What we care about as scientists determines what we look for and provides us our perspective. Hence, a population geneticist and a political anthropologist, viewing the same members of a community, will not "see" the same community because they care about different aspects of it. When a researcher's perspective is organized by a well-developed orientation, we refer to what is "seen" as a *system*; it follows that researchers with different orientations see different systems.

The Nature of Systems

Systems and their properties. A system is a conceptual construct made up of a set of categories and their mutual interrelations. For some writers (e.g. Boulding 1968, Meehan 1968) the term "system" is indistinguishable from "theory" as defined in Chapter 1—that is, an abstract calculus and a set of operations or correspondence rules. In keeping with the focus of this book on "orientations" rather than theories, I prefer to regard a system as the description of reality—necessarily simplified and imperfect—implied by a particular orientation. We must keep in mind that when speaking of systems, "properties" of systems, or "types" of systems, we are really speaking of conceptual schemes. Systems theorists (e.g., Bertalanffy 1968), and others who use the term "system" fairly casually, often write as though systems existed per se, awaiting discovery. They even make a distinction between "real" or "natural" systems and "conceptual" systems. From my definition above, the reader can see that there are no "natural" systems according to my perspective, only constructions of the analyst (see Meehan 1968:32–56).

The concept of system implies a holistic concern for the complex relations among many categories, or "parts." In an analysis of these relations the obviousness of our categories has a way of breaking down. For example, the categories "frog" and "pond" appear natural and discrete, and the statement "the frog is in the pond" seems clear enough. But when we study an actual frog and pond, we discover that the frog contributes features to the pond, and vice versa. The frog, by feeding and reproducing, helps determine at any moment the composition of the pond. In a similar way the frog is determined by the pond's unique configuration of nutrients, and breeding places, and other organisms. Further, in the long-range evolutionary perspective the frog and all the pond's other organisms evolve together as mutually interacting elements of an ecosystem. Where does one end and the other begin? When the frog emerges from the water onto dry land, has it left the pond, or has the pond been extended?

The complexity of the relations between these two categories shows the importance of limiting the elements to be included in a system. After all, we have hardly begun to examine the notion of a "pond" in this example: plants draw upon its moisture, other animals feed and drink from it, bringing contributions from beyond the pond's apparent border and carrying part of it away. There are practically an infinite number of observations that could be made, grouped into categories, and used to describe "pond" in this system. But only a small number of these possibilities will actually be selected. Thus, a system is always *closed*: what is included is determined by the specific approach and methods of the researcher. By

contrast, reality is always *open*, because there are always more attributes and relations among a set of events than can be described
within any single orientation.

Systems and functionalism. In a profound but not very useful
sense, everything in nature is related to everything else. The version of this truism that has been most apparent in cultural anthropology has been named "weak functionalism" (Gouldner & Peterson
1962:2). A close relationship exists between what physical and
biological scientists call "modern systems theory" and what has been
an intrinsic part of cultural anthropology under the name of
"functionalism" for nearly two generations. The functionalist position is that the analytical parts of a sociocultural whole are "functions" of one another in the mathematical sense that as one varies,
the others will also vary. The doctrine of "wholeness" in modern
systems theory asserts the same functional interrelation of parts. So
basic is this reasoning to social sciences that functionalism (and general systems theory) are not to be considered as particular kinds of
social science, but rather as integral to all social science (Harris
1968:521).

Social science, then, coincides with the general systems view. But
it is not always clear that the new terms of systems theory represent
real scientific gains. Many terms now in use refer to kinds of processes that anthropologists have long recognized under different
names. For example, Wolf's (1957) "levelling hypothesis" of Meso-
american religious hierarchies would now be named a "homeostatic
mechanism," whereas most cultural evolutionary arguments, including, for example, Geertz's *Agricultural Involution* (1963),
would now be named cases of "positive feedback." The real advance
represented by systems analysis is not in terminology but in emphasis, primarily a more rigorous formulation of functionalism. To
avoid the trap of weak functionalism, two kinds of rigor are needed:
first, a theoretical orientation that clearly identifies the relevant variables and predicts the expected relations among them; and second,
a more quantitative sense of the strength and direction of the
influences exerted by each variable upon each of the others in the
system.

The modern systems approach also tempers the traditional emphasis on the *structure* of a system as a fixed relation of the parts with an equivalent emphasis on the *process* by which systems come into being, are maintained, and are transformed into other kinds of systems. To say that a system exists, therefore, implies less a static structure than an aggregate of correlated variables, constantly in motion yet remaining within specified limits. To say that one system as changed into another system means that one or more variables have exceeded the limits allowed under the old concept of the system, and that a new concept of the system now applies.

Systems and causality. Systems theorists are fond of saying that the systems viewpoint goes beyond mere "linear, one-way causality in bivariate situations" to a multivariate view that admits of complex mutuality and feedbacks among variables (Bertalanffy 1968:10–17, 44–46; Rapoport 1968:xiii–xxii). They rarely state explicitly what follows from this—that causality as we understand it ceases to apply.

A familiar example concerns the related processes of population growth and technological change. In a traditional evolutionary argument, improvement in the efficiency of food producing techniques was taken as the independent, or causal, variable that made possible increased population densities and complex social orders (see Childe 1951; L. White 1949; Braidwood 1967). On the other side, Boserup, arguing as an economist, has stated that technological improvements associated with population increase usually decrease efficiency; in general, marginal productivity declines while more food per acre is produced. Since on *a priori* logical grounds we would not expect people to accept lower efficiency, we must conclude they were caused to accept lowered technological efficiency by increased population pressure (Boserup 1965:11). Both the above arguments share the form of bivariate causal analyses common in the laboratory sciences. It is a fact that research in such fields as biochemistry, for example, explores determinate relations between only two variables at a time, expending great ingenuity to control the influences of all other variables on these two. This simplification is a most powerful means for learning how to predict changes in nature.

Transfer of the bivariate laboratory model of science into cultural anthropology is generally unjustified, however, because our discipline deals with naturalistic situations that cannot be reduced to laboratory scenes. Technological evolution and population pressure are a case in point. Our only evidence is what we think happened in history, and that introduces two uncertainties. First, it becomes impossible to observe which changes came first; indeed, the most plausible view is that there was a continuous feedback between the two processes, as extremely small increases in food production allowed small numbers of additional children to be born and raised, later creating additional population pressure (and labor supply) for increasing food productivity per acre. The causal argument here turns circular. And, second, many other variables undoubtedly influence the behavior of the two we are concerned with. For example, all human populations have means of birth control, implying that population increase is not an autonomous process but some sort of *decision*; so is the adoption of technological change. These decisions are taken against a background of considerations that include terrain and climate (Carneiro 1970), local concepts of "adequate standard of living" (Hassan 1974), and relations to markets (Smith 1975).

The inclusion of feedbacks between many variables befogs the clarity and direction of a causal analysis. In order to avoid the opposite extreme of weak functionalism, we must aim for quantitative descriptions that will permit more accurate predictions of the *set* of circumstances under which, in the present example, changes in technology and population take place. As a matter of fact, the main terms of this argument ("population pressure" and "productive efficiency") are currently ambiguous, because no set of operations has been widely accepted for describing either variable; operations that do exist, such as measurements of "population density per square mile" or "productivity of garden labor," have serious defects as measures of the theoretical terms. The same is also true of subsidiary terms in the argument, like "carrying capacity" or "subsistence level" (more on this in Chapter 4). This is no small difficulty. It means not only that there is no existing way in which theoretical predictions can be tested, but that we do not even know how to provide an adequate description of the phenomena we are arguing about. For example, in a recent volume of papers devoted to this issue (Spooner 1972) none of the authors provided an operational definition of population pressure (cf. Hassan 1974). The potential for wasted words and general confusion in such situations is enormous.

Does it follow that causality is a lost cause? Students who have recently discovered a systems viewpoint are especially often ready to discard causality altogether. Yet the concepts "cause" and "system" each compensate for weaknesses in the other. The weakness of bivariate causal arguments is that they oversimplify complex natural situations; analysis of systems of many variables provides richer, more realistic descriptions without necessarily ignoring the strength and direction of mutual influences among variables. The weakness of systems arguments is their tendency toward vague unwieldy complexity; causal arguments direct our attention to intervention and control, reflecting the inevitable purposes that lie behind the research, and allowing us to order variables according to their importance in predicting changes in the system.

System Orientations in Cultural Anthropology

In this book I have grouped many particular research procedures into a small number of research orientations. These orientations raise different questions and propose different methods for answering them. In order to avoid confusion, it is best to break a research project down into its component orientations, to be clear about how specific questions are being developed and how answers are to be sought. At a later stage of the research, data gathered within specific orientations can be reintegrated into holistic descriptions that will be more precise, and probably more genuinely rich, than would otherwise have been possible. In this section I describe in outline form five orientations, and make explicit my sense of how they fit into a general scheme of cultural ecology. In the next section I will illustrate the usefulness of orientations in research by providing a model research proposal employing all five orientations.

The orientations. I have labeled the five orientations I treat in this book "input-output," "exchange," "culture and personality," "max-imization," and "cognitive/structural." Other orientations certainly exist within cultural anthropology today, but only these five have generated substantial bodies of well-designed, quantitative field re-search. A few examples exist of quantitative research that cannot clearly be assigned to one or another of these five orientations, but in those cases it appears that the theoretical statement has been left out altogether.

The presentation of the orientations in Chapters 4 through 8 flows from "behavioral" descriptions toward "normative" or "structural" descriptions. The former refer to descriptions based on the field-worker's own observations of what people actually do, or on in-formant recall of actual events; the latter refer to an informant's interpretative statements about what *ought* to happen, or about the correct or appropriate structure of the world. This distinction is of fundamental methodological importance, because the two types of descriptions are based on entirely different kinds of research opera-tions that ought to be clearly separated in ethnographic reports. But, although this requires nothing more than "a consciousness of the relationship between formal rules, operating situations, and awkward facts" (Mead 1966:111), it has taken cultural anthropolo-gists a long time to develop that consciousness. In the past, perhaps in an attempt to provide the most readable and orderly accounts of confusingly strange societies, ethnographers centered attention on normative rules. Cases of individual variation and rule-breaking be-havior were given less display. This has often led young anthropolo-gists preparing for their first research to the erroneous conclusion that "culture" is similar to language in orderliness; in fact these ethnographers simply limited their descriptions of culture to those aspects that possessed the orderliness of language. Recent trends within cultural anthropology are balancing structural descriptions with descriptions of individual behavior and "intracultural di-versity" (Harris 1968:601–3; Pelto & Pelto 1975).

The input-output and exchange orientations are primarily be-havioral in method; the maximization and cognitive/structural orien-tations are primarily normative; and the culture-and-personality orientation is somewhere in the middle. Each orientation contains three parts: (1) *an orienting statement*, which filters certain aspects of the research problem into prominence and temporarily excludes others; (2) *a core variable set*, which isolates the measurable phenomena identified by the orienting statement; and (3) *a set of operations*, which indicates how we are going to measure the core variables. Here I will briefly set out the orienting statements and sets of core variables they identify for each orientation; specific operations are left for discussion in the appropriate chapters below.

The input-output orientation, also known as "noncultural ecology" (Vayda & Rappaport 1968), is rooted in biology. The term input-output is used by economists to refer to an economy analyzed as a flow of goods and services between "sectors," and by ecologists to refer to an "organism of focus" as linked to other organisms and resources by means of exchanges of energy through feeding, reproduction, and defense. In anthropology this orientation takes human beings as the organism of focus and holds that humans are biological organisms whose behavior is aimed at meeting biologically defined needs. Core variables include time and energy inputs to subsistence tasks, outputs of goods and services, patterns of consumption, and rates at which natural resources are exhausted.

The exchange orientation is generated by the orienting statement that exchange is an aspect of all social relations, from such obvious matters as a parent feeding a child or two political allies exchanging confidences to such less apparent ones as a person lying to another, stealing from another, or even just grimacing at another. Exchange therefore refers to actual observable transactions between individuals; it does not refer to attempts to maximize satisfaction through "social exchange" (Homans 1958), which I consider under the maximization orientation. All social life can be seen as flows between individuals; the core variables are exchanges of any sort between people, measured in terms of the frequency, direction, and content of the exchanges.

The orienting statement of culture and personality focuses on what motivates individual adults to make their community persist, and how these motivations are inculcated during the socialization of children. The core variable set includes both cultural variables, such as subsistence technology, socialization practices, and residence patterns, and psychological variables, such as feelings revealed by expressive behavior, and attitudes discovered from interviews, analysis of dreams, and other sources.

The maximization orientation assumes that individuals act to maximize their own satisfaction. The orientation comes from economics and is used commonly by economic anthropologists, but it can be applied to any process of decision-making. Core variables include the range of choices open to individuals in given circumstances, the value or *utility* of each outcome to the individual, and informants' descriptions of the manner in which they make their choices. The orientation raises methodological problems in anthropological fieldwork because money value, such as successful measure in economics, is not always an acceptable measure of utility in the settings where anthropologists work.

The cognitive/structural orientation owes most to the science of linguistics. Its orienting statement is that cultural behavior, on analogy with linguistic behavior, follows rules, or "mental forms," that define appropriate and inappropriate behaviors in specified environments. The core variables are informants' statements concerning the categories of things that exist in their world, and how those categories relate to each other. The occurrence of implicit or nonverbal structures ordering the categories may be inferred from these variables, even when informants show no direct awareness that such structures exist. Methodological emphasis is on procedures that come as close as possible to describing "native views" or "psychological reality." With the possible exception of culture and personality, this orientation most directly attacks the problem of ethnocentrism.

Each of these orientations by itself contains a large body of theory and method. A whole career could be, and occasionally is, devoted to working within just one orientation. More often, though, anthropologists—even those with a dominant interest in a single orientation—incorporate issues and methods from others in their work. Given the importance of holism to cultural anthropology, such borrowing may be beneficial—provided we are careful and self-conscious about the way we mix "findings" developed from distinct perspectives employing methods that are not comparable.

Intersections. By combining orientations we can develop comprehensive descriptions without losing methodological clarity. In what follows I have combined the five orientations in a single overarching "macro-orientation" that both reflects my own preferences and appears to represent, at least loosely, the dominant perspective under which most quantitative research in cultural anthropology is now being conducted—cultural ecology.

In a cultural-ecological perspective, the input-output orientation takes on a central importance; the other orientations are relevant insofar as they relate directly or indirectly to the fulfillment of biologically identifiable basic needs. In Steward's formulation, which is the most influential and useful one, the object of central interest is the *cultural core*, defined as "the constellation of features which are most closely related to subsistence activities and economic arrangements. The core includes such social, political, and religious patterns as are empirically determined to be closely connected with these arrangements" (Steward 1955:37). Now this definition, like those of the five orientations discussed above, lacks theoretical and methodological precision. We are not told how to discover or describe what "subsistence activities" are, and yet this is not an obvious matter, as we will see in Chapter 4. Nor are we told how one "determines empirically" the closeness of the connection between subsistence activities, economic arrangements, and various "patterns." All Steward has to say is that "although technology and environment prescribe that certain things must be done in certain ways if they are to be done at all, the extent to which these activities are functionally tied to other aspects of culture is a purely empirical problem" (Steward 1955:41). In fact, it is both a theoretical and an empirical problem, but Steward's overview provides us with the starting point we need.

Standing alone, the orientations are too generous in scope; they become more definite under the cultural-ecological macro-orientation, which focuses on the intersections between input-output and each of the other orientations. The exchange orientation, for example is concerned with any observable transactions between individuals; this may include anything from handshakes to avoidance. The intersection with input-output, however, is specifically concerned with the behavioral side of the "social relations of production." Exchanges immediately relevant to biological needs include such obvious examples as food sharing, farm-produce marketing, and labor exchange. We need not rule out such less obvious examples as gossip and gift exchange, but their relations to biological need-fulfillment should be specified according to some acceptable procedure. The culture-and-personality orientation already blends an ecological sense of what individuals must do to survive with a concept of personality formation as the process by which individuals acquire the motivation "to do what they must do" (see the discussion of the "Whiting Model" in Chapter 6). Of particular interest in the intersection with input-output are such topics as how people feel about the work they do, how they react to the social relations arising from work situations and the distribution of what is produced, and how they view food, hygiene, property, combat, and reproduction. The maximization orientation, with its stress on "utility" in choice-making, intersects with input-output when utility is defined in terms of biological needs. Whatever the "native's view" of the purposes of his or her decisions, the observer seeks to demonstrate their relevance to fundamental life processes. The cognitive/structural orientation, which seeks the "mental forms" lying behind behavior, intersects with input-output when the implications of various mental forms for the solution of basic life problems are made clear. Many formal structural analyses that have been criticized as "trivial"—for instance, analyses of disease terms or kin terms—take on a new significance when their practical relevance in the daily lives of people is spelled out.

The interrelations among the orientations are summarized in Figure 2.1, which represents a pyramid, viewed from above, with input-output at the apex and the other orientations at the four corners of the base. As the figure also reveals, all the orientations at the base intersect with each other. Exchange intersects with culture and personality in the realm of "interpersonal relations," meaning those

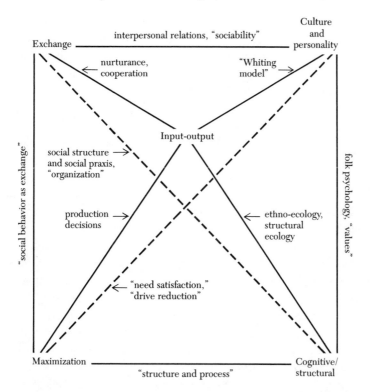

Fig. 2.1. The interrelations among the five orientations in a cultural-ecological framework.

interactions between individuals (gift-giving, deference, aggressive play, etc.) that reflect personality dispositions like trust, dependence, or competitiveness. Exchange and maximization intersect in the arena of "social exchange," including such individually manipulated social relations as friendships and coalitions. Exchange and the cognitive/structural orientation intersect in the comparison between the rules of social "structure" and the actual social behavior or "organization" that is observed. The culture-and-personality and maximization orientations together define the notion of "psychic economy," as a process of individual decision making to balance competing "drives" or "motives" in an individually satisfying manner. The culture-and-personality and cognitive/structural orientations meet in the realm of folk psychology, the native concepts of emotional life and mental health. And the maximization and cognitive/structural orientations intersect when the shared structures of the community become "process" as individuals use (and transform) structural elements in making their daily decisions in all spheres of life.

It should be noted that there is no reason why we could not construct other pyramids with different orientations at the apex. I chose the cultural-ecological perspective here for two reasons. First, when I was assembling materials for this book I found, to my initial surprise, that the great majority of quantitative research within cultural anthropology had been done, often explicitly, within a broadly ecological framework. This is probably nothing more than the result of the common-sense aspect of the approach, which states the obvious: that individuals who are alive must be taking steps to stay that way, and that in most of the communities where anthropologists work these steps occupy the greater part of the individuals' daily lives. Anthropologists who try to make their descriptions faithful to their informants' thoughts and acts will inevitably end up with a marked ecological component, simply because the exchanges of highest frequency, the most common decisions, and the desires and anxieties of a group are generally concentrated on the various means of staying alive.

The second reason reflects my belief that many significant issues of our time are at base ecological ones. It is not accidental that the huge transformations being effected in the world by industrial technological systems are directed by individuals whose daily lives are almost entirely spent in carefully controlled environments that by their very nature exclude, as they are (culturally) intended to do, any direct, intuitive sense of what other organisms are like or how our fates are bound up with theirs. The stimuli we receive from our fellow humans, and from books, magazines, movies, and above all television, generally reflect the unnatural isolation our culture has brought about. This "unnatural" world of ours is, of course, ecologically comprehensible. Modern technology provides ample, secure diets, controls disease, lengthens life expectancy, and provides means for comfort and ease. But it carries other implications as well: for example, that all other organisms are inferior to humans and may as well be extinct unless they are directly useful to us. Our "work" is increasingly removed from the biological world; muscular effort is increasingly replaced by energy-consuming mechanical effort; we are losing track of what we produce at the same time that what we consume comes to us by increasingly mysterious means; and we are becoming ever more individualized and dependent upon an abstract process of production we do not in any demonstrable sense control.

Much of the malaise of our times can be examined within a cultural-ecological perspective. We need a broader, cross-culturally adequate sense of the human condition: What brings satisfaction in work? Under what circumstances do people maintain close personal ties, and what costs and benefits do these bring? What are the ecological bases of war? By what processes do communities arrive at the awareness that they have dangerously exceeded the tolerance of their ecosystem, and how do they decide what to do about it? These questions are as complex and difficult as any that scientists have learned to ask, and a good deal more urgent than many.

Research Design

The art of research design is to develop projects that are at once relevant and feasible. This is indeed an art, but there are some basic components that belong in any good research proposal. The following outline is a useful starting point in preparing a proposal:

1. General statement of the problem
2. Specific statement of the problem
    i. History of the problem
    ii. Orientation of the research
3. Description of the population
    i. Relevance to the problem
    ii. Access
    iii. Sampling procedures
4. Methods: Timetable and operations

The following example of a proposal for research on a case of cultural change illustrates both the use of this outline and the role of orientations in research design.

1. *General statement of the problem.* The proposal is to study the process of technological change in a community of subsistence farmers. Of central concern will be the circumstances surrounding the increased production of foodstuffs for sale. The research will contribute to our understanding of two interrelated processes of widely acknowledged importance: first, how a community's food production can be increased; and second, how traditional subsistence producers come to take on greater involvement with the markets and other institutions of modernizing national societies.

2. *Specific statement of the problem.* The purpose of the subsection "history of the problem" is not simply to cite all the available literature on the topic but rather to show command of the part of the literature that has made the most significant contribution to identifying the main issues and defining the problem. In the present example, we might choose to identify the following issues: the relationship between population and technological change (Childe 1951, Braidwood 1967, and Boserup 1965); the "rationality" of subsistence farmers (Frank Cancian 1972); and the nature of the difference between household subsistence economics and the modern "firm" (Chayanov 1966, Sahlins 1972). All these issues are closely related to one broad question: How do traditional subsistence farmers become *motivated* (or not motivated) to increase their market production of foods?

Having described the history of the problem, we turn to the orientation of the research. In this proposal we assume that the starting place of the inquiry ought to be the search for biologically rooted motives for change (this assumption could neither be proven nor disproven). Will the change increase (or decrease) the quantity or quality of the foods available to the household? Will it increase access to medical care? Does it enhance the security of old age? Does it reduce the danger or drudgery of work? The answers to these questions are not automatically assumed to be yes; research may disclose that increased cash-crop production leads to decreases in the biologically defined quality of life within the community, and that other purposes are being served instead.

A description of the input-output system provides a first-level response to the research problem. The time and effort expended under the traditional regime to produce foods and other necessities can be compared with the inputs and outputs characteristic of the new regime. It is then possible to ask, for example, if the productivity of labor is improved, or whether the range of necessary consumption goods available to the household has changed. If, for example, the new change requires large increases in capital inputs (e.g. fertilizer), the income available for home consumption may actually decrease even though the productivity of labor has increased.

Description of the exchange system indicates changes in cooperation and distribution. For example, anthropologists often find that traditional production systems are based upon frequent labor exchange, food sharing, and resource pooling, all of which may decline during technological change. What do these exchanges *accomplish* for people under the old practices and why are they abandoned (if, in fact, they are) under the new?

The culture-and-personality orientation calls for study of the attitudes and emotional values that provide strong, often unconscious motivation preventing or encouraging technological change. Such matters as food preferences, security drives, attraction to cooperative work settings, deeply felt obligations to relatives, and so on may support the traditional system and discourage change, or may predispose individuals toward change.

The description of maximization processes lays out the framework within which individuals make their decisions to change or not. In fact, the whole problem might be reduced to the question, What are people trying to maximize? Do they want increased labor productivity, security rooted in reliable exchange relationships, or are they perhaps unable to abandon "outmoded" emotions only suited to the traditional system? We would like to show the "calculation" (conscious or not) which leads to the decision to change.

The cognitive/structural description provides an account of the situation as far as possible in the terms the participants themselves see it. How do they describe the traditional and modern systems? What do they regard as appropriate or inappropriate techniques? What are the kinds of persons they recognize and how should they relate to each other? What account do they give of the decision process? This approach does not merely fulfill an abstract anthropological requirement for structural analysis; above all, it recognizes the community member as the most informed person in the matter, by virtue of life-long personal, practical experiences that outside agents of change, no matter what their "expertise," can never acquire. One of the main lessons of participant-observation is that people are rarely ignorant about their self-interest, and are usually capable of discussing at great length and with great understanding how they meet their basic needs.

Description of the change process using each of the five orientations provides a well-rounded approach to the definition of the motivation for change. Before turning to the specific methods of description, we need to identify the community where the research is to take place.

3. *Description of the population*. This section of a proposal generally opens with an introduction to the group to be studied, including a review of the available literature, a broad description of the environment, an analysis of the group's linguistic or other affiliations with neighboring groups, and a brief characterization of its economy, social system, political relations, and religious beliefs.

Next we would describe the relevance of our chosen group to the problem: in the present case we would need to demonstrate that the community in question provides an opportunity to observe both traditional subsistence producers and individuals changing their production to increase cash-crop (food) outputs. The manner of the change is important: is it gradual or sudden, does it require capital inputs, is it voluntary? Aspects of the traditional system that would influence motivation to change should also be identified: how productive is traditional agriculture, how do prevailing lines of exchange affect it, and what is the local concept of an adequate standard of living? On these matters the literature is nearly always vague and spotty, and expectations based upon the literature are often contradicted in the field.

After this comes the matter of access. Whether a scientific researcher will be allowed to enter the community identified in the research proposal or not has become the biggest practical barrier to anthropological research. For reasons that do not always seem justified to us, governments of countries in which professional anthropologists wish to do research have become highly restrictive. This is so even though (and perhaps because) the great majority of anthropologists have always adopted sympathetic positions in defense of the rights of local populations to integrity and self-determination. Anthropologists should now demonstrate in their proposals that they have permission, or at least the prospect of permission, from the relevant agencies in the host country. Anthropologists who are preparing to do research in the region for the first time must expect long delays and considerable suspicion before their permission is granted, and should begin to introduce themselves and their research to the appropriate persons at least a year in advance of their planned departure for the field. Senior anthropologists, experienced in their areas, improve the situation by translating their own works into local languages and seeing to their distribution within the host countries, thereby maintaining ties and showing a commitment to giving something in return for what they have taken during past field projects.

Finally, sampling procedures should be spelled out. There are no "natural," clearly delineated populations. Households, villages, and regions are always characterized to some extent by flows in and out of residents, and by exchanges with the "outside." Part of the definition of the population to be studied requires a statement of the way observations on individuals are going to be made to apply to a whole population. This is discussed in detail in Chapter 3.

4. *Methods.* Each of the orientations provides a unique set of questions subsidiary to the main question of what motivates change; each also has a set of unique research operations associated with it for answering those questions. A convenient way of arranging this section of a proposal is around a timetable of research activities. Since the body of this book is concerned with discussing specific research techniques in association with orientations, only a few kinds of techniques are indicated.

The research will take place over an eighteen-month period. The first three months will be spent in a regional survey. The purpose of this survey is (1) to find the most appropriate single community for long-term participant observation, and (2) to develop a sound sense of the similarities and differences among communities in the region. The survey will collect general data about village size, household composition, land-use practices, and other general sociocultural phenomena. The extent to which the community ultimately chosen is representative of the region can then be judged with some accuracy.

The next twelve months will be spent in participant observation in a single community over a full annual cycle. Direct observations and interviews will be devoted to describing (1) basic production processes (mapping resources, measuring agricultural inputs and outputs), (2) the major lines of exchange (frequencies of labor exchange, visiting patterns), (3) attitudes and values (attitude questionnaires, analysis of stories), (4) decision making (cost-benefit analysis, decision criteria), and (5) the normative structure (eliciting frames, cognitive testing). The goal is as complete an account as possible of the implications of the traditional system, and the coming changes, for evaluating the (biologically conceived) well-being of individuals in the community.

The remaining three months will be spent preparing a preliminary writeup and identifying gaps in the data. This phase of the research is generally ignored in practice, because by this time the research is just beginning to gain momentum and it is painful to think that it will shortly come to an end. Thus, at this point organization is often abandoned in a mad effort to get as much data as possible before leaving the field. As a result, the conceptual unity of the research comes apart and large holes in the data that could easily have been filled in the field are not discovered until some time after the return home. Much more productive in the final months of research is to gradually wind down the sheer data-gathering in favor of making a first-order integration of the data. At this point it is useful to try to outline the shape of the ethnographic account (thesis, book, articles) that is being aimed for. How do all the disparate bits of information, gathered by separate techniques, fit into some sort of whole? It is clear that the various orientations feed into one another. The search for maximization processes, for example, must take into account the actual facts of input-output, the experienced benefits of social ties, the feelings of individuals, and the structural definitions concerning what is "natural," "right," and so on. In spelling out these interrelations, one becomes aware of kinds of information that will be needed to develop a more complete argument later; if this is done before the field has been left far behind, then one of the most painful sources of disappointment with fieldwork can be substantially diminished.

Each researcher must find a creatively satisfying solution to the problem of research design, and this must be done anew for each research project. Research has its origins in commitments that are part of the individual's own makeup, and only the researcher can give a project the unity and purpose it must have if it is to be successful. Yet research in cultural anthropology is too broad and too ambitious in its goals ever to be completely satisfying. Actual fieldwork always threatens to whirl out of control, and the only way to keep this from happening is to develop a research design that will be flexible enough to bend with the unexpected pressures of field realities and yet sturdy enough to hold the research within definite bounds. This can be done by clearly identifying the central questions the research is geared to answer, and by keeping those questions central throughout the research. Since informants rarely understand fully what the research is aiming at, and since fieldwork must, if it is to be successful, make the researcher doubt his or her own cherished beliefs, including the commitments that brought the research into being, the research design often stands as the only relatively stable benchmark in an amorphous, shifting landscape.

CHAPTER THREE

Quantifying Cultural Data

M EASUREMENT, IN THE general sense of "taking the measure of a thing," is a characteristic process of living systems; at this level, "measure" is a synonym for "percept." All descriptions, therefore, no matter what their specific forms, result from some measurement activity, and the adequacy of the measures used depends in the final analysis on the purposes for which the description is being provided. In this chapter we explore the implications of adherence to scientific standards of description for the measurement of cultural phenomena.

In cultural anthropology, standards of description are rarely made explicit; if they were, we would frequently find them contradictory. It is not unusual, even in the acknowledged masterworks of ethnography, to find a descriptive potluck of careful documentation alongside sweeping generalizations in the same monograph. An especially important difference in standards of description divides "humanists" from "scientists" in anthropology. The former call for rich, personalized descriptions, whereas the latter emphasize parsimony and comparability. The bias against humanism is that it is soft-headed and ineffective; the bias against science is that it is depersonalized and mechanistic. The two camps find little common ground, yet anthropology historically seems to have encompassed about equal proportions of each.

Quantitative descriptions, which at the highest level achieve fully numerical precision, would seem to fall squarely within the scientific camp. The defense of quantitative measurement that follows can thus be seen as a defense of scientific procedures against the humanist critique. The reasons for increasing the quantitative aspect in ethnographic description, however, are not solely scientific; they have more to do with generating effective knowledge, where the meaning of "effective" has both scientific and humanistic connotations. The humanist critique of science and quantification is further considered below, as is the history of quantification in anthropology.

Why Quantify?

Quantitative measurement can increase the effectiveness of anthropological description by increasing reliability; increasing comparability; retaining negative cases; expressing intracultural diversity; increasing the precision of theoretical propositions; and increasing the power of statistical tests. Most anthropologists, whatever their particular purposes, would agree that these advantages of quantification are worth having, if they do not cost too much.

Reliability. A measure is reliable to the extent that two or more observers of the same event take the same measure of it. For example, most members of our culture are able to make reliable use of thermometers to measure temperature. The numerical scale of the thermometer and its proven consistency in the hands of many separate observers are the basis of its reliability. Verbal descriptions, such as "cool" or "steaming," have the power to evoke rich subjective impressions of an event, but are inherently ambiguous; they cannot guarantee that the community of readers, given individual preferences for one temperature over another, will understand the terms as they are used by the original observer. In general, when an argument is expressed in precise quantities, readers can be certain of the author's meaning without having to infer shades or qualities of the event.

Comparability. An increase in the reliability of most anthropological descriptions will also result in an increase in their comparability.

The progress of cultural anthropology depends directly upon our ability to develop theories of cross-cultural scope, and the low comparability of existing data severely constrains cross-cultural theory construction. As a result, the comparative theorist is forced to accept the lowest common denominator of measurement, which is usually an absolute classification of a broad typological sort, such as the division of the world's societies according to residence types (patrilocal, neolocal, etc.) The breadth of the classification buries important distinctions and nuances (for example, two societies labeled "patrilocal" might be shown through more sophisticated measurements to be 60 percent and 90 percent patrilocal, respectively—a considerable distinction). The traditional individualism of cultural anthropologists—the sink-or-swim approach to research, whereby mere survival for a long-term field project makes us experts—must be modified to include a professionally shared methodology for the purpose of cross-cultural comparisons.

Negative cases. Consciously or unconsciously, we are always seeking patterns in the course of research; the value of quantitative measurement lies in the fact that it preserves an accurate record of the negative cases that do not fit the patterns we are trying to establish (Mitchell 1967:21). In the beginning of a field research project, certain events take on special importance as we attempt an initial understanding of the behavior we are observing; later on, even in the face of contrary evidence, the initial impressions remain. The experience of anthropologists who have collected and analyzed quantitative data is that many early impressions are confirmed, but others are found to be largely or entirely false.

Intracultural diversity. Just as selective forgetting after leaving the field homogenizes the memory of what the field setting was like and leads to the suppression of negative cases, so a kind of implicit mental multivariate analysis takes place and reduces the welter of contradictory impressions to a few "types" of persons and of events. One form of this has been an overreliance on the description of rule systems, which has left the impression among some nonfieldworkers that individual behavior in non-Western societies is as strictly determined and unconscious as language is (e.g., Dalton 1969:67). If people were in fact as rule-abiding as some ethnographies imply, they would be no more than proper-minded simpletons. Quantitative observations of many individuals provide a record of diversity that allows comparisons within a cultural unit between such subgroups as young and old, male and female, or kin and nonkin; these, in turn, may be compared to predictions flowing from the rule system.

Theoretical precision. Theoretical statements that refer to vague attributes of the world are not particularly helpful in guiding research. We have seen that the difference between scientific statements and statements of faith rests ultimately on the notion of falsifiability. To be falsifiable, a proposition must be susceptible to measurement (must be able to be tested); hence quantitative precision of measurement contributes to the improvement of theory. The only theoretical issues that can ever be resolved are those that predict precise, observable differences in the outcomes of specified events.

Statistical power. The resolution of theoretical issues generally hinges on evidence that differences between two or more groups of individuals are large enough to be *significant*. Statistical inference is one way of testing for significance, and the more quantified the data, the more powerful the statistical tests that can be applied in an analysis. This is discussed further in the section below on statistical testing.

Quantitative data, then, contribute in a variety of ways to the strength or trustworthiness of an analysis. As a rule, the collection of quantitative data does not take more time than impressionistic research. The researcher in the field often spends long periods idly waiting for something to happen, or simply watching, in an "eyes open" fashion, what is going on; these times can be filled with counting and measuring procedures of a simple sort that neither interfere with the events being observed nor take the researcher away from the scene of activity. By concentrating the researcher's attention, quantitative procedures undoubtedly do detract from direct apprehension of the scene as a whole; but one need not be counting every minute to collect useful quantitative data. And experience shows that quantitative data not only offer better solutions to the problems with which the research began, but also reveal unexpected facets of the field situation just because, compared to intuition, they are less under the control of our prior expectations.

Quantification and Mathematics

Students beginning to learn about the application of formal methods to anthropological problems are generally uncertain about what difference, if any, there is between mathematics and quantification. Although the two subjects are intimately related, the distinction between them should be kept clear. Within cultural anthropology, mathematical approaches have been more effectively developed and communicated than quantitative approaches, which are fragmentary and disorganized. Quantification is concerned with the numerical description of empirical situations, whereas mathematics is concerned with the abstract symbolic representation of concepts and their relationships; in terms of scientific theory as described in Chapter 1, the abstract calculus of a theory is usually mathematical and the research operations are usually quantitative. Mathematical thinking imposes clarity and rigor on analysis by eliminating unnecessary concepts and making explicit the order that is thought to exist among the concepts: "mathematics is the language *par excellence* in which it is difficult to say something you do not intend" (Kay 1971:xii).

As we learned in Chapter 1, the belief that a researcher can go into the field and simply describe "what is there" is a self-deception; all description is conceptual. Subjecting the conceptual structure behind a particular description of reality to mathematical scrutiny is the most powerful means of exposing that structure to public criticism. The attraction of mathematics lies in its generality, though that is also its limitation: "because in a sense mathematics contains all theories it contains none; it is the language of theory, but it does not give us the content" (Boulding 1968:3). The risk of mathematical analysis is that the mathematics will be taken as good in and of themselves, regardless of the content of a specific theory and the real-world purposes to which it is directed: for example, it has been argued that "if it is unrealistic to assume that the universe conforms to mathematical principles, then we must search for those aspects of the universe which admit of mathematical formulations" (Buchler & Nutini 1969:2–3). What would be the purpose of such a program, except to serve mathematics for its own sake?

In most cases mathematical formulations serve us best when used in conjunction with empirical descriptions. A mathematical analysis can reveal aspects of the data that do not make sense. As an example, we may take the Natchez Paradox (Douglas White 1973). The Natchez Indians of what is now the Southern United States were originally described as having four inherited classes—three of "nobility" (Suns, Nobles, and Honored People), and a fourth of "commoners" (Stinkards). Members of all three noble classes were required by rules of exogamy to marry Stinkards. Descent was matrilineal, except that the children of Sun fathers became Noble, and the children of Noble fathers became Honored. As this rule system came under scrutiny, it became apparent that over time the class of Stinkards would increasingly diminish relative to the noble classes. A mathematical analysis revealed the paradox clearly: under these rules the system was demographically unstable, and after a period of time it would become unworkable.

Some attempts were made to conserve the basic model by reference to processes that had not been included initially. For example, it was suggested that the class of Stinkards was continuously replenished by assimilation of outsiders from "lesser tribes". It was also held that women of noble classes reproduced more slowly than Stinkard women. Unfortunately, neither "solution" was supported by adequate data.

D. R. White et al. (1971) returned to original French records to see if the proposed model corresponded to the empirical descriptions. They found to the contrary that only male children of Noble fathers became Honored; female children became Stinkards, and the only Honored women were the wives of Honored men. Furthermore, after three generations, descendants of Nobles were demoted to the next lower class, that is, from Suns to Nobles, and from Nobles to Honored People and Stinkards. Developing a new mathematical model incorporating these modifications, the authors found that such a marriage system would be compatible with reasonable demographic assumptions.

In this book, the focus will be not on the formal mathematics associated with specific methods but on the designs for the collection and description of the data themselves. Kay (1971) has presented the case for mathematics in anthropology clearly, and Burton (1973) and Douglas White (1973) provide excellent recent reviews. The advantages of building mathematical models in close conjunction with empirical data, as seen above in the Natchez example, are also shown in Romney's (1971) paper on the measurement of endogamy, and in Smith's analysis of central places in Guatemala, discussed in Chapter 7 of this book.

Quantification and Statistics

One reason for quantifying anthropological data is that the more powerful statistical procedures call for quantification. For this reason, I require students in my course in research design to have had an introductory course in statistics. Most of them find this requirement frustrating because courses in statistics are rarely taught by anthropologists and rarely take into account anthropological problems. Such courses tend to focus on specific statistical procedures, whereas what anthropologists usually need is a general background in probability theory and an introduction to the wide variety of techniques useful for holistic researchers who might be doing a regional survey, behavioral observations, and cognitive interviews all in a single project. In this section I will explore some of the relationships between quantitative research design and statistical hypothesis testing. For readers who need a "bare-bones" introduction or a refresher in statistics, I recommend McCollough and Van Atta (1963); for more depth there are D. Thomas (1976), written especially for anthropologists, and Siegel (1956); and for probability theory there are Kemeny et al. (1966) and Parzen (1960).

Statistical tests of significance. We usually think of the "significance" of a finding as its meaning within our theoretical frame, that is, whether it can be construed as "supporting" our particular theory or not. But *statistical* significance has a clear and precise meaning, and is substantially independent of the *theoretical* significance of a finding. Social scientists are especially prone to confuse these concepts.

The term "statistics" can refer simply to descriptive measures, such as "mean" or "quartile," that can be used to summarize the character of a research population; but more commonly it refers to the results of *statistical inference* where the properties of a population are inferred from the properties of a *sample* of that population. The statistical significance of a finding is an indication of the likelihood that a given description of a sample is characteristic of the population from which the sample was drawn. Let us review how a specific hypothesis is subjected to a statistical test of significance.

First, we must determine the hypothesis. The general form of a hypothesis is a statement of the expected relationship between two or more variables. The process of hypothesis formulation, in which the variables are identified and expected relations predicted, is a theoretical one that occurs *prior* to statistical manipulation. As an example, we might want to know whether in some kinds of peasant villages the social standing of the father has something to do with the marriages of the offspring; we could put forth the hypothesis that "marriage occurs between offspring of fathers of similar social standing."

Second, we must be able to measure the variables in empirical settings so that the hypothesis is at risk of falsification. In this case, we assume that we know what "marriage" is and that we can determine the "social standing" of the fathers of the partners to specific marriages.

Third, the observed cases must be a *representative sample* of the population to which the findings will be generalized. The hypothesis predicts a relationship between variables; the *test* of the hypothesis is whether a relationship discovered in the sample is likely to be true of the population at large. The present example predicts that, from the standpoint of marriage practices, there are two different populations: the offspring of high-status fathers, and the offspring of low-status fathers. The test of the hypothesis answers two questions:

(1) do we observe differences between two groups in the sample; and (2) if we do, are these observed differences likely to be true of the whole population? Cancian, from whom we have borrowed our present hypothesis, tested it in a Mexican village (Frank Cancian 1965). He found that offspring of high-prestige fathers did in fact marry each other more often than they married offspring of low-prestige fathers, and vice versa. Now the second question really asks, What are the chances of getting this result from a random sample of a population in which father's prestige does *not* influence marriage? This is the question that statistical inference answers. In the current example, Cancian computed that the chances were less than 5 percent, making it likely that the populations of low-status and high-status offspring were really different from one another.

Before proceeding further, let us examine two issues that arise at this point. First, the statistical significance of a finding does not automatically ensure its theoretical significance. That the population of high-status offspring is statistically different from that of low-status offspring does not necessarily mean that this is of theoretical importance. What about those marriages that did cross status boundaries (over one-third of the marriages in Cancian's sample)? The reported trend toward "within-status marriages" would not support a theory predicting that all marriages, or all but a few, would be between "same-status" offspring. The demonstration that a finding is statistically significant does not relieve us of the responsibility for deciding whether that finding also has theoretical significance. The opposite is also true: a pattern discerned from a set of data may have theoretical significance, whether or not statistical tests of significance have been computed. For example, statistical significance tests are rarely computed for multivariate analyses, which often have undeniable theoretical significance.

Second, we have seen that before statistical tests of significance can be used to test a hypothesis, several steps have to be taken. Specifically, we had to identify the set of variables to be tested; we had to make measurements; and we had to follow proper sampling procedures. Let us examine each of these steps more closely.

Variables. A variable is a theoretically relevant attribute that can assume any one of a range of values. A variable is not an entity, but rather an observable aspect of an entity; if we were strict operationalists, we would have to say that an entity is defined by the variables for which it has been measured. The entity "person," for example, can be described by hundreds of variables, from eye color to social role. Entities are not defined, however, by the simple listing of variables; rather, variables are organized into theoretical systems, either theories or orientations, which specify mutual interrelations. A person, for example, can be defined by a number of different systems of variables, such as the "physiological" system or the "personality" system. No variable exists apart from such a conceptual system.

Theoretically relevant attributes of a system do not always vary. Attributes that are variable within a broad perspective may, in the boundaries of a particular orientation, become constants. For example, genetic attributes are known to vary between human populations, and variation in gene frequencies is used by physical anthropologists to describe similarities and differences between populations. But for cultural anthropologists, genetic attributes of human populations are held to be constants; this follows the basic postulate of cultural anthropology that the genetic bases of culture (e.g., language capability, skill with tools, memory) are evenly distributed among human populations; individuals may vary but populations do not.

Measurement. A variable faces in two directions at once: in addition to its theoretical face it has a methodological face, and the connection between the two is neither automatic nor direct. The theoretical meaning of a variable is determined by its place within the "nomological net" of concepts and relations. Its methodological meaning is determined by the specific research operations used to measure it. Within the social sciences there is nearly always some doubt about the *validity* of research operations as measures of theoretical variables; "scientists think in the theoretical language and make tests in the operational language" (Blalock 1972:14). As we saw in Chapter 1, intersubjective research operations can enhance the *reliability* of data by giving a reasonable assurance that another researcher using the described methods would attain similar results. But reliable data are not necessarily valid as measures of a theoretical variable. For example, culture evolution theory makes much use of the variable "population pressure"; but the most common operational measure, and it is a fairly reliable one, is "population density" (persons per unit of area), which is not at all satisfactory from the theoretical viewpoint. The same population density can represent very different population pressures depending on resources and technology; thus, a population density of 10 persons per square kilometer in a fertile valley yields a different pressure depending on whether we are dealing with hunter-gatherers or farmers.

In such cases, where no "single criterion" (e.g., thermometer as measure of temperature) serves as a valid measure of the variable, it is often necessary to develop a sense of "construct validity" (Cronbach & Meehl 1956) by integrating a number of different measures. An acceptable concept of population pressure, for example, would have to be constructed out of a number of variables, including population density per unit of area, availability of basic resources (water, wild foods, fertile soils, etc.), amounts of time individuals spend obtaining food, nutritional content of the diet, and many others. Since the concept is multivariate and requires a systematic integration of variables, more intuition enters in than in a single-criterion variable. As Pelto (1970:41–44) observes, validity in this sense has been of more central concern to anthropologists than reliability; we have depended heavily on intuitive concepts and shown suspicion of single operational measures. But the one should not be sacrificed for the other:

> The writer must note what portions of his proposed interpretation are speculations, extrapolations, or conclusions from insufficient data. *The author has an ethical responsibility to prevent unsubstantiated interpretations from appearing as truths.* A claim is unsubstantiated unless the evidence for the claim is public, so that other scientists may review the evidence, criticize the conclusions, and offer alternative interpretations (Cronbach & Meehl 1956:197; emphasis added).

Levels of measurement. The usefulness of a measure depends in part on the "level" at which it is taken. The "level of measurement" (or degree of quantification) refers to the kind of information a measure conveys about the relations between variables according to a scale (see Siegel 1956:21–30; Forcese & Richer 1973:53–75; Pelto 1970:183–86). Not all measurement has a numerical form. At the lowest level is *naming*, whereby observed phenomena are placed in classes (nominal scale of measurement). This is the most common form of measurement employed in cross-cultural theory construction: communities are classed as "matrilineal" or "patrilineal," as rearing children to be "dependent" or "independent," as having Dravidian kinship terminology or some other kind, and so on. The judgment is one of class inclusion; no judgment of *degree* is made.

When it is possible to *rank* the observations according to some scale, a higher level of measurement is achieved (ordinal scale). It is possible to say that one community differs from another not merely by the presence or absence of an attribute, but also by the degree to which it possesses that attribute. Many measures used for comparing cultural units, such as the evolutionary typology of Band, Tribe, Chiefdom, State, and the Folk-Urban "continuum," permit such "more-or-less" judgments to be made. But there is still lacking a means for saying exactly *how much more* of the attribute one community has than another.

The *numerical* level of measurement permits this precise relative judgment (interval and ratio scales). At this level we can know that an object rated "three" is not only "more" than an object rated "one," but also that it is exactly three times as much as the object rated "one."

Although there are circumstances in which it is not good to force the issue, higher levels of quantification are generally better than lower ones. The low levels of measurement commonly used in ethnographic reporting do much to hinder the improvement of anthropological theory, and the limitation of cross-cultural analyses to nominal data has been a source of continuing frustration since the earliest comparative work was done. Moreover, with more anthropologists aware of the need to provide statistical tests of significance in support of many of their arguments today, it is well to keep in mind that the more powerful statistical techniques—those that guarantee a smaller margin of inferential error—are those that require higher levels of measurement. Reluctance to quantify anthropological data should be carefully founded, therefore, on evidence that the costs of quantification will exceed the clear benefits it brings.

Sampling. The problem for statistical inference is to generalize from a sample to a population. All scientific generalizations are statistical in the sense that they are based on a limited number of observations of particular phenomena: from these observations, inferences about every occurrence of the phenomenon are drawn. To put it another way, data are gathered from samples, but theories refer to populations.

In this regard it is useful to distinguish three levels of sampling unit. First there is the *theoretical population*, the unit referred to in theoretical statements. Anthropological theory generally refers to ill-defined "cultural units" such as "marginal peasants," "egalitarian societies," "horticulturalists," and so forth. Next there is the *empirical population*, or "community of focus," the unit in which actual research is conducted. The cultural anthropologist works in a definite community, which may be as small as a hamlet of closely related households or as large as an entire region. The empirical population is bounded and defined by the actual extent of the fieldworker's efforts, and thus is far more restricted than the theoretical population, which in practice seldom has clear boundaries. Last there is the *sample*, the set of individuals or groups on which actual measurements are taken. In small communities the sample and the empirical population may be identical, but in larger communities only a portion of the total membership is ever observed or interviewed. Even in small communities, fieldworkers typically rely on certain individuals more than others, so that some kinds of measurements refer only to samples even though other measures may refer to the entire empirical population. From the standpoint of statistical inference, the usefulness of a given set of measures for generalizing about a whole population depends on representativeness at two levels. First, in what sense is the empirical population representative of the theoretical population? And, second, in what sense is the sample representative of the empirical population?

The typical problem for cross-cultural theory is to account for similarities and differences among types of sociocultural units. One difficulty is that we have no information about the universe of "all sociocultural units"; we only have information about communities that have been studied. Since there is no way to get information about communities that have not been studied, we do not even know how many there are, let alone what their characteristics are. The problem of whether "known societies" adequately represent "all societies," therefore, has no solution.

A problem to which modern researchers can offer a solution, however, is that of the representativeness of the empirical population within the region in which it occurs. Anthropologists seldom select their empirical population at random; such matters as ease of access, prevalence of diseases, availability of letters of introduction, and other considerations of convenience always intervene. For this reason, ethnographers sometimes include a caveat in their publications to the effect that their findings apply only to the specific community in which the study was done. This head-in-the-sand solution merely ignores the problem, though, by implying that no generalizations can be drawn from the study. It is certain that generalizations will be drawn, and some sense of the unusual features of the community in comparison with others in its region can be very helpful to those who will be doing the generalizing.

A practical solution to this problem is to include a regional survey as a preliminary part of any research project. For example, suppose the study is to be done in a river valley in which about 50 villages with cultural and linguistic similarities are situated. It is probable that villages differ in size, access to alluvial land, location relative to such central places as markets or municipal seats, and so on. A representative sample of, say, twenty villages might be selected and visited, with the goal of describing a number of relevant general characteristics of each. Such a survey gives a reliable indication of the range of variation of communities within a region, and helps in the selection of an appropriate community for traditional, in-depth participant observation. Instead of arguing loosely that the community of focus is "typical" in some sense, it then becomes possible to specify what an "average" community looks like and to compare the chosen community with the average, point by point. Regional surveys thus have a useful role in good research designs.

The second level of sampling problem is the relation between the empirical population and the sample of informants. Anthropologists cannot be everywhere at once, even in very small communities; and, like other people, they prefer being certain places and in the company of certain individuals more than others. Individuals differ by age, sex, wealth, and skill; these and other differences influence their beliefs and behavior. Representative sampling is required to ensure that some sense of the full range of individual differences is preserved in the final description. Strictly speaking, the only representative sample is a *random* sample. The concept of randomness is so important to an understanding of sampling that it is surprising how often students emerge from a general statistics course without any clear notion of what randomness is (and is not). Parzen (1962:2) gives this definition: *"A random (or chance) phenomenon is an empirical phenomenon characterized by the property that its observation under a given set of circumstances does not always lead to the same observed outcome (so that there is no deterministic regularity) but rather to different outcomes in such a way that there is statistical regularity."* For example, in tossing an unbiased coin, there is no deterministic regularity, since either a head or a tail may occur on any particular throw; but there is statistical regularity because the proportion of heads (or tails) will tend toward 0.5 in a large number of trials. A "random sample" is a random phenomenon constructed by the researcher so that there is no deterministic regularity in the selection of individual cases for the sample. This is done by ensuring that every individual in the population has an equal chance of being selected for the sample, and that the selection of one individual does not in any way affect the probability that any other will be selected.

Statistical inference is entirely based on mathematical probability theory regarding regularities in random phenomena. When a sample of individuals is drawn at random from a population, then certain relations between measurements of the sample and the measures that would (theoretically) be true for the whole population become predictable. But if the sample is not random, then its relation to the whole population cannot be predicted. A statistical test of significance is only meaningful if the sample is random (but cf. Naroll 1970:1230).

Whatever the central purposes of a particular research project, it is advantageous to introduce random sampling techniques at focal points in the study. If the focus is on economic activities, for example, then random surveys of gardens, work routines, personal holdings, etc., are called for; if the focus is on the rights and duties of kinsmen, then people should be interviewed at random concerning the rights and duties they recognize. The most convenient method for drawing a random sample is to use a table of random numbers. Random number tables are constructed so that each digit appears with equal probability, and without any known determinate regularity; the numbers are in random sequence no matter where we begin in the table, or whether we read from left to right, up to down, or in some other sequence. Other randomizing techniques, such as drawing lots from a hat or shuffling playing cards, are also acceptable, but a table of random numbers is both easier to use and less subject to undetected determinants (e.g., playing cards may stick together) than other methods.

There are many ways in which the samples anthropologists draw are not random, but some kinds of nonrandomness are less justified than others. The least justified sample of all is a *haphazard* one. Researchers may draw haphazard samples in the field, then return to claim that their samples are "representative" because they cannot think of any bias operating in the selection of subjects. The fact is, however, that we human beings are not built to generate random sequences; on the contrary, we are ordering devices, consciously or not. Haphazard samples are almost certainly influenced by taste, convenience, or a nonrandom sense of what is representative. For example, I have drawn from a handbook of statistical tables (Kendall & Smith 1939) the following sequence of random numbers: 77, 17, 94, 47, 47, 57. If we were asked to generate a random sequence, it is highly unlikely that we would string together so many sevens, because we think of strings of numbers as intuitively (but erroneously) nonrandom; what is random about this string of sevens is the way it was produced: in each of those positions, any digit between 0 and 9 had an equal chance of appearing.

Systematic sampling, such as every fifth house or every tenth name in a register, is often used in sociology, but for anthropologists I do not recommend it. A systematic sample is not random because the individuals appearing next to the one chosen have no chance of being included. For example, in a community where patrilineal relatives live next to each other, sampling every fifth house would systematically ensure that none of the members of the sample had any close patrilineal relatives in the sample. If we then wished to generalize about the degree of patrilineal affiliation in the population at large from the incidence of patrikin in the sample, the results would be a complete distortion of the true situation.

Informant self-selection out of the sample is a nonrandom influence in all social research (see Rosenthal & Rosnow 1975). Some people refuse to be observed or interviewed, as is their right. Aside from making an effort to draw random samples and to encourage every member of the community to participate, there is little to be done about this problem. All subjects of anthropological research must be volunteers informed of the purposes of the research and of the probable effects of the research on their lives—anything else is ethically unacceptable.

Incidentally, when samples are drawn at random it is often difficult for community members to understand why they were chosen or not chosen; the natural tendency is to imagine that one is chosen for a reason. Speculation about the reasons can lead to suspicion and hurt feelings. Saucier (1974) solved this problem by asking all members of a village in Rwanda to meet together in a central location to draw lots from an urn; their lots determined their inclusion in the sample in a way perfectly obvious to them all.

At times, a *stratified* sample may also be justified. In a stratified sample, relevant subgroups of the population are identified and random samples of specified sizes are drawn from each; the purpose is to ensure that no group is underrepresented owing to a random fluke (such as the string of sevens seen above). For example, if we were doing research on concepts and treatments of disease in a community of 500 members only 25 of whom had special medical knowledge, random selection of a sample of 40 people for careful observation and interviewing might result in the total exclusion of the 25 people with specialized knowledge. To avoid this, we would take random samples from each group (e.g., 30 nonspecialists and 10 specialists) in order to be sure to include enough specialists. Nonspecialists still must be included, of course, because unique characteristics of the specialists can only be identified against the background of nonspecialists.

Since many statistics courses do not devote sufficient time to sampling problems, readers may wish to consult Kish (1965) or Blalock (1972:509–30) for detailed discussions of sampling problems and methods.

Statistics in cultural research. Since so much of anthropological description concerns what is shared, or "typical," about behavior and beliefs in a community, correct procedures of statistical inference are necessary if limited observations and interviews are to be taken as applying to a whole community. In the past, we have had to take the representativeness of the data in ethnographic accounts on faith; we should do better in the future.

We have seen that the powers of statistics are dependent on the research methods employed: the higher the level of quantification, the more precisely a statistical test can determine whether an observed distribution is likely to be true for the population as a whole. Furthermore, the whole process of statistical inference only works on the assumption that the sample is randomly selected. Departures from randomness do occur, but only the refusal of an informant to participate in the sample is genuinely unavoidable. Haphazard samples are unacceptable because they leave too much room for unexamined biases to enter, and because in most cases a random sample could be selected just as easily.

Perhaps we should end on a note of caution against overdependence on statistics: a single, "well-informed" informant is often the only available or efficient source of certain kinds of information, and the development of personal ties is of the greatest importance in successful fieldwork. There is also a tendency to use a statistical test as a mechanical substitute for reasoned judgment about the "significance" of a finding. Sometimes numerical differences between two groups are so small that even if they are statistically significant it is difficult to see what their theoretical significance might be. Similarly, numerical differences can often speak for themselves without statistical significance values attached. Statistical tests add rigor to judgment and focus attention on all-important sampling problems, but the final responsibility for deciding what to believe rests with the researcher, not with automatic procedures.

The History of Quantitative Approaches in Cultural Anthropology

Science and humanism in cultural anthropology. In Chapter 1 we saw the usefulness of scientific method in achieving anthropological goals. As cultural anthropologists, we have a responsibility to confront our own ethnocentrism, and that of other members of our society, with empirically tested cross-cultural theories of human behavior and thought, if the categories of social scientific thought are not to remain culture-bound. Participant observation for long periods in culturally unfamiliar settings is the primary means for combating ethnocentrism, but it does not alone ensure that erroneous expectations will be discovered and corrected. A scientific attitude requires above all that prior expectations, and the research operations used to test them, be explicit and public; this often leads to analyses phrased in the "dehumanized" language of numbers and algebraic expressions.

The terms "science" and "humanism" stand for two intellectual camps whose centers are so far apart that C. P. Snow was moved, in a classic argument, to refer to them as "the two cultures" (Snow 1959). Snow differentiated humanists and scientists not only according to their techniques of analysis, but also according to some of their most profound predispositions. For example, he found that an optimistic and "progressive" outlook characterized scientists whereas a pessimistic and "conservative" outlook characterized humanists.

Because the differences between the two groups are deep and pervasive, they fail to communicate effectively, regarding one another across a no-man's-land of misapprehension and suspicion. Though we might dispute the details, Snow's distinction is real and the points of contact between the two groups are emotionally charged and abrasive.

Scientists and humanists approach the understanding of specific events from opposite directions. For the scientist, events are defined by the measurement of a limited set of "relevant" variables of wide generality and comparability; for example, the variable "mass" may theoretically be measured for any manifestation of matter, and provides one general basis for the comparison of one event with another. Any given event is understood in relation to other events, as one instance of the operation of principles (laws) that apply to all events in the same domain.

Humanistic understanding concentrates on the specific event itself, taking into account as many of its different aspects as possible in the effort to achieve a rich, holistic appreciation of it. For example, the concept of the Renaissance in Florence has this particularistic, holistic character. Understanding of the event is achieved less through comparison with other events than through integration of its many aspects into an intuitively felt whole.

Any event—an automobile accident, for example—may be viewed in these two differing ways. From a scientific perspective, a given automobile accident is immediately related to a large number of automobile accidents by measuring the "relevant" variables: time of day, weather conditions, age of driver, drunkenness. Explanation of the accident amounts to showing which attributes of the accident made it "likely" given our knowledge about the conditions under which accidents occur in general.

Inevitably, some accidents will occur when they are not expected. A scientific analysis will classify such cases as "exceptions" of the sort expected in any statistical distribution. It is recognized that many factors regarded as "contingent" because they are poorly understood or are believed to influence very few accidents have been left out of the scientist's analysis. Such contingent factors may take on commanding significance in a humanist analysis of the same event. This will be especially true for aspects of the accident that individuals involved in it *feel* are important. The driver's own impatience, another driver's impoliteness, an unexpected reflection of light may all become part of understanding of the event, even though they may enter into no general scientific theory of traffic accidents. Even "exceptional" cases can be understood in terms of contingencies such as these.

At the core of the humanist critique of science is the notion that human individuality tends to be obscured in ordinary scientific practice. An individual comes to be defined by measures on a variable set (age, sex, occupation), and is understood as following a trajectory determined by the play of natural laws. By contrast, individual creativity and purpose are central to the humanist perspective. "Here there emerges, as the *fundamental feature of all human existence*, the fact that man is not lost within the welter of his external impressions, that he learns to control this sea of impressions by giving it *ordered form*, which, as such, stems in the final analysis from himself, from his own thinking, feeling, and willing" (Cassirer 1961:21–22; emphasis in original). The point comes at which scientific method cannot deal with such "transcendental" concepts as "soul" or "self" without voiding them of substance (Stent 1975). Humanism is thus a necessary complement to science in cultural anthropology.

The aspect of science that has drawn the heaviest humanist fire is the perspective known as "mechanistic materialism," which "presupposes the ultimate fact of an irreducible brute matter, or material, spread throughout space in a flux of configuration. In itself such a material is senseless, valueless, purposeless. It just does what it does do, following a fixed routine imposed by external relations which do not spring from the nature of its being" (Whitehead 1925:17). Creativity and meaning appear as secondary aspects of the universe, epiphenomenal outcomes of natural law operating on evolving matter. Natural processes are assumed to be as predictable as the workings of a piece of machinery, as in the philosophy of Laplace.

The very precision of Newton's laws led, . . . to new problems of a philosophical order. For, as these laws were found to be verified in wider and wider domains, the idea tended to grow that they have a *universal* validity. Laplace, during the eighteenth century, was one of the first scientists to draw the full logical consequences of such an assumption. Laplace supposed that the *entire universe* consisted of nothing but bodies undergoing motions through space, motions which obeyed Newton's laws. While the forces acting between these bodies were not yet completely and accurately known in all cases, he also supposed that eventually these forces could be known with the aid of suitable experiments. This meant that once the positions and velocities of all the bodies were given at any instant of time, the future behavior of everything in the whole universe would be determined for all time. (Bohm 1957:36).

Though some individual scientists probably hold views that are in practice indistinguishable from this outmoded philosophy, in fairness to modern science it must be said that philosophers of science have led the way in criticizing mechanistic materialism. The Laplacian view of nature as composed of discrete parts and their determinate relations is now criticized because it neglects the influence of the whole on the parts. The *organization* (or environment) in which entities occur is no less fundamental than the entities themselves, and this becomes more apparent the more we deal with entities that may be said to have *minds* (see Whitehead 1925:79). The future behavior of matter is not mechanically predictable because it may change in new, as yet unanticipated, environments. Recognition of this "qualitative infinity of nature" (Bohm 1957:137–40) has provided science with an escape valve for the pressure to acknowledge creative elements in nature, and particularly in human behavior.

In this light the goals of science, especially the human sciences, appear a bit more modest than they did before. In place of the (unprovable) assumption that all human thought and activity can be explained with reference to natural laws, we say that scientific method offers a way to discover patterns in human behavior that will be helpful in predicting aspects of the world. Creativity and a residue of unpredictability are taken for granted.

There are dangers, especially for the anthropologist, in either the scientific or the humanist position. Rapoport (1968:xxii) has said of scientists and humanists: "The former stand in danger of trivializing the study of man and, what is often worse, of placing their expertise at the service of groups having power to manipulate man for their own purposes. The latter stand in danger of obscuring the study of man in free-wheeling speculations without sufficient anchorage in facts or testable hypotheses." If it is our judgment to emphasize science over humanism, or vice versa, that is a proper exercise of responsibility: "We do not want ethnologists so balanced that they have no humanity. We want a balanced profession, a varied lot of anthropologists" (Redfield 1953:157). We should only recognize what a monumental waste of energy it is to deny acrimoniously the validity of approaches selecting a different balance from our own.

Quantitative approaches in early cultural anthropology. The traditional anthropological report, or ethnography, attempts to mediate the contradictory tendencies of humanism and science in anthropology. Ethnographers aim for objective, "factual," comprehensive accounts of cultural behavior that simultaneously will be holistic descriptions of particular cultural units *and* sources of data for comparison with other cultural units. Ethnographies in the past were, for reasons not entirely obvious, decidedly nonquantitative in their presentation of data (Firth's *Malay Fisherman* [1946] is a striking exception). This does not appear to be the result of any simple prejudice against counting cases; judging from the numerical tables that occur sporadically in older monographs, it would seem that anthropologists often counted the things that interested them in the field. But their results were generally published with a minimum of numbers.

Two reasons can be given for this. First, ethnographers were strongly influenced by the belief that descriptions of cultural behavior could be given without an explicit theoretical perspective. This meant there were no priorities concerning which data most urgently needed quantitative measurements and tabular description. We can see this reflected in the haphazard occurrence of quantitative tables in ethnographies: one author quantifies labor put into cash-crop production but neglects the output data; another does the reverse; and still a third ignores both input and output but provides a table of local market prices. Approaching an ethnography for the first time, it is impossible to predict which tables will be present and which lacking.

Second, before digital computers became widely available, the usefulness of spending long, tedious hours compiling numerical descriptions by hand was not very clear. The main goal of most ethnographers was a general-purpose, holistic description of a cultural unit that was probably about to disappear forever. Furthermore, the multivariate statistical procedures most suited to describing functional, systematic relations among a set of variables either had not been developed or were too time-consuming to attract researchers, whose colleagues were in any case far from insisting on quantitative demonstrations.

Looking back, it is hard not to sympathize with the dilemma earlier ethnographers faced between comprehensiveness and quantification; we still face it today. Nonetheless, we need to be aware of the limitations of traditional ethnographic reporting. Where the conclusions of these ethnographers were not demonstrated with quantitative data, it is legitimate to ask, "just how were field data processed into published descriptions?" The answer is, "in the tutored mind of the anthropologist." Given enough "eyes open" research, with notes as *aides-mémoire*, and a lengthy period of cogitation and collegial discussion, one produced a description. Although some numerical data might be summed up along the way, the route from direct observation to final ethnography was hidden from view in mental processes of pattern-seeking and selective forgetting.

The reluctance of anthropologists to agree on standards for ethnographic reporting has taken a great toll at the level of cross-cultural theory. Since single ethnographies are strong on some points and weak on others, comparative theorists have had their troubles compounded by having to accept, in order to compare at all, the lowest level of measurement found in a given group of "acceptable" reports. It is always possible to come down a level of measurement, but it is almost never possible to go up (without new data). From the beginning, cross-cultural comparisons have entailed severe reduction in information content, and even then considerable guesswork has been required to bring many ethnographic reports up to the low cross-cultural measurement levels.

Curiously, cross-cultural research (based on the published research of others rather than on ethnographic analysis of one's own data) has attracted the most quantitative anthropologists. Despite weaknesses in the data, some valuable and influential cross-cultural analyses have been written (Naroll 1970). To a considerable degree, however, cultural anthropology is judged by the success of its cross-cultural theories, and it is unlikely that future improvements will be purely theoretical, without newer data in more useful forms.

Cross-cultural research has long been associated with scientific goals and procedures. Lewis Morgan and Edward Tylor, for example, were distinguished from the majority of their nineteenth century contemporaries primarily by their strong commitment to basing conclusions on many carefully weighed descriptions of separate societies. Tylor, especially, was prone to support his search for cultural patterns with numerical data (see Tylor 1889).

A surprisingly advanced study of cross-cultural patterns was reported in 1915 by Hobhouse, Wheeler, and Ginsberg in their book *The Material Culture and Social Institutions of the Simpler Peoples*. Taking as their primary variable "the advance in man's control over nature," they ranked "tribes" along a developmental progression from "lower hunters" to "Stage III Agriculture" and sought correlations of this prime variable with other variables. For example, Figure 3.1 shows one such correlation: the expected transformation of "justice" from the private sphere at the lower stages of the progression to the public sphere at the upper stages.

Hobhouse, Wheeler, and Ginsberg were well aware of the limitations in their data. Their observers, usually traders and public officials, were untrained; the less contacted societies were underrepresented in their sample; and their basic unit of comparison, the "tribe," had no clear meaning. The first of these limitations was the most serious: if original observers were untrained, then on what basis could it be maintained that concepts such as "public justice"

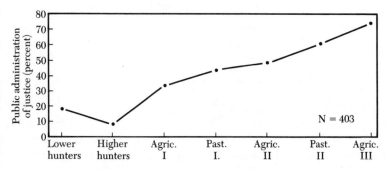

Fig. 3.1. The correlation between progress in man's control over nature and the development of public justice. The plotting points represent the percentage of societies (N = 403) at each stage for which justice is administered by a public institution. Source: Hobhouse, Wheeler, & Ginsberg 1915:73–74.

referred to the same thing in different societies? Largely because of this fundamental weakness in the data, Boas led a movement away from cross-cultural generalization, arguing that it was premature until more intensive field studies by trained anthropologists could be undertaken. The lasting importance of this phase of Boas's influence lies in his emphasis on the fact that the very social systems we want to theorize about are disappearing while we argue over inadequate data. Unfortunately, though Boas initially hoped research would result in the generation of better cross-cultural theories, his concern with theory receded as the actual collection of data got under way (Eggan 1961:115).

An instructive outgrowth of the atheoretical nature of the Boasian program was Kroeber's "Culture Element Survey." In Kroeber's view, cultural units could be analyzed into component elements, or traits. Traits were generally specific, as illustrated by the following list from Driver and Coffin (1975:67–72), selected with a table of random numbers from a recently modified list of 392 traits applicable to North American Indian cultures.

Trait number	Trait
40	Dogs used in hunting
287	Semitailored hide, nineteenth-century westward expansion
56	Composite fishhooks
75	Wooden hoe blades
85	Burning used for better wild crop

Trait number	Trait
4	"Buffalo" subsistence area
338	Pottery oil lamps
299	Soft-sole moccasins
385	Hawaiian sister and female cousin term of reference

A given cultural unit was described by specifying whether each trait was present or absent (nominal level of measurement). Kroeber assumed that traits were generated in centers of creativity and were then carried away, like pollen; like pollen, too, the farther one went from the generative center, the less frequent the trait. Cultures could be described as more or less similar according to the number of traits they possessed in common.

Kroeber began to devise his trait lists in order to describe similarities and differences among North American Indian groups, but the paucity of data that could be compared led him to initiate new fieldwork. "The prime purpose of the Survey was to insure greater comparability of cultural information than existed in the published work of ethnographers. It was not so much a case of previous field ethnographers having been in conflict, as of their not meeting in their work, and not getting around to many smaller groups. They started with diverse interests, went off in different directions, rarely made clear whether traits not mentioned were actually absent from the culture or had not been inquired into, and so on" (Kroeber 1952:263). Over a period of years, thirteen different fieldworkers were involved in the Culture Element Survey. Using the common framework of the trait lists, they produced data of greatly increased comparability (Driver 1962:18).

To Kroeber's disappointment, however, the results of the Culture Element Survey were largely ignored by his contemporaries. Kroeber believed that this indifference resulted from his colleagues' being "averse to quantitative expression, averse to questionnaires, . . . averse to presence and absence data, averse to single informants per tribe or band, even when the number of bands [ran] into the hundreds" (Kroeber 1952:263). Aversion to quantification per se can hardly have been a major factor, since presence and absence data are the lowest level of measurement, and the "quantitative expression" Kroeber refers to is the sums of columns of presence or absence measures. A more likely explanation is that Kroeber's approach was basically nonsystemic at a time when the feeling was growing among anthropologists that cultures are "patterned" or functionally integrated wholes. Kroeber assumed that culture could be adequately described as the addition of discrete elements, each of which could apparently exist with or without any of the others. His approach, with its echoes of Laplace's mechanistic philosophy, thus stood in opposition to the holistic approaches of Tylor and of Hobhouse, Wheeler, and Ginsberg—though all worked at the nominal level of measurement.

For Kroeber, traits might be found together only if they were *genetically* related by having spread from a place of common origin. His predecessors, however, had assumed that cultural characteristics would have *functional* relations so that the existence of one would simultaneously require and reinforce the existence of others. The extensive research problems posed by this difference between "functionalist" and "diffusionist" approaches have been examined under the name of "Galton's problem" (see Pelto 1970:296–99; Naroll 1973).

Kroeber's trait lists treated each separate trait as equal to each of the others, drawing special attention to none. Functionalist theories of sociocultural systems, however, develop expectations regarding which traits will be found together with which others. Traits that do not appear to be functionally related to others come in time to be dropped from consideration. The problem is a little like that facing modern radio astronomy: not exactly sure yet what to listen for, radio astronomers direct their antennas at a large number of stellar objects and scan a wide range of frequencies. As a result they pick up mostly noise, from which patterns are exceedingly difficult to discern. Kroeber's trait lists, lacking a theoretical position against which the traits might reveal patterns of relationships, suffer the same deficiency: too much "noise" is retained to permit the pursuit of orderly analyses.

A recent attempt by Driver and Coffin (1975) to find "functional" or "evolutionary" patterns in the data from the Cultural Element Survey exemplifies these problems. The authors, working with a set of traits (the "Driver-Massey sample") from the original trait list, used multivariate statistical techniques to seek clusters of variables that would reveal some of the patterns predicted by functional and evolutionary theory. Their overall results were negative: "Perhaps the most important finding is that most of the intertrait correlations cannot be explained or interpreted in functional or causal terms, but rather must be attributed to unknown causes, events, accidents, and agents of history" (Driver & Coffin 1973:3). The few clusters that were found did not make very much sense, aside from a tendency for clusters of traits to reflect broad environmental adjustments, and Driver and Coffin finally concluded that "Lowie's . . . famous phrase that culture is 'that planless hodgepodge, that thing of shreds and patches' is still good and applies to most of the relationships within the Driver-Massey sample" (p. 66).

To be sure, there appears to be much confusion in the data; but we need to consider the locus of the confusion. The ten traits listed earlier, selected at random to give a fair representation of the nature of the trait list, are themselves something of a hodgepodge, and any sample of the traits leaves a similar impression of numerous bits of information, mainly concerning material culture, that do not fit in any significant way into the current theories Driver and Coffin are rejecting.

For example, the first cluster emerging from the multivariate analysis contains the following seven traits (Driver & Coffin 1975:32):

Trait number	Trait
47	Only small hand nets for fishing
239	Rectangular, gabled house, thatched
188	Black drink
144	East houselike storage structure
103	S.E. acorn preparation process
342	Unpoisoned dart blowgun
161	Green corn ceremonies

The authors conclude that, aside from a possible relation between the house type and the storage structure, "all other traits in Cluster one may be said to be related to each other in a non–functional-causal manner. . . . The dominant explanation of Cluster one may be phrased as unknown geographical and historical factors, not some internal cohesion that fits a functional, evolutionary, or cyclical developmental scheme" (p. 32).

But why would anyone have expected such traits to be related in the first place? Why were they selected for analysis? Above all, why were the theoretically relevant variables not included? For example, current evolutionary theories generally relate such variables as community size, intensity of food production, complexity of social order, and technological achievements. In the Driver-Massey sample of traits, none of these variables appears. In what sense has evolutionary theory, or any other theoretical perspective, been tested? Orderly analyses do not simply "fall out" from masses of data; the order must begin with the research design, wherein a restricted set of variables is selected with a clear purpose. If there is no particular expectation that the variables will correlate, then they probably will not. The outcome of the analysis by Driver and Coffin should be seen as a confirmation of this principle, and not as the criticism of functional-causal theory it claims to be.

The set of cross-cultural data most analysts have relied on has been the almost single-handed responsibility of George Peter Murdock. Murdock began compiling a "cross-cultural survey" in the 1930's whose purpose was to make the widely scattered ethnographic record conveniently accessible to scholars, particularly those from other fields such as psychology and sociology (Murdock 1940). He took complete textual descriptions, translated them into English when necessary, and cross-filed them according to geographical and topical headings. Scholars interested in a particular subject could look in the files to see what ethnographic data existed for many different societies. The result was not a trait list but rather a cross-referencing system in which whole descriptive passages were retained intact.

From this evolved the idea that the tedious job of comparing large numbers of different societies would be made simple if the information in the files could be expressed in alphabetical and numerical codes suitable for computer processing. The result of years of coding, over 90 percent of which was done by Murdock himself, was the *Ethnographic Atlas* (Murdock 1967). In it were listed 862 societies for which data were regarded as adequate, along with coded values on each society for approximately 50 variables ranging from subsistence economy to marriage, community organization, and aspects of religious belief and practice. Anthropological response to Murdock's efforts was substantial; Naroll's (1970) survey of cross-cultural research found over 150 studies, most of which appear to have used some version of the *Ethnographic Atlas*.

The codes Murdock used are more closely related to anthropological theory than were Kroeber's traits. In seeking evidence of cultural evolution, for example, users of the *Ethnographic Atlas* find that Murdock's codes specify the degree to which the subsistence economy depends on agriculture as compared to gathering, hunting, fishing, and animal husbandry; give mean community sizes, along with indications of degree of nucleation of settlements; and give information on social complexity and technological capabilities. Naroll shows that a number of specific cultural-evolutionary hypotheses have been supported by cross-cultural data (Naroll 1970:1242–49).

Two related problems continue to vitiate the potential of the *Ethnographic Atlas*. First, the level of measurement represented by the codes is very low. Whole social systems become characterized by single typological designations such as "patrilineal exogamy" or "bilateral descent." The codes refer to practices presumed to be "prevalent" in the society, which weakens the precision of theoretical propositions that might be tested using the codes. And second, even where the codes are numerically precise (e.g., "dependence on hunting is 16–25 percent"), there is real doubt about the reliability of the data. Most ethnographic reports, as we have noted, do not specify community patterns with numerical precision. Murdock has had to infer the numbers from verbal descriptions, which often amounts to an artificial and perhaps unwarranted elevation of the level of measurement.

It is an odd footnote to the history of quantitative cross-cultural research that two great anthropologists, Driver and Murdock, whose long dedication to scientific principles has had important and beneficial influence on cultural anthropology, on reaching the status of respected elders have both expressed pessimism and even disillusionment about the relationship between anthropological theory and anthropological data. Murdock, in his 1971 Huxley Memorial Lecture, criticized the bulk of anthropological theory for its lack of operational definitions: "I therefore feel no hesitation in rejecting the validity and utility of the entire body of anthropological theory, including the bulk of my own work, which derives from the reified concepts of either culture or social system, and in consigning it to the realm of mythology rather than science" (Murdock 1972:20). Coupled with Driver's conclusion that culture really *is* a thing of shreds and patches, we are left with the impression that attempting to bring "scientific rigor" into anthropology has hardly been worth the effort.

On balance, however, it is fair to say that both Driver and Murdock are underplaying the amount of advance in the reliability of cross-cultural knowledge over the last generation. Reviews of cross-cultural findings, such as Textor 1967 and Naroll 1970, are much more constructive in this regard. What has happened, in fact, is that the work of Murdock and Driver and others like them has prepared the way for what Naroll (1970:1230–31) has called a new "generation" of cross-cultural research employing conceptual frameworks that require different codes and higher levels of measurement than those achieved before. New field research, among culturally distinctive peoples, is the source from which the new cross-cultural data will have to come.

In tacit recognition of this fact, a new style of ethnography has been emerging that emphasizes problem-oriented descriptions of more limited focus than that characteristic of the old holistic ethnographies. This new focus identifies certain variables as central and others as peripheral, with two results: first, the quality of data on the central variables is improving; but, second, the quality of data on peripheral variables (which might be of central concern in other analyses) is no better than before, and may even be declining. The dilemma between holism and detailed measurement which formerly was resolved in favor of holism is now being resolved in favor of detail. A balance between the extremes can be struck by involving several ethnographers in the study of a single society, as in the Chiapas Project (see Vogt 1969). But individual fieldworkers will have to continue to take the responsibility both for making broad data-gathering efforts and for adopting the most precise methods of measurement possible if cross-cultural theory is to make further strides.

CHAPTER FOUR

The Input-Output Orientation

Ɪɴ Cʜᴀᴘᴛᴇʀ 2 the notion of an orientation was discussed and the five orientations that make up what I call the cultural-ecological macro-orientation were briefly listed. In this chapter and the four that follow I take up each of the five orientations I have identified in turn, discussing them in detail and giving examples of productive quantitative research carried out with them.

I begin in this chapter with the input-output orientation, which is the starting point for all ecological research in cultural anthropology. Research using an ecological approach is common in a number of scientific disciplines besides anthropology. This general ecological orientation emphasizes two points: first, following evolutionary theory, that biological organisms are striving to meet those "basic needs" essential to their survival and reproduction; and second, that any organism we choose to study (the "organism of focus") is part of an encompassing environmental system of other organisms and nonliving resources that the organism of focus adapts to and also changes with its behavior.

Input-output analysis in ecological research is a way of describing environments of interacting elements (organisms and resources). We label such complex environments *ecosystems*. The commonest form of input-output analysis describes an ecosystem as a flow of energy between elements (Odum 1971). For example, in a simple model of a forest ecosystem, we may isolate four elements: plants, microorganisms, nutrients, and the sun. Plants use the sun's energy to assimilate nutrients (water, minerals) for growth and reproduction; as leaves fall and plants die, microorganisms decompose them, deriving energy in the process. The decomposed matter then becomes available for further plant nutrition. Since all organisms require energy in order to feed and reproduce, the flow of energy in an ecosystem is a basic, quantifiable measure of interactions within it.

The ecosystems we analyze are usually more complex than this forest of four elements described solely in terms of energy flows. One way to increase the complexity of the system is simply to include a larger number of elements: instead of "plants," we may distinguish trees, vines, epiphytes, etc. Interactions between elements can still be described as energy flows, though summarizing them mathematically, for example in a small number of algebraic equations, becomes more difficult the larger the number of elements in the ecosystem. A second way is to consider what in addition to energy is being exchanged in the ecosystem. Bees obtain food energy from the nectar of plants, and in turn help pollinate them. Although this, too, involves energy flow, the pollen a bee carries from one plant to another is not merely a packet of energy— indeed, food energy is an irrelevant aspect of the pollen compared to the genetic information it carries in the reproductive process. Similarly, the "dance" bees do in order to inform other bees of the location of nectar, though it costs energy to perform, provides no energy directly in return, but rather information that is then used to obtain food. These interactions cannot be fully described in energy terms, since something besides energy is being exchanged between organisms.

This second kind of ecosystem complexity makes quantitative analysis difficult, for the precision the energy measure provides is difficult to attain in discussions of flows that cannot be described in energy terms. In biology, this difficulty is sometimes resolved by distinguishing between "ecology"—the study of energy flows and the development of mathematical models of ecosystems—and "natural history"—a more holistic approach that allows many "measures" of interaction (e.g., vocalization, display, parental care), but that provides little opportunity for quantification or mathematical modeling.

Input-output analysis is also used in economics (see Leontieff 1966; Richardson 1972), where a similar measurement problem arises. Economists analyze an economy into sectors, such as the agricultural, manufacturing, and household sectors. But sectors produce different commodities for exchange; hence it is difficult to say anything very precise about an economy in which foods, manufactures, and household labor *as such* are exchanged because, like apples and oranges, these items are not comparable. The economist resolves this problem by expressing all items in terms of cash value and then analyzing the economy as flows of cash between sectors (Leontieff 1966:136), dropping along the way all aspects of the exchange that cannot be described in cash terms.

When Steward (1955) defined the cultural core of a society in terms of "subsistence activities" and "economic arrangements" (see Chapter 2), he was implicitly starting with a biological sense of what "basic needs" are. Avoiding biological reductionism, however, Steward carefully extended the concept of a cultural core to include those behaviors—whether culturally transmitted technologies or religious beliefs such as food taboos—whose connection to subsistence activities could be empirically demonstrated. Earlier, Malinowski (1941, 1945), who more than any other anthropologist attempted to develop a theory of basic needs, had also argued that biological reductionism did not follow from a biological beginning. He wrote, "[we] started from the axiom that culture is an instrumental reality, an apparatus for the satisfaction of fundamental needs, that is, organic survival, environmental adaptation, and continuity in the biological sense. To this we have added the empirical corollary that, *under conditions of culture, the satisfaction of organic needs is achieved in an indirect, roundabout manner*. Man uses tools. . . . He does this not alone but organized into groups. Organization means the tradition of skills, of knowledge, and of values" (Malinowski 1945:44; emphasis added).

Now it is well that we stress how anthropology inevitably draws us outward to include social organization and values in the concept "subsistence," but the difficulty is to know where to stop. For it has been repeatedly found that any human act, belief, or artifact can be described as "ecological" because it always relates to some "environment" (context) and is somehow functionally part of community *survival* (i.e., existence; see Anderson 1973:182). We seem to be confronting again the problem of weak functionalism discussed in Chapter 2.

Partly in response to this problem, it has been argued that an ecological perspective in anthropology should be "noncultural" (Vayda & Rappaport 1968:492–93), that is, should remain within a biological framework emphasizing what humans share with all living organisms—needs for food, shelter, defense, and reproduction. Indeed, a legitimate starting point in any sociocultural research is to ask how human behavior succeeds or fails in meeting biological needs. But the limits of a biological approach are soon reached, if for no other reason than that biologists do not have suitable methods for studying many phenomena, including norms and values, that we cannot avoid when dealing with human subsistence systems. A further limitation on noncultural ecology is that the emphasis on culture "in" nature obscures the ways in which culture is "opposed to" nature (R. Murphy 1970:168). This latter notion is one that the accelerating human destruction of complex biological ecosystems forces on us.

Measuring Input and Output

The problem of deciding what aspects of a cultural system are to be included in an input-output analysis can be handled at least partially at a methodological level. We may decide to study only those aspects that can be demonstrated to have a relation to subsistence, where by "demonstrated" we mean with reference to an acceptable body of data. Why this is only a partial solution can be seen more clearly if we take some examples. To begin with a relatively straightforward one, we review Cancian's careful analysis of corn farming in Zinacantan, a community in Chiapas, Mexico (Frank

Cancian 1972). Input-output analysis lends itself to the comparison of alternative production strategies according to "profitability" or "efficiency"; Cancian's goal was to discover whether peasant farmers would be responsive to more "profitable" alternatives, as "rational" decision-makers in the Western economic sense. The question is of considerable interest to economic anthropologists in particular, and to all who want to understand the circumstances influencing agricultural change and increased world food production.

Cancian's input data were cash values for the costs of production, including the rental cost of the land and expenditures on hired labor, seed, and transportation. Output data were the cash values of the corn produced. The net return to the farmer could be calculated by subtracting the input costs from the output value for a specified unit of land. Differences in farming strategy led to differences in net return, so that each strategy open to a farmer could be characterized by a unique "expected net return."

Cancian described differences in farming strategy along two main dimensions—the *scale* of production, and its *location*. The scale of production varied from as little as one *almud* (15 liters) of corn seeded to as many as eight *almudes*; the larger the scale of the operation, the greater the amount of land the farmer would have to rent and the greater the number of laborers he would have to hire. The location of production varied from fields in the immediate vicinity of Zinacantan to locations at such a great distance that farming was impossible without truck transportation. Cancian's conclusion from the input-output analysis was "that farmers with larger operations make more profit, and that farmers in the more distant zones make more profit" (pp. 105–6). This is evident from Table 4.1.

According to Table 4.1, "rational" farmers should show a preference for agricultural strategies that are large in scale and distant from Zinacantan, for these offer the highest net returns. Comparison of the expectations founded on this table with the actual farming behavior of Zinacantecos is discussed with the maximization orientation in Chapter 7. Here I want to stress that the analysis is especially effective because all inputs and outputs could be phrased in cash terms. If zone 9 produced items different from those zone 2

TABLE 4.1

Expected Net Returns to Zinacanteco Farmers
Under Normal Conditions, in Pesos

Amount of corn seeded	Distance from Zinacantan			
	zone 1	zone 2	zone 6	zone 9
1 *almud*	428	571	691	714
2 *almudes*	637	834	1,268	1,385
4 *almudes*	638	988	1,950	2,217
6 *almudes*	608	1,154	2,647	3,015

SOURCE: Frank Cancian 1972: 101.

NOTE: The higher the zone number, the greater the distance from Zina-cantan.

produced, and if the two could not be compared using cash value, then Table 4.1 could not have been constructed. On the other hand, Cancian's decision to quantify with cash values involved a certain sacrifice in cross-cultural comparability. First, not all the relevant inputs were included: Cancian found he could not count a farmer's own time in field labor and management as "input" because the labor was not priced and because intangibles such as ability and diligence entered in complex ways. This means that comparisons of Zinacanteco food-production strategies with those of other communities can only be made if in other studies the farmer's own labor is also excluded. Second, Zinacantan cannot be compared with production systems where cash value cannot be measured, as in many tribal economies where markets are of small importance. Neither of these limitations detracts very much from the value of Cancian's data, but I mention them as illustrations of the unavoidable fact that the benefits of any method of quantifying input and output are always accompanied by costs, and that such costs should be acknowledged and weighed against the benefits.

A way around the second limitation (cash as a measure) is to use energy, since even people who lack money and markets still spend energy getting food and other subsistence needs. A solution to the first limitation (how to include all the relevant inputs and outputs) is more difficult to find, as the next example shows.

In Chapter 2 we raised the issue of the role of population growth and technological efficiency in cultural evolution. Proponents of each side of the controversy assume that the "efficiency" of a production system can be measured and compared with that of other systems. Elsewhere I have attempted to analyze the efficiency of food-producing techniques among tropical forest horticulturalists of the Peruvian Amazon (A. Johnson 1977). In a community of Machiguenga (Arawakan) Indians, using techniques to be discussed below, I estimated the energetic efficiency, defined as the calories of food-energy output per calorie of labor-energy input, of each of four food-producing strategies: gathering wild forest foods, riverine fishing, poultry raising, and horticulture. The analysis showed that the production of wild forest foods, such as game meat, grubs, fruits, and nuts, produced only about 0.8 calories of food value for each calorie of work energy expended; that is, the efficiency of getting forest foods was so low it did not even "pay" for itself in calories. The efficiencies of the other techniques were fishing, 2.0; poultry raising, 9.3; and horticulture (maize growing), 45.4. Clearly, maize produced in gardens was the most efficient source of food energy.

These data are especially interesting because evidence indicates that the Machiguenga are shifting their food production system from hunting, fishing, and gathering to poultry raising and gardening. This would seem to be a clear empirical case of technological change in the direction of increased energy efficiency. Because of problems that arose in the analysis, however, I am not sure this simple interpretation really accounts for what is happening.

For example, it is not always clear which human efforts are to be called labor inputs. Some inputs are unambiguous, such as those taking place directly at the site of food production (e.g., stalking game, planting maize), but others are not. Machiguenga men occasionally worked (expended energy) for coffee growers in the contact zone in exchange for a steel axe, which was used in turn as an input to clear new gardens (clearly a subsistence input), to cut wood for arrowheads (an input, but somewhat indirectly), and to shape the outline of a drum for beer parties (not obviously a subsistence input). The axe had many other uses as well.

The main problem is to find an operationally clear yet theoretically satisfying basis on which to distinguish input effort from other kinds of effort. Even the manufacture of a drum can be related to food production by some such logic as this: the drum heightens the pleasure associated with a social event (a beer party), which in turn increases the solidarity of the participants, which in turn increases their ability to cooperate in subsistence activities. A fully explicit theory of "basic needs" would help us here by allowing us to decide whether the drum is close enough to the subsistence process to be included in our calculations. Working with the bits and pieces of such a theory that were available, I finally decided on the methodological solution of counting only those efforts put in at the site of food production; this effectively cut out drum production, but it also cut out labor expended at home in making bows and arrows, fishing nets, and harvesting bags. This indeterminacy regarding inputs makes comparison of different food-producing strategies less simple a matter than it seemed at first.

In this example, the problems raised in measuring output are perhaps even more serious than those concerning input. If wild foods are such an inefficient source of energy, why do the Machiguenga in fact spend over 15 percent of their daylight time getting them? The answer is that forests and rivers provide more than food energy to the Machiguenga. Outputs of these nondomesticated resources include animal protein, fruits, nuts, vegetables, fibers, and hardwoods. Travel to hunting and fishing spots brings people into contact with the changing rivers and forests, so that unknown resources can be discovered and information about them shared throughout the region by gossip. Comparing the caloric efficiency of wild and domestic food sources, therefore, tells us little about Machiguenga subsistence activities, because the latter are aimed at providing much more than mere calories. Since these other outputs in many cases are closely related to basic needs of the people, they should be as carefully described as the energy outputs, and need to be included in any analysis.

In sum, input and output are not obvious matters, but rather can only be investigated with reference to a definition of basic needs.

Human effort has consequences, only some of which can be shown, at least at present, to fill basic needs; these we call outputs. Inputs, by implication, are the antecedents—like labor, resources, and skill—that can be shown to be necessary to produce the outputs. We anthropologists are far from agreeing on what the basic needs of mankind are and on how to demonstrate the necessary connections for defining inputs and outputs rigorously and in a cross-cultural framework. Thus concepts like efficiency, which depend on measures of input and output, must be used cautiously. When identifying certain activities and products as inputs or outputs, we should make public the criteria of selection by explicitly stating what we have taken as our set of basic needs.

Population, Work, and Health

In the remainder of this chapter I discuss a number of methods in input-output research. Many are commonplace or are well described in other literature, and are mentioned only in passing; interested readers are referred to the original sources for more complete information. The methods are grouped for convenience into three roughly distinct categories: (1) *the population of humans*, particularly in relation to the other humans, other organisms, and material resources it encounters in meeting its basic needs; (2) *work*, or the nature of the effort expended by humans in meeting their basic needs; and (3) *health*, or the extent to which basic needs are in fact being met.

Population. Despite recent advances in demographic theory and knowledge, reliable data on non-Western populations are still very limited. This is especially true of historical data (McArthur 1970), but many anthropologists do not even report basic current population data, and others who do have not always been careful about quality. Yet patterns of production and exchange, and innumerable other features of community life, can only be understood in terms of the distribution of people according to age, sex, and modes of residence and settlement.

A short census is a good way to begin a field research project. It gives the researcher an opportunity to become acquainted with community members and the externals of daily life, and it gives the people a chance to meet and observe the researcher. At a minimum, a census should determine the sex, age, and place of residence of each member of the community, or of each person in a random sample of the community. In communities where birth records are not kept, determination of age becomes very difficult. For children, tooth emergence is a useful clue (see Weiner & Lourie 1969:17–23). Otherwise, birth order of siblings and reference to external events of known dates, such as floods or eclipses, can be used to increase the accuracy of age estimates (Howell 1976:230–34).

The matter of place of residence is more complex, since it is intimately linked with household composition and settlement patterns for the community as a whole. Hence it is of the utmost importance that the researcher specify precisely what he means by "place of residence." Is it the place where the informant habitually sleeps, or eats, or stores possessions? Is it perhaps a place that the informant merely claims to live in? Moreover, it is likely that some members of the community, especially those in their early teens, will shift their residence at least once during the course of the research; how we determine when such a shift occurs will depend on how we operationalize the term "residence" in our initial census. Once place of residence is determined for the members of the community or the sample, household composition can be established. In general, a household is a spatially discrete dwelling, but this term also needs operational specification because ambiguous households, such as multifamily dwellings or dwellings for each spouse in polygamous societies, are often found. Relations among the various members of the household should also be specified (kin, servant, boarder, etc.).

With the results of the census, the researcher can prepare a map of the community's settlement pattern, showing residence locations relative to such resources as agricultural land, wells, stores, and roads. If settlement is influenced by seasonal migrations, this also should be reflected. Since people generally become fatigued after a half hour or so of census questions, it is advisable to administer short censuses rather than a single "big" one. In this context it may be noted that recensusing after a period of time lends a diachronic perspective generally lacking in anthropological reports (Hacken-berg 1973:290–91; Otterbein 1970).

The regulation of population numbers relative to environmental resources and technological capacities is a major concern of eco-logical anthropologists, and thus some evidence of reproductive practices should also be collected. The reproduction histories of a representative sample of women should include age of menarche, estimated dates of all known conceptions, the number and sexes of the births (live or not), the causes and ages of mortality of offspring, and the present whereabouts of living offspring. This can be tied to an inquiry about the deaths of adult relatives in an effort to estimate the life expectancies of community members and to develop in-formation concerning the most common causes of death. Howell (1976) and Chen and Murray (1976) provide good introductions to the problems encountered in demographic research; Bogue (1970) provides a "model interview" for fertility research; and Hackenberg (1973) discusses methods of genealogical research. Birth-control methods are widely practiced in human populations, and informa-tion on local methods and the frequency with which they are used is needed. Women are often reluctant to talk about such matters, however; male anthropologists working alone are especially liable to find data on reproduction difficult to collect from women. Baker and Sanders (1972), Nag (1974), and Marshall and Polgar (1976) should be consulted before the start of the research.

The environmental resources available to a population have much to do with its settlement pattern and mode of subsistence. In many cases, a good sense of the resource base may be obtained simply by observing the rewards to labor; for example, if we observe fisher-men in one location working twice as hard as those in another loca-tion for the same size catch, this is a good indirect indication of resource availability. Direct measurement of the abundance of fish requires the specialized skills of the field biologist, and would not normally be attempted by the anthropologist. Assuming that the people themselves are not overlooking useful resources, we can take their own patterns of resource use as an acceptable guide to the environment.

At times, however, this is not an appropriate assumption. In many societies, certain animals, fishing spots, or areas of land are taboo; the reasons given for not using them are spiritual, yet we would like to know if the taboos have ecological implications. For example, Ross has argued that comon game taboos in lowland South America protect easily endangered species from extinction (Ross 1977). In such cases the character of the resources themselves, as distinct from the human activities for exploiting them, becomes important. Since the resources of interest to any particular researcher can be as various as the environments people live in, we must be content here with a few rules of thumb. First, resources should be sampled frequently and randomly; a poor catch on one day does not mean the fishing spot is always poor. Second, we should quantify wherever possible; qualitative descriptions such as "rare" or "abundant" are not as helpful after the fieldwork is over as we might have hoped while still in the field. And, third, we have to learn to consult: agricultural economists and soil analysts have developed standards for collection of soil samples, marine ecologists have procedures for estimating fish populations, health experts know how to measure the incidence of parasite infections, and so on; whenever a research project leads into specialized areas such as these, interdisciplinary consultation becomes necessary.

Work. Once the population has been described, we face the question of how the population maintains itself. In the most general sense, "work" can be defined as the "human effort" expended in biological "maintenance." As we just saw, this raises practical difficulties in measurement because what kinds of human activities we say are necessary for maintenance hinges on what we call "basic needs." Finding a cross-culturally acceptable measure for human *effort*, however, is not so difficult. Either time or energy can be used as a common denominator measure of effort. Analysis of time expenditure is useful because it has a kind of innate cross-cultural comparability: there are only twenty-four hours in a day, and it makes sense to assume that people everywhere value their time and allocate it to different activities according to priorities that include biological needs. Though anthropologists have usually given ethnographic descriptions of how time is spent under such headings as "the daily round" or "the annual cycle," time allocation has not been described with the care it deserves.

Two kinds of description are needed. First, the amount of time spent in completing whole tasks or segments of activity can be measured. Examples of such tasks include bathing an infant, cooking a particular food, curing a patient, visiting a neighbor, or making a basket. In practice, not all activities occurring in a community can be timed this way since the anthropologist cannot be everywhere at once; so only those that are close to the central purposes of the research will generally be timed. For this reason, a second way of describing time expenditure is needed that will sample among individuals, places, and times of day to give a representative overview of patterns of time allocation in the community.

In the past, anthropologists studying time allocation have chosen a certain period, such as four days (Lewis 1951:63–71) or four weeks (R. Lee 1968:36–39), and have attempted to observe how a small number of individuals spent all their time during that period. For two reasons, however, their results cannot be considered representative: first, because a small number of days cannot represent the whole year, during which seasonal variations, chance illnesses, etc. will play a big role; and second, because a small number of individuals cannot represent a whole community, in which individual differences are frequently large. Simply lengthening the period of observation is not a practical solution, since the amount of field time spent in this way would rapidly reach a point of diminishing returns as the broad research goals came to be sacrificed to this one limited (though fundamental) set of data.

A convenient solution to this problem is to take a random sample of the activities of community members throughout a complete annual cycle. The ideal sampling procedure would be to select a community member at random and a time of day at random, and then to "spot-check" the person's activities at the selected moment. In actual fieldwork this can be wasteful, since it might involve walking frequently from house to house at scattered moments just to observe single individuals. Not too much randomness is lost if households

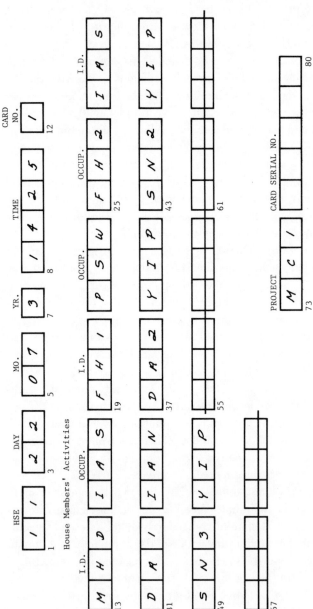

CODING SHEET – HOUSE MEMBERS PRESENT

Fig. 4.1. A sample coding sheet. The sheet is based on an 80-column IBM card, with each box representing one column on the card. With the identification and occupation codes spelled out, the sheet would read as follows: "Household 11, July 22, 1973, 2:25 P.M., card 1. Male househead, idle, awake, drinking beer; female head one, preparing food, straining manioc beer; female head two, idle, awake, drinking beer; daughter one, idle, awake, doing nothing; daughter two, youth, idle, playing; son two, youth, idle, playing; son three, youth, idle, playing; no other members present." At the base of the sheet are spaces for a three-entry project number and for consecutive numbering of all data sheets.

are selected rather than individuals, or even if clusters of households are observed at the same time on any particular day. The important point is that the time of observation and the households to be observed on any particular day should be randomly selected, so that the people will be unable to predict when a spot check will take place and adjust their behavior accordingly (e.g., prepare a meal, get dressed up, etc. for the anticipated visit).

This research technique was applied in a community of Machiguenga Indians in the Peruvian Amazon (A. Johnson 1975). Owing to the scattered settlement pattern, only thirteen households were accessible for regular observation, and these made up the sample. Hours between 6 A.M. and 7 P.M. were chosen at random, and activities of all sample members during these hours were recorded; difficult mountain terrain made visits at night impossible. Observations were made on an average of about once per week for an entire annual cycle, resulting in some 3,500 individual observations. The activities recorded were ideally those each person was engaged in just before he or she became aware of the observer (in practice, ideals such as this one are not always met, but they are nonetheless useful in maintaining the overall quality of the data). When members of households were absent, their activities as reported by their relatives, or by themselves later in the day, were recorded. Later, activities were coded on coding sheets (see Figure 4.1) and then were processed by computer. Data for the first several months of research were processed during the fieldwork and were available for guiding the later phases of the fieldwork. An example of the data is given in Table 4.2.

Random activity samples are not a substitute for intensive studies of production activities, but they are relatively easy to conduct and take comparatively little time. The data they provide in return are rich—covering not only input-output activities (however defined) but all ways of spending time, including religious practices, leisure time, and social interaction (an example of the latter will be given in the discussion of exchange relations in Chapter 5). For input-output purposes, they provide the basic framework within which descriptions of productive labor can be set. They can also provide checks on

TABLE 4.2
Mean Daylight Time Allocations of Machiguenga Adults

	Men (N = 15)		Women (N = 20)	
Activity	Time spent, in minutes	Percent of 24 hours	Time spent, in minutes	Percent of 24 hours
Eating	71	4.9%	55	3.8%
Food preparation	12	0.8	141	9.8
Child care	1	0.1	69	4.8
Manufacturing	81	5.6	124	8.6
Woodworking	52	3.6	5	0.3
Cotton cloth making	1	0.1	105	7.3
Other	28	1.9	14	1.0
Wild food getting	122	8.5	51	3.5
Collecting	22	1.5	19	1.3
Fishing	45	3.1	18	1.2
Hunting	45	3.1	0	0
Other	10	0.8	14	1.0
Garden labor	144	10.0	51	3.5
Clearing, burning, planting	29	2.0	1	0.1
Weeding	45	3.1	2	0.1
Harvesting	47	3.3	39	2.7
Other	23	1.6	9	0.6
Idleness and recreation	141	9.8	149	10.3
Hygiene	20	1.4	35	2.4
Visiting	62	4.3	45	3.1
Other	126	8.8	59	4.1
TOTAL	780	54.2%	779	53.9%

SOURCE: Adapted from A. Johnson 1975, Table 4, p. 308.
NOTE: Totals vary slightly owing to rounding.

the accuracy of the direct labor-time estimates. For related research, with interesting data from other cultures, see Erasmus (1955) and Szalai (1972).

Time alone, however, is not necessarily a valid measure of "effort" because tasks differ in the amounts of energy they require, and persons in different cultures may work at different rates. Energy expenditure has thus become an alternative measure for comparing human activities across cultures.

In the past, anthropologists provided only indirect estimates of energy-expenditure rates because of the technical problems of measurement in naturalistic field settings. Harris, for example, adopted the expedient of assuming that energy expenditures in work are everywhere constant at 150 calories per hour (Harris 1975:234). Recently, technological developments have made it possible for anthropologists to measure energy expenditures directly in the field. R. Thomas (1973) has described the use of a lightweight gas meter, worn on the back, that measures the volume of air expelled by the subject and determines the percentage of oxygen in the expelled air. A comparison of the latter measure with the actual percentage of oxygen in the atmosphere allows a direct computation of the calories burned during work.

Energy expenditures may be calculated by task and person in the same way that time allocations were in Table 4.2. Table 4.3 presents such figures for the Machiguenga. Rates of energy expenditure per minute at given tasks are multiplied by the average minutes per day spent at those tasks (from Table 4.2) to compute the estimated average daily expenditures of energy for adult males and females. Because random sampling procedures were used, and because observations were made at the site of activity rather than in

TABLE 4.3
Mean Daylight Energy Expenditures of Machiguenga Adults

	Men (N = 15)			Women (N = 20)		
Activity	Cals. burned per min.	Daylight energy expenditure in Cals.	Percent of total energy expended in 24 hrs.	Cals. burned per min.	Daylight energy expenditure in Cals.	Percent of total energy expended in 24 hrs.
Eating	1.9	135	4.2%	1.3	71	3.7%
Food preparation	1.9	22	0.7	1.9	268	13.9
Child care	2.2	2	0	1.4	96	5.0
Manufacturing	3.7	300	9.4	1.7	211	11.0
Wild food getting	5.3	645	20.1	4.4	227	11.8
Garden labor	5.0	722	22.5	2.6	134	7.0
Idleness and recreation	1.3	184	5.7	1.0	149	7.7
Hygiene	2.4	47	1.5	2.5	88	4.6
Visiting	1.3	81	2.5	1.0	45	2.3
Other	3.2	404	12.6	1.8	107	5.6
TOTALS		2,542	79.2%		1,396	72.6%

SOURCE: Montgomery & Johnson 1977: 102.
NOTE: 24-hour energy expenditure totals were 3,202 Cal. for men and 1,924 Cal. for women.

artificial laboratory settings, the data are less vulnerable to the biases that have limited the usefulness of previous studies.

However useful time and energy measures may be, input cannot be fully described in terms of any single measure. There are many inputs that contribute to the quality of the output, or to the ease and enjoyment with which it is produced. The social organization of work, through division of labor and economies of scale, affects input; so does the motivation and skill of the individual worker. Many inputs of this sort can be studied with techniques discussed in later chapters, but there will always be inputs that cannot be quantified.

As suggested in our "efficiency" example above, output is still less susceptible to common-denominator measures than input. Output may refer to any measurable consequence of work. If cash value is the measure adopted, then output simply refers to any commodity produced for sale. But just as with input, this raises problems of cross-cultural comparability: prices vary by region, there are still communities on earth whose market involvement is rather slight, and there are outputs that are not bought and sold in any economic system. Anthropological descriptions of output, therefore, usually provide lists of products measured in standard units, such as liters of grain, yards of cloth, or, simply, the number of items. Frequently, local measures are given, but this is generally inconvenient for purposes of cross-cultural comparison. The most useful form of output data, at least at present, is in quantities of whatever is produced, along with estimates of local market value, where applicable. This leaves us with the apples-and-oranges comparisons that ecologists and economists have sought to avoid, but, given the breadth of the anthropological perspective, this appears to be the only acceptable alternative. If other analysts wish to express outputs in purely cash or energy terms, these data can be converted for their purposes. Leaving the data in naturally occurring units maximizes the possibilities for future analysis, in which use of other common denominators, or combinations of them, may be attempted.

An issue that links population processes to general ecological and economic considerations is the value of children's labor. Might it be the case that large households are common in peasant societies because of the benefits children's labor brings to the household? This hypothesis, though plausible, is very difficult to investigate cross-culturally because existing data are often good concerning either population or production processes but rarely both at the same time. B. White's (1976) study, *Production and Reproduction in a Javanese Village*, can serve as an excellent model for such research in the future.

Health. The concept of "health" lies at the heart of an ecological approach in anthropology. Again, the framework of biological needs is useful to prevent the notion of health from open-endedly embracing everything bearing on well-being in the general sense. Under our orientation, health can be defined as the state of the individual in which the variables monitoring biological need-satisfaction (e.g. body weight, blood pressure, serum protein) are being maintained within theoretically acceptable, or "healthy" limits. The ecological approach, as far as possible, explains observed patterns of human behavior as outcomes of attempts to maintain health in this sense. Although people everywhere have cultural ways of dealing with debilitating diseases such as malaria, amebiasis, and schistosomiasis (Alland 1968:88–89), nutritional health is the main interest of ecological anthropologists, primarily because so much human effort and ingenuity is expended in getting food (Montgomery 1973). "Mental health" poses separate problems not addressed here, though indirectly touched on in Chapter 6.

Most anthropological fieldworkers cannot hope to achieve the high standards of data that are met in the health sciences, both because of lack of training and because field sites are generally far from laboratory facilities. They can, however, collect basic demographic data as indicated earlier in this chapter, and investigate the following matters as well.

A sense of the "average" diet, and the variations in the diet according to social position, should be obtained. Nutritionists often use "24-hour recall" questionnaires to estimate the amounts and kinds of food ingested, but the most reliable technique is to be present for all meals and to weigh everything that is eaten. Awkward as this seems, especially since food is such a sensitive matter for most people, this has been done in a number of studies. Generally, the food is weighed during preparation, not as it is being eaten by family members, whose individual share of the meal must be estimated by eye (see Gross & Underwood 1971; Montgomery 1972; and Weiner & Lourie 1969:469–503). A representative sample of the research population is highly desirable here so that a sense of the adequacy of food intake for different segments of the population can be obtained. For example, in their study of Brazilian plantation workers, Gross and Underwood found that in poorer families children suffered at the expense of their bread-winning fathers in the allocation of scarce family food supplies (1971:735–36).

The nutritional health of individuals can be measured by a variety of means, including anthropometry, clinical observations, and biochemical tests (the indispensable guide to this subject is Jelliffe 1966). Heights, weights, and other measures can be used to identify undernourishment or retarded growth. The occurrence of nutritional diseases of the gums, skin, skeleton, and other body parts can be observed through clinical inspection. And biochemical analysis of blood can test for a wide range of possible nutritional deficiencies. Most students will need to consult professional nutritionists before making their own observations in the field.

A good example of an anthropological study employing the above techniques is Montgomery's research on nutritional health in a village in southern India (Montgomery 1972). He was investigating the expected relationship between socioeconomic status and nutritional well-being in a stratified society. Using explicit operations, he described a local population (age, sex, household composition, caste membership, occupation, etc.) and its income from agriculture and other sources. He observed dietary practices, weighed foods, and did nutritional anthropometry, enlisting the aid of medical researchers for clinical observations and blood sample analyses. From the numerous quantitative data he collected, he was able to report a large number of findings related to the issue of health and stratification. For example, he found community health on the whole to be "relatively satisfactory" (p. 131), with an absence of severe protein-calorie malnutrition (kwashiorkor). Yet anthropometry indicated that 60 percent of the community was more than 10 percent below standard in weight, which may raise questions about the usefulness of such "standards." Moreover, though family economic rank showed a moderate correlation ($r = .57$) with dietary intake (p. 144), it was not correlated with nutritional status as determined by anthropometry, clinical observation, or biochemical analysis. Instead, nutritional status was related to differences in sex and age, with adult males, youths between ages 12 and 15, and infants aged 0 to 2 being best nourished (p. 147).

Montgomery's study is of value for documenting the actual extent of undernourishment in a traditional agricultural community, and for showing the ways in which socioeconomic status does and does not influence nutritional health. The finding that the correlations between income and nutritional status are not very strong challenges us to be less naive about how stratified agrarian societies work "on the ground."

It is to be regretted when cultural anthropologists with an interest in community health concentrate their research on health attitudes and concepts in the community to the exclusion of the biological facts of health. As in Montgomery's study, there is usually ample room for "biomedical," "ethnomedical," and general ecological research. As noted before, however, this will call for either special training before starting fieldwork, or close cooperation with trained medical personnel during fieldwork, or both.

Nonetheless, though we can agree that people need protein and shelter from the cold, we probably cannot agree on exactly how much protein, or how much warmth, is minimally necessary for health. A practical sense of what "health" is, therefore, is not acquired by memorizing an authoritative list of "basic needs." Our own provisional lists are best constructed by reading widely until a reliable sense of the areas of professional agreement and disagreement is developed; useful recent guides to the literature can be found in Rappaport (1971); Heider (1972); Anderson (1973); Montgomery et al. (1973); Netting (1974); Alland (1975); and Vayda and McCay (1975).

CHAPTER FIVE

The Exchange Orientation

THIS CHAPTER is concerned with social relations as they are manifested in interpersonal exchanges. As Belshaw (1965:4) writes, "all enduring social relations involve transactions, which have an exchange aspect"; quantitative descriptions of patterns of exchange within a community are therefore of the widest possible cross-cultural interest. A problem arises, however, in determining what "exchange" is. Nearly everything, from tangibles such as goods or money to less tangible items such as approval or doubt, can be exchanged between people. The problem of deciding which exchanges are relevant for scientific analysis is embedded in the larger problem of deciding what is meant by the concept of a social relationship.

For many decades, the anthropological study of social systems was dominated by a normative, structural perspective primarily based on principles of kinship (Eggan 1955:503); in practice, the perspective often narrowed even further to systems of kinship *terms* (see, for example, Murdock 1949). Analyses of "primitive" and "tribal" social systems typically listed kin types, such as "mother" or "sister's son," and then described the rules of appropriate behavior that were said to govern their interrelations in actual social life. This dependence on kinship rules in the analysis of traditional social life probably had much to do with convenience: relative to the complicated cross-currents of everyday behavior, kinship terms and rules of appropriate kin-behavior are structured and comprehensible. Nonetheless, this absorption with kinship has contributed to the development of a normative bias in ethnographic description—a bias that has intensified with time (Firth 1975:11). Even recent efforts to introduce greater rigor into the comparative study of exchange have tended to emphasize mathematical analysis of normative structures over quantitative description of exchange behavior (Buchler & Selby 1968; Mitchell 1974:279).

Specific research designs for developing normative descriptions are discussed in Chapter 8, but it is my belief that accounts of actual behavior as observed by the ethnographer and trained assistants are needed if the analysis of social systems is not to remain wholly confined to descriptions of how informants think the social world *ought* to operate. The normative approach "applied to our own culture . . . would conjure up a way of life in which men tip their hats to ladies; youths defer to old people in public conveyances; unwed mothers are a rarity; citizens go to the aid of law enforcement officers; chewing gum is never stuck under tables and never dropped on the sidewalk; television repairmen fix television sets; children respect their aged parents; rich and poor get the same medical treatment; taxes are paid in full; all men are created equal; and our defense budget is used only for maintaining peace" (Harris 1968:590).

In this chapter we look at social relations from the standpoint of the "work" they do for people—in the primary sense of the material flows they generate that help people meet basic needs. Individuals seek or are forced into exchanges with other individuals that, far from being isolated from need-fulfillment, are "in reality the very organization of economy" (Sahlins 1965:139). In recent terminology, we are interested in social networks, particularly those that are "personal" (egocentric), ecologically oriented "field-sets" (Whitten & Wolfe 1973:724). But whereas most work on social exchange and networks has dwelt on theoretical and typological issues, we are concerned here instead with how those theoretical perspectives can be operationalized through behavioral descriptions.

The main limitation on normative descriptions is that they generally use nominal measures. This is true whether or not kinship is the language in which social relations are described. For example, Bott's study of the relationship between the social networks and "role relations" of married couples in London was based entirely on nominal data (Bott 1971). She was interested in explaining differences in the degree of segregation of roles between husbands and wives: for some couples roles were strictly separate, whereas for others there was considerable overlap.

Bott's notion of a role-relationship referred to the "expectations" of each spouse regarding proper behavior rather than to the behavior itself; moreover, she did not speculate on what relation these expectations might have had to actual behavior. She did try to relate differences in role-relationships to a number of other variables, such as occupation and class, but her strongest and initially surprising finding was that role-segregation was closely related to the kind of social networks in which the marriage partners participated.

The networks in question were the personal networks of husbands and wives. The extent to which members of a network are linked with all other members is the degree of *density* (Barnes 1972:13); in Bott's terms, a low-density network was "loose-knit," and a high-density network was "close-knit." Her findings associated a high degree of role-segregation with those husbands and wives who participated in high-density networks and a high degree of role-overlap with those who participated in low-density networks. Her explanation for this finding was that individuals who had close-knit personal networks with school friends, kin, and neighbors were less inclined to look to their spouses (through role-overlap) for loyalty, collaboration, and mutual interdependence. Husbands and wives whose networks consisted of loose-knit groups of friends and acquaintances were more likely to spend time helping one another and in recreation together, since their outside social ties were more fragmentary.

Bott's data consisted of informants' statements regarding which persons they spent time with, and whether they were kin, friends, or neighbors. The extent to which her argument is borne out by her data is impossible to judge, however, since she does not present her

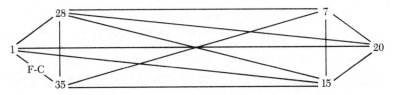

Fig. 5.1. Pilaga food exchange: presence or absence of links. F-C = father-child. Source: Henry 1951:214.

data. Yet given the nominal level of measurement, in which a person either *was* or *was not* a member of a specific network with no indication of *degree* of membership, we could not expect the data to have provided strong support for her hypothesis in any case. Indeed, Bott lamented the lack of quantification in her own study and called for future quantitative research (p. 61).

The contribution quantitative measures of exchange can make to the analysis of social relations is clear from Henry's classic study of the Pilaga Indians of Argentina (Henry 1951). During research in a Pilaga village, Henry kept records of exchanges of food between six family groups. The network of relationships he discovered is represented in Figure 5.1, in which a line links any households known to have exchanged food on two or more occasions. Since only two possible lines are missing (between families 7 and 1 and families 20 and 35), network analysts would regard this as a densely connected graph. But as it stands, Figure 5.1 gives us a view of Pilaga social organization corresponding to the "weak" form of functionalism because it omits two especially important facts: first, the *strength* of each food-exchange, relationship; and, second, the predominant *direction* of the flow of foods. Fortunately, Henry collected sufficient quantitative data in his study to determine the relative strength and direction of these exchanges.

Table 5.1 shows, for example, that the ties between families 15 and 28 and families 7 and 35, which are represented as identical in Figure 5.1, are actually very different: the tie between 15 and 28 is strong, based on a total of 20 observed cases of food exchange (nine from 15 to 28, and eleven from 28 to 15); on the other hand, the tie between 7 and 35 is nearly nonexistent, based on the minimum two cases of exchange (one in each direction). Henry discussed many

TABLE 5.1
Frequencies of Food Exchange Between
Pilaga Families

From household	To household						Total
	28	7	20	15	35	1	
28	X	14	17	11	8	29	79
7	19	X	4	2	1	0	26
20	26	9	X	3	0	1	39
15	9	0	1	X	7	17	34
35	4	1	1	6	X	F-C	12
1	0	0	0	2	F-C	X	2
TOTAL	58	24	23	24	16	47	

SOURCE: Adapted from Table VI in Henry 1951, p. 214.
NOTE: F-C = father-child.

cases of such differences in strength and showed that in general they resulted not from differences in genealogical closeness, but rather from idiosyncratic circumstances of a complex order. In addition, Table 5.1 reveals marked asymmetry in the direction of flow between some households. Household 1, for example, never gave to 28, whereas 28 gave 29 times to 1. Ethnographic data showed that 28 was the chief's family, which Henry calls "the unifying factor in the village" (p. 214). Family 1 was dependent on the chief because the male head of 1 was absent for wage labor much of the time. Asymmetry in both strength and direction of food exchanges was the rule rather than the exception among the Pilaga, generating tension and hostility between families. The clear implication from this is that mechanical descriptions of "exchange" focusing on single cognitive aspects such as genealogical relations will not be useful in predicting actual exchange behavior.

The main limitations of Henry's data are, first, that he did not employ any representative sampling procedure (he gives the impression that his record is complete [p. 192], but it seems doubtful that it could be if he was doing any other research at all during the months of food-exchange observation), and, second that he did not include measures of the quantities and kinds of food exchanged, thus failing to distinguish between small and large gifts or between ordinary and special foods (see pp. 191–92). Nonetheless, Henry's study is an outstanding early example of the value of quantifying exchange relations beyond the presence-absence level in order to preserve a record of intracommunity differences in strength and symmetry of relations.

Another influential early approach to the quantitative study of social relations was developed by Chapple and Arensberg in their article "Measuring Human Relations" (1940). In contrast to most earlier researchers, Chapple and Arensberg concentrated on techniques appropriate to studying not recollected or recorded cultures but "live" cultures—those subject to direct, careful observation. Their goal was "a science of human relations."

According to their notion of science, research was to be centered on directly observable phenomena and not on inferred states of being, such as emotion or consciousness.* The authors proceeded to outline a series of units of observation, including *action* (essentially, a change in muscular activity), *interaction* (a set of actions by individual A followed by a set of actions by individual B), and *event* (all the actions from start to finish of a set of interactions between the same persons). They then proposed to measure these units along a number of dimensions, the most important of which was to be duration, but among which were also initiation, termination, and specific muscular change. These measurements were to be used to describe differences between individuals, and in particular to describe hierarchical patterns of interaction. This early approach was an important precursor of modern interest in careful behavioral descriptions (e.g., Harris 1964); moreover, the authors' identification of time as a measure of exchange activity has been not replaced but rather supplemented in recent years.

Exchange Relations

In the present context, the study of interpersonal exchanges is a way of asking what social relations *do* for people. This resolves into a number of specific questions about observed transactions:

*This limitation, though appropriate insofar as it insisted that research units should be measurable, gave a strong overall behaviorist cast to the research program.

What is exchanged?

How much of it?

Flowing in which direction?

How often is it exchanged?

How long does the transaction last?

How long have such exchanges been going on?

These dimensions of identity, quantity, direction, frequency, duration, and history give far more detailed information than the presence-absence descriptions of normative analysis.

Individuals work to maintain social relations because the exchanges they encompass are valued. Quantitative descriptions of actual exchanges shed light on how exchanges do or do not contribute to individual well-being, which from an ecological perspective is viewed initially in terms of biological need-fulfillment. Though much exchange behavior is directly related to the satisfaction of biological needs, many other kinds of exchange also occur (e.g., gossip), and the burden of proof of their ecological relevance is on the ethnographer. If particular social structures are somehow to be explained in terms of cross-cultural regularities, and not simply assumed to exist *sui generis*, then the place to start is in the ecological analysis of exchange behavior, where the implications of the social structure in people's daily lives become apparent.

Dyads, kinship, and friendship. From a behavioral standpoint, the analysis of a social system begins with individual dyads and expands to the level of a group through interlinked statements about numbers of dyads. The existence of a group of many members is easy to demonstrate *normatively*, if it is named and said by informants to have identifiable properties. For example, lineages in many societies are named and are believed by their members to regulate access to resources. But from a behavioral standpoint, demonstration of a group's existence requires that the members of the group behave toward one another in observable ways that distinguish a dyad within the group from a dyad between a group member and an outsider. For example, if group members address one another by exclusive terms, or if they cooperate significantly more with one another than with outsiders, then a group can be said to exist behaviorally. Very few of the groups that occupy anthropological analysis have had their existence demonstrated with quantitative behavioral data.

The basic form of dyadic relations has been described by Foster in important papers (1961, 1963, 1967) that have not generated as much interest as they merit, perhaps because of the restriction of his discussion to the Mexican village of Tzintzuntzan, and because of his failure to relate his argument to current sociological theory. According to Foster, social relations in Tzintzuntzan, in contrast to the model of social structure developed for unilineal kin groups (Fortes 1953), may be described as a series of "dyadic contracts" with the following five properties.

1. Relationships are dyadic.

2. Relationships are informal and "unenforceable through authority" (1961:1173).

3. Following from 2, the existence of a dyadic contract must be continuously validated through exchange; when the exchanges end, the relationship begins to fade.

4. Exchanges are generally out of balance at any particular moment, with the debt continually shifting back and forth between the dyadic partners.

5. There is an expectation that over the long term the value of the exchanges will balance out, so that the partners' income will be roughly equal to their outflow (Foster 1961; see also A. Johnson & Bond 1974:61–62).

The intellectual roots of Foster's approach lie in a view of human beings as "rational decision-makers" allocating scarce means among competing ends (see Chapter 7, The Maximization Orientation). Individuals in a social context are assumed to be maximizing some kind of value by manipulating the human resources around them (see Homans 1958: Blau 1967). The contrast Foster draws between Tzintzuntzan and unilineal descent groups, however, is based largely on a difference in approach: structurally, social behavior appears to be determined by the positions of individuals within a cognized rule structure; but in the dyadic model, individuals appear to be in charge of their own social lives, shaping their personal networks in terms of their perceived self-interest. Somewhat accidentally, this dichotomy has been reflected in practice by a structural

emphasis on normative data in contrast to a dyadic emphasis on behavioral outcomes of individual decisions.

The structural and dyadic positions do not define different kinds
of society; rather, they refer to the poles of the universal dialectic
between individual and society (Tönnies 1955 : 12; R. Murphy 1971 :
76–79). As an example, we may take a quantitative analysis of meal
exchange among the Bantu-speaking Yombe of Zambia (A. Johnson
& Bond 1974). The 300 villagers of Muyombe subsist by horticulture on land acquired from the chief (according to rights established
at birth); they are organized into exogamous agnatic lineages (patri-
lineages) that hold corporate authority over the members and property of the lineage. At the normative level, the Yombe believe their
social system to be structured primarily by agnatic principles. Members of the same lineage are expected to have intimate, cooperative
relations, sharing willingly within a common enterprise. The Yombe
express highly critical opinions of the Westerners they have encountered, who (they feel) are self-serving and ignore the needs of
their kinfolk.

At the behavioral level, the Yombe mark their ties of warmth and
cooperation by sharing meals together. Yombe men do not eat with
enemies or those with whom they are involved in serious disputes.
Meal-sharing is a sign of intimacy and trust, a visible symbol of an
underlying current of day-to-day favors. In the course of his research, Bond observed 543 meals involving one or more of the 37
adult males in the community. If the Yombe acted on the basis of
their normative beliefs, the highest frequencies of meal-sharing
should have occurred between agnates. Yet the actual distribution
of meals shared, as shown in Table 5.2, revealed that patrilineal kin
ate together only 22 percent of the time. Furthermore, the data
show that nearly all patrilineal meal-sharing was between men and
their unmarried sons or grandsons; adult brothers shared only 4
percent of all meals, and no married men ate with their fathers. Yet
nearly half of all meals were shared with non-kin friends. Does this
mean that men *avoid* their close patrikin in establishing ties of
cooperation and trust, or does it mean that they are merely *extending* their friendly relations to strangers? Analysis of other data indi-

TABLE 5.2
*Yombe Meal-Sharing, by Relation
of Partners*

Relation of partner	Percent of meals shared
Patrikin	22%
Matrikin	19
Affines	5
Non-kin "friends"	43
SUBTOTAL: Shared meals	89%
No partner	11%
TOTAL	100%

SOURCE: A. Johnson & Bond 1974: 59.
NOTE: The table is based on observations of 543 meals involving one or more of 37 adult males.

cated that Yombe agnates, despite their strong ethic of cooperation, are actually in competition with each other over many highly valued resources and for this reason do not trust each other. They deliberately choose their meal partners from among men who are not close agnates in order to have allies to help them in their competition over resources and in the conduct of everyday affairs (A. Johnson & Bond 1974:58–59).

The quantitative analysis of Yombe meal-sharing does not so much contradict the normative view of kin-based society as provide a complementary understanding. Yombe men do recognize and honor kin obligations. On the other hand, food, which fills a most immediate biological need, is also a "nurturant" gift in the broader sense; Yombe men do not need meals from their friends, since they have food at home, but sharing a meal builds confidence in the relationship. In Muyombe the work of friendship is to buffer the individual against the inordinate and powerful demands of the lineage, and against competition from coequals within the lineage.

In the same study, the Yombe data were compared with patterns of food exchange in a community of Brazilian sharecroppers, whose norms about exchange emphasize the very individualism that the Yombe disapprove in "Westerners." Yet the Brazilian data in fact show a strong behavioral preference for exchange with kinsmen

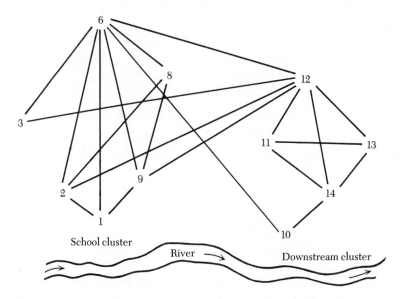

Fig. 5.2. Presence and absence of visiting between Machiguenga households.

(A. Johnson & Bond 1974:60). In both the Yombe and the Brazilian cases, therefore, quantitative data on exchange behavior add a dimension of understanding not available from the normative data alone.

Machiguenga networks. Time-allocation data, based on random visits to households as described in the previous chapter, can yield useful insights into interpersonal relations. Turning again to the Machiguenga for our example, a visit by a member of one household to another may be regarded as an exchange. In practice, visits may be for gossip, gift exchange, or barter; but for the present we will focus on the frequency with which visits of all kinds occur between members of different households. Operationally, frequency of observed visits is taken as an indicator (among several worth considering) of the strength of social relationships between households.

Figure 5.2 presents a network diagram showing the cases in which at least one visit was observed between pairs of eleven Machiguenga households that were observed. The households in this community happen to fall into two neighborhoods, the "school clus-

TABLE 5.3
*Frequencies of Machiguenga Household
Visits: Households 11, 13, 14*

Visit from	Visit to		
	11	13	14
11	X	2	7
13	18	X	37
14	39	1	X

ter" and the "downstream cluster." The figure shows a dense pattern of connections, but it is based simply on presence-absence data and does not reveal strength or asymmetry of the relationships. Yet both of these factors are important to an understanding of Machiguenga social behavior. To see why, we will examine first only households 11, 13, and 14 in the downstream group. Members of these households visit one another frequently, but not symmetrically. Table 5.3 gives the actual frequencies with which members of each household were observed to visit the others.

From the table we can see that the overwhelming majority of visits go in one dominant direction, with household 11 receiving (57/9), household 14 both receiving and paying (44/40), and household 13 predominantly paying visits (3/55).

The asymmetry thus expressed is understandable in terms of the relative positions of the male and female heads of the three households. The male head of household 11 is the older brother of the male househead of 14; the female head of 11 is the mother of the female head of 14; and the female head of 13 is the sister of the two brothers. Household 11 is the center of social activity of this extended-family group; it is the largest household, and the place where special foods such as fish, meat, and grubs are usually prepared and distributed, and where beer parties are held. The two brothers are close companions who often tease their brother-in-law, in a light-hearted way. The latter gets along with his brothers-in-law, but is dependent on them because his own gardens are small and theirs are large. The pattern of visiting reflects these asymmetries of age, kinship distance, and economics in the relationships of the male househeads. The composition of the three households is shown in Figure 5.3.

These kinds of asymmetry characterize all Machiguenga social relations to some degree, as we can see when we turn our focus back again to the larger community. Figure 5.4 presents the visiting patterns among the same eleven households of Figure 5.2, but shows the degree of strength and asymmetry in the visits. Household links are characterized as "weak," "moderate," or "strong" according to the number of visits exchanged, and arrows show "one-sided" flows in the direction of visits (defined as a degree of asymmetry of roughly 4:1 or greater). When we consider that our definition of one-sidedness excludes all "weak" links but one (that in which four visits are paid in one direction and none are returned), we can see from the number of arrows in Figure 5.4 that Machiguenga visiting patterns are very asymmetrical indeed. Households 6 and 11 are the focuses for visits in their respective neighborhoods. We have already seen the reasons for the ascendancy of household 11. Household 6 is also dominant, but for different reasons. The head of household 6 is a Machiguenga Indian with several years of education who now is the government-paid bilingual schoolteacher in the region. With his pay he can buy trade goods to exchange for garden labor; in this way he can maintain the largest gardens and hold the

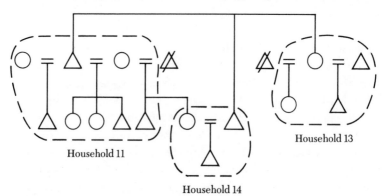

Fig. 5.3. Machiguenga household composition: households 11, 13, 14.

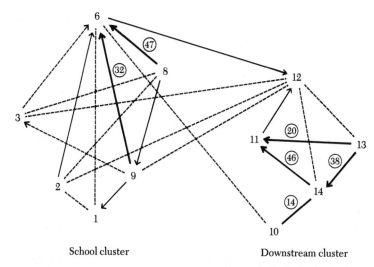

Fig. 5.4. Machiguenga visiting patterns. Relationships occurring with a frequency of less than 5 visits are shown by dotted lines; those with frequencies of 5 to 10 visits, by thin solid lines; and those with frequencies of over 10 visits (very strong relationships) by heavy solid lines. Arrows are added where the asymmetry in visiting frequencies is approximately 4:1 or greater. Numbers in circles represent frequencies larger than 10.

most beer feasts. In the past, unusually strong or intelligent individuals could attract scattered households to live near them and help them give beer parties. Now, however, the schoolteacher is able to substitute money for the personal eminence he does not fully possess, and is taking over the older "headman" role.

The Machiguenga, who are a politically egalitarian people used to living in small, extended family clusters such as the one involving households 11, 13, and 14, nonetheless regard hierarchy as a natural feature of all interpersonal relationships. Under the traditional system, such attributes as age, kin relation, courage, and hard work led to hierarchical relations of the kind that appear here as asymmetrical visiting patterns. In the changes that are following from people's increased participation in national society, the same behavioral asymmetries are extended to the instrumental relations of an emerging patron-client system.

The randomness of the time-allocation data gives a reliable sense of frequencies of interaction. In the Machiguenga case this was advantageous because informants were reluctant to express preferences for certain households over others, or to rank individuals according to prestige, authority, or other hierarchical notions. In general, informants cannot be expected to remember their own exchanges either, at least with this kind unbiased accuracy; nor will they be aware of all the patterns likely to emerge from behavioral analysis.

Accra networks. Under many circumstances, direct observation of human activities is impossible, or may be too disruptive to be defended as a workable field technique. This is especially true of research in cities, where interviews are often the only recourse. Sanjek's (1972) study of personal networks in a neighborhood of Accra, Ghana, illustrates the value of interview-based quantitative network descriptions in urban settings. Earlier studies of African cities had agreed that ethnic or "tribal" affiliation was the major determinant of interpersonal relations from marriage to recreation. Sanjek hypothesized that economic class influenced social networks more than ethnicity did. As a first step toward testing this hypothesis, he developed a technique for determining the relative importance of ethnicity in personal interactions.

Sanjek's research among tenants of eleven apartment buildings in a single neighborhood convinced him that ethnicity was a very confusing and diffuse factor in interpersonal relations here. Answers to the question of which tribes could be found in Accra today turned up 136 different ethnic terms; residents of the eleven buildings alone represented no fewer than 22 different ethnic identities. Yet these people visited one another, chatted together in the courtyard, and intermarried. "People of the same ethnic identity in the neighborhood could not be considered groups. . . . People of one ethnic identity often did not know of, let alone interact with, others of their same identity" (p. 187).

Sanjek sought through an analysis of personal networks to make quantitative statements about the extent to which "single-ethnic" or "multiethnic" interactions characterized the daily lives of the community members. The analyses of African urban networks that had shown ethnicity to be an important variable had not been based on quantitative studies of many individuals, and thus Sanjek felt that "their methods [were] insufficient to support their conclusions" (p. 205). Epstein's (1961) study of networks in an African city, for example, based on the activities of one informant for a five-day period, was an important methodological innovation; but having just one informant meant that there was no way of judging the representativeness of that informant's network. Was the study not at base intuitive? "Epstein's failure to pose the question of the typicality or representativity of Chanda's network is responsible for his own uncertainty as to whether the network is a discovery procedure or an apt illustration of what Epstein knows beforehand of Ndela and Copperbelt social organization" (Sanjek 1972:208).

Sanjek's solution was to study the personal networks of 40 individuals for four days each. It would have been ideal to conduct such studies through direct observations, but in this case the indeterminacy of the disturbance to individual routines would have been too great; consequently, Sanjek asked his informants each day where they had been, and noted for the purposes of the network analysis all individuals with whom they remembered exchanging words. The result was 1,239 "multiactor scenes" involving conversations between two or more people. Of these scenes, 55.9 percent involved members of different ethnic identities, whereas only 44.1 percent involved members of the same ethnic identity. Was this percentage of interethnic exchange high? Sanjek noted the difficulty of evaluating his results in the absence of similar studies. But, since the "pluralists" and the network analysts had written as though the percentage of single-ethnic scenes should have been very high, Sanjek concluded that his data did not support an "ethnic analysis" of interaction.

Sanjek's conclusion will probably surprise those who have maintained the importance of "ethnic" or "tribal" identity in African cities. However, it is important to note that it is not "conclusive" as it stands, for it does not satisfy a general requirement in presenting quantitative data—the construction of a model of the distribution that would have been expected by chance (the null hypothesis).

Only by comparing the distribution of ethnic interactions expected by chance and the actual distribution can we judge the validity of Sanjek's conclusion.

The advantage of a methodologically explicit study is that it is possible to reevaluate the data. In this instance we can pose the question, If all the individuals in Sanjek's sample were interacting purely by chance with respect to ethnicity, what percentage of the total interactions would be expected to occur between members of the same ethnic identity? We know that for his study Sanjek chose ten individuals from each of three ethnicities—Kwawu, Ga, and Ewe—plus another ten from several remaining ethnicities (for a total of 40). The three major ethnic identities were chosen because they were the most common ones in the eleven study buildings. We may estimate the expected frequency with which single-ethnic scenes would occur at random by computing the expected frequency with which a member of each group would meet someone else from the same group, and adding the figures for all groups together. The frequencies with which various "tribal identities" occur in the Accra census for 1960 are Kwawu, 27 percent, Ga, 39.8 percent, and Ewe, 14.7 percent (Sanjek 1972:76–77). Within the sample, of course, Kwawu, Ga, and Ewe each occur with frequencies of 25 percent. Table 5.4 shows our computation of the expected frequency of single-ethnic scenes in Sanjek's sample. From it, we can see that about 14 percent of all interactions should involve members of the same ethnic group by chance.*

Now Sanjek's calculations showed that the actual occurrence of single-ethnic scenes was 44 percent, which is considerably higher than the 14 percent we have just computed would occur at random. Some of the difference, as Sanjek pointed out, stems from the fact that individuals interact with relatives more than would be expected by chance, and that relatives are generally (but not always) of the same ethnic identity. Still, ethnicity is clearly an important factor in determining frequencies of interaction, even though the absolute

---

*This figure would be slightly higher if we included the probabilities for all of the other ethnic groups, but their frequencies of occurrence would add only a small additional amount.

TABLE 5.4
Expected Frequencies of Single-Ethnic Scenes, Assuming Randomness

(1) Ethnicity	(2) Ego	(3) Alter	(4) Expected Frequency (2 × 3)
Kwawu	.25	.027	.007
Ga	.25	.398	.100
Ewe	.25	.147	.037
Other	.25	(very small)	—
Total expected frequency of single-ethnic scenes			.144+

frequency of single-ethnic interaction Sanjek found was less than 50 percent.

Behavior on film. The measures we have reviewed so far, of meal-sharing, visiting, and conversing, though detailed by comparison with the typological categories of normative ethnography, are still too insensitive for many purposes. Social behavior is built on specific acts, such as touching, scolding, or smiling, that are often subtle and difficult to observe. The quantitative investigation of microbehavioral patterns that Chapple and Arensberg proposed a generation ago has become feasible today with the availability of computers and modern portable film equipment. Film has advantages in that scenes may be reviewed as often as necessary and may be viewed by other observers to increase the reliability of the behavioral codes employed in describing even the fleeting exchanges that the camera can isolate. Although a camera is intrusive and may be viewed with suspicion in some cases, it is not qualitatively different from a tape recorder or even a pencil and notebook. As with all anthropological research, the informed consent of the participants is the only ethical basis on which filming can be done. Once completed, however, a film opens very rich and as yet little-explored possibilities for behavioral research.

DeHavenon and Harris (1976) used videotape records of family interactions in New York City to describe patterns of hierarchy in the family. They taped one full week in the lives of each of four families chosen from a similar economic background but differing in that (1) two were white and two were black, and (2) one "husband-father" was absent and one was present in each color group. Coders observed 130 hours of tape, concentrating on the occurrence of requests and commands and on all activities that could be construed as responses (or failures to respond) to those requests and commands. Comparisons within and between the four families were then made to determine differences in amounts of requests made and degrees of compliance. Among their many findings, supported by quantitative data, the following may serve as examples.

> Both black mothers are the least compliant on their families' request-receiver hierarchies while the two white mothers are most compliant. The youngest child in each of the black families is the most compliant. The youngest child in each of the white families is the least compliant. In both black families the request-receiver hierarchy of compliance is 100 percent age ranked; i.e., the youngest is the most compliant and the eldest the least. The husband-father–absent white family is also 100 percent age ranked for compliance . . ., but in a direction . . . opposite to that of the black husband-father–absent family; i.e., the mother is the most compliant, the youngest child the least (DeHavenon & Harris 1976:8–9).

The above example emphasized differences between black and white American households, but these differences are seen to be comparatively small in the next example. Orna Johnson has taken videotapes of family interactions in Machiguenga households, demonstrating that videotape techniques can be used also in rural settings where electricity and other amenities are absent. In Table 5.5, figures give the "cost" of receiving compliance to requests for action, such as "pass the salt" or "be quiet," for white and black American and for Machiguenga households. The cost is computed as the ratio of requests that are not complied with to requests that are (i.e., cost = number of noncompliances ÷ number of compliances). The cost of compliance (in repeated requests) grows with the number of noncompliances. As we can see, the two kinds of American households are similar in having an average cost of compliance of about 1.4. Compared to the Machiguenga, members of both kinds of American households (in which father is present) must issue many commands in order to receive compliance. Requests for action are often ignored in the American households, but rarely ignored among the Machiguenga, especially when an adult is making the

TABLE 5.5
Average Cost of Compliance in American and
Machiguenga Households

Household member	White American	Black American	Machiguenga
Husband	1.4	1.1	0.4
Wife	1.4	1.3	0.3
Children	1.8	1.4	0.8

SOURCES: DeHavenon & Harris 1976, Figure 1; O. Johnson 1977, Appendix F.
  NOTE: In the American households, only father-present households are included in this table, because no Machiguenga father-absent households were observed; all data are averages, except for American husbands and wives, of which
there are only one each in both black and white households. The computation
of "cost" is explained in the text.

request. In one respect all groups seem similar, however: children
have the highest cost of compliance. Behavioral analyses from
videotapes lend themselves very well to cross-cultural comparisons
such as these.

Our last example illustrates the use of behavioral analysis of exchange in a more traditional area—that of the relationship between
kinship structure and interpersonal behavior. Again, Orna Johnson's
videotape data are used, this time to demonstrate large behavioral
differences between Machiguenga kinsmen during food exchanges
at meals (O. Johnson 1977: chap. 8). In extended-family households,
the sexes separate into two clusters at mealtimes. Women serve the
men, but there are frequent exchanges between individuals both of
the same sex and of the opposite sex; food is broken into morsels and
exchanged as gifts, which in turn are often broken into smaller
morsels and redistributed yet again. These small exchanges obviously give pleasure and are a regular part of any meal.

But these exchanges are not random, as may be seen in Table 5.6.
Women, for example, exchange among themselves more than would
be expected by chance, whereas men exchange with each other
less than expected; this is in keeping with other data showing Machiguenga women to be more "sociable" than men (O. Johnson &
A. Johnson 1975). The pattern of exchange between individuals of
the opposite sex is even more striking, and is related to the marriage
rule prescribing cross-cousin marriage. Husbands and wives show a

TABLE 5.6
Machiguenga Food Exchanges

Type of exchange	Observed exchanges	Exchanges expected by chance
Same-Sex		
Women	32	23
Men	19	27
Opposite-Sex		
Husband/wife	37	13
Unmarriageable	23	34
Unmarried cross-cousins	0	14
TOTAL	111	111

high frequency of exchanges—more than expected by chance. Exchanges between other men and women are less than expected by chance, but with a further important difference: men and women who are "unmarriageable" within the kinship system, and between whom sexual relations would be regarded as incestuous (that is, they are not cross-cousins), exchange only somewhat less often than expected; but cross-cousins who are not married to each other, yet who fall into the category of potential sex partners or spouses, are never observed to exchange food. Johnson suggests that this reflects the tension introduced into a relationship by possibilities for sexual relations that are not being acted upon; since food exchange implies intimacy, and may at times even symbolize sexual relations, unmarried cross-cousins avoid food exchanges just as they are expected to avoid sexual relations.

Society as a Behavioral System

People experience social relations as a set of exchanges, which may be few or many and of highly diverse content. Yet the anthropological study of social systems has concentrated on normative structures to the detriment of quantitative descriptions of observed behavior. This may have been justified once, when computers had not yet taken the drudgery out of patterning masses of observations, but the continued neglect of behavior indicates that what may once have been a necessary expedient may now have become an unexamined and retrogressive bias.

Functional and causal analyses of social process generally assume that the behavior being explained has some purpose. Social relations are described as providing economic security, sanctioning behavior, contributing to group solidarity, and so on. But the data for testing these explanations refer almost exclusively to norms rather than to the actual quantitative content of the social relations. If the data refer to norms but the theoretical propositions refer to the behavioral impact of the norms, then the test of the hypotheses assumes a perfect correspondence between norms and behavior that certainly does not exist in reality. The simplest remedy would be to test behavioral hypotheses with behavioral data.

Behavioral descriptions using such operational categories as frequency and duration offer indispensable data for cross-cultural comparison. Just as at the center of input-output analysis is a core of "noncultural ecology," so also a variety of "human ethology" lies at the heart of exchange analysis. Rather than assume that cognitive structures determine behavior, we now recognize that "cognition" is one kind of description and that "behavior" is another; the congruence of the two is a matter for empirical determination. From an ecological perspective, it is not concepts and rules that have effects but human actions. Thus the normative bias reverses ecological priorities, and the behavioral study of exchange is an attempt to redress the balance.

CHAPTER SIX

The Culture-and-Personality Orientation

Psychological anthropology is a large and diverse subfield of cultural anthropology. The theoretical interests of its practitioners range from the evolution of human behavior and the discovery of "human nature" to the exploration of cross-cultural patterns of perception and cognition, and even to aspects of culture change: in short, psychological anthropology is as diverse as the field of psychology itself (Bourguignon 1973). What characterizes this branch of anthropology is its concern to distinguish the psychological processes common to all human beings from those that vary from one cultural setting to the next, and its attempt to predict the circumstances under which these variations occur. The efforts of psychological anthropologists have been so plagued by methodological problems, however, that most "findings" reported in cross-cultural research are accepted only provisionally, and with much discussion and equivocation (Edgerton 1970:338; Kennedy 1973: 1121–22; LeVine 1973:13).

In this book, I have divided my discussion of psychological anthropology into two chapters—the present one on the culture-and-personality orientation, and Chapter 8 on the cognitive/structural orientation. Here we will focus attention on the cross-cultural study of emotional states and their correlates in society and economy; in Chapter 8 we will consider patterns of perception, categorization, and meaning. Though this division does not fully encompass the field, it does emphasize important methodological differences. Moreover, most of the quantitative, operationally explicit research that has been done so far can be described under one or the other of these two orientations. Because the main problems raised in these two chapters concern *reliability* and *representativeness*—problems confronting all researchers in psychological anthropology—the solutions suggested should be helpful in the elaboration of research procedures on psychological topics in the most general sense.

Culture-and-Personality Research

The name of this orientation suggests one of the fundamental tenets of Freudian theory—that personality is the product of the interaction of the biogenetic nature of the human individual ("instinct") and the often incompatible demands of cultural life ("civilization"). Freud believed that the mediation of the apparent contradictions in this interaction occurred within the structure of the family, and that the human personality emerged through a necessary progression of stages more or less universally repeated in the common experiences of family life. Psychological illness, by this view, resulted when the orderly progression of personality development was interfered with; psychological health was restored when the source of the interference was uncovered, through analysis, and removed.

Freud's theory was phrased in explicitly universal terms, and it fell to anthropologists, because of their cross-cultural concerns, to debate whether the extension of Freudian theory outside the Northern European framework of its originator was justified. Malinowski early argued that because family forms had been shown to vary widely across cultures, the personalities emerging as a result of experiences within the family would also differ widely—to the point, perhaps, where what was considered normality in one culture might be defined as abnormality in another (1927:17–21). This argument has seemed intuitively reasonable to many, yet despite further suggestive evidence gathered over the years, many psychologists and anthropologists remain committed to the universalistic

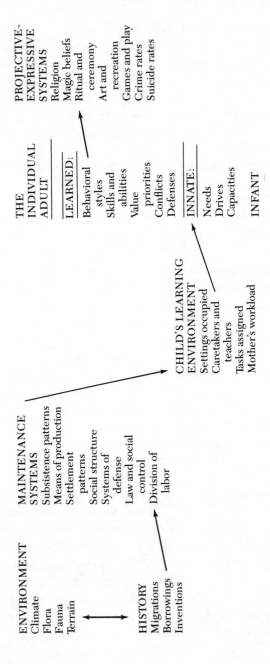

Fig. 6.1. The Whiting Model. Source: B. Whiting & Whiting 1975: facing p. 1. Compare J. Whiting 1973:3; Fromm & Maccoby 1970:124; LeVine 1973:57.

propositions enunciated by Freud. A recent debate occurred among anthropologists, for example, over whether the concept of mental "health" can be defined only for single cultures or for humanity as a whole (J. Murphy 1976).

The point of intersection between the culture-and-personality orientation and the input-output orientation under our ecological framework is how individuals come to be motivated to help meet the biological needs of their social group rather than simply of themselves. The consensus among culture-and-personality theorists is that culture (including social organization) confers such clear biological rewards over and above those the individual would be able to attain alone that its benefits outweigh its costs to the individual; nonetheless, those costs, produced by "cultural frustration," must be compensated (Freud 1961:36; Kardiner 1939:17,471; Fromm 1941: 305,310; Mead 1954:6–8; LeVine 1973:57; J. Whiting 1973:3).

Figure 6.1 presents a general view (adapted from the "Whiting Model" in B. Whiting & Whiting 1975) of the socialization process from an ecological perspective. We can see that particular systems of production, arising from environmental and historical givens and aiming at the satisfaction of "biochemical" needs, shape such human activities as work routines and social relations during work, patterns of settlement and daily interpersonal interaction, and control over natural resources and wealth. This organized productive activity provides an environment within which the young are socialized. To be effective, socialization must mediate the sometimes contradictory impulses of individuals in the face of socially defined standards of appropriate behavior, and it must do so in such a way that the individual comes to maturity *wanting* to behave in the appropriate way.

Through a process about which no one is entirely clear, individuals appear to react to the stresses of the socialization experience by producing what have been called in the literature "secondary institutions" (Kardiner 1939), "cultural reactions" (Malinowski 1939: 940), "projections" (J. Whiting 1973), or "ideology" (Fromm & Maccoby 1970:124). Examples of these secondary products include rituals, myths, values, taboos, art, and games. Analysis of these "projections" can permit both description of personality characteristics and investigation of those processes of individual "adaptation" that bring personality differences into being (Harrington & Whiting 1972:472; LeVine 1973).

This theory, as seen in the Whiting Model, can be tested by determining whether personality, as assessed by analysis of projective materials, covaries with productive arrangements. The importance of developing and improving such a theory, as Kardiner early recognized, lies in the need to "furnish a critique of social forms in order to enable us to predict their stability, to locate more precisely the discomforts they create and the compensatory efforts they set in motion" (Kardiner 1945:1–2). An understanding of how production activities influence individual personality will enable us to judge production systems, including our own, in terms of comparative costs and benefits to the human participants in them.

From the idea that personality is influenced by subsistence arrangements has arisen the assumption that communities with similar subsistence systems should produce adults with similar personalities, that whole communities should reflect a "basic personality type" (Linton 1939:vi–vii; 1945:viii). Although the idea appears sound, the level at which shared personality characteristics was sought in the past was undoubtedly too general. Even within the most homogeneous communities, personality differences have been found based on variations in personal abilities and responsibilities of the sexes that led to patterned differences in work and relations of production. In this chapter we will review several studies supporting the general idea of a relationship between productive activities and personality, but also showing that personality traits are not necessarily shared at the level of whole communities or "cultures."

Before turning to these studies, a word is in order on a conflict that pervades current culture-and-personality research: it is the conflict between science and humanism, in essence, that we reviewed in Chapter 3. On the one hand, Harrington and Whiting (1972:472) define "personality" in holistic terms as "the model of what the individual assimilates and of how he organizes what happens to him"; their approach to culture-and-personality research stresses the individual as an integrated and active being who responds creatively to environmental circumstances. In contrast to this is the "elementistic" approach of behaviorism, which conforms fairly closely to the operational standards of the "hard" sciences by insisting that the concepts of analysis refer to directly observable behaviors (see Deutsch & Kraus 1965:78–79).

Though there is certainly a real need for more behavioral observation in culture-and-personality research, most anthropologists avoid a thoroughgoing behaviorist position because they believe that the intuitive notion of the "self" is part of the means by which we can understand members of other cultures; as Margaret Mead put it, "disciplined introspection and empathy are essential to the study of the unique characteristics of humankind" (Mead 1976:905).

An Intuitive Approach

In the remainder of this chapter we will examine several attempts at quantitative research relating ecological and personality variables. We will begin with a study that is ecological, quantitative, and holistic, but that presents serious problems of operationalism; we will then look at several less ambitious, but operationally sounder, studies.

Fromm and Maccoby (1970) studied 417 adult members of a Mexican Village in an attempt to relate social character to both socioeconomic and ideological variables. Fromm had developed an approach to personality formation closely related to the "Whiting Model" of Figure 6.1, and it is summarized here as Figure 6.2. In the "Fromm Model" the phrase "ideology and values" replaces

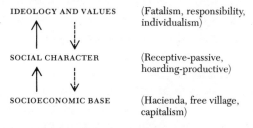

Fig. 6.2. The Fromm Model. Adapted from Fromm & Maccoby 1970:124.

Whiting's "projective-expressive system," though both mean about the same thing. As far as the heading "social character" is concerned, Fromm means by it "that part of their character structure that is common to most members of the group" (Fromm 1941:304).

In their study, Fromm and Maccoby provided extensive information about their research procedures. Their descriptions of individual social character were based largely on the results of an "interpretative questionnaire" in which informants were asked to respond to a number of specific and general questions, for example:

20. What is your work and what does it consist of?
21. a) What do you like most about it?
    b) What do you like least about it?
    . . .
40. What experience in your life has been the happiest?
    . . .
81. For what purpose do you believe we were born into this world?

The purpose of administering a standard questionnaire to an entire community was two-fold: first, to find the degree of sharing of character traits among members of the population: and second, to find other variables, such as economic status and religious practice, that were associated with character differences in the population.

In order to judge their success, we must first ask how, from the varied responses to the interpretative questionnaire, Fromm and Maccoby arrived at a character description for each person. Now in their view, any individual can be described by a unitary "orientation" reflecting dominant, as opposed to "secondary," tendencies. In this scheme, individuals are assigned to nominal classes along a number of dimensions: for example, one dimension classifies individuals as "receptive," "exploitative," or "hoarding"; another dimension labels them "productive" or "nonproductive." An individual is defined by position on the combined dimensions; thus we may find "nonproductive-exploitative" orientations, "productive-hoarding" orientations, etc.

Unfortunately, despite an open and extensive discussion of methods, Fromm and Maccoby do not give a very informative description of the actual operations by which informant responses were transformed into a single dominant orientation for each individual. Their treatment of the problem is revealing of the basic methodological difficulties in culture-and-personality research. On the difference between a "conventional" questionnaire and their "interpretative" one they write:

> In the conventional questionnaire, the answers are taken as raw material or coded according to behavioral categories, and the task is to analyze them statistically. . . . The main effort is directed toward the choice of an adequate sample of relevant questions and toward the most fruitful statistical elaboration. All these steps have to be taken in the interpretative questionnaire also, but they seem relatively simple in comparison with that element characteristic of the interpretative questionnaires only, and that is the interpretation of the answers with regard to their unconscious or unintended meaning. The task of interpretation is, like any other psychoanalytic interpretation, difficult, and takes a great deal of time. It requires knowledge of psychoanalytic theory and therapy (including the experience of one's own analysis), clinical psychoanalytic experience, and, as in everything else, skill and talent. Psychoanalytic interpretation—of associations and dreams as well as of answers to a questionnaire—is an art like the practice of medicine, in which certain theoretical principles are applied to empirical data (1970:26).

The problem here is to maintain standards of reliability. Fromm introduced an element of reliability control by training a group of professional social scientists to score the questionnaires. Scorers were trained by scoring actual questionnaire results for Fromm, who corrected them when their scores disagreed with his own. This itself seems quite a subjective procedure, but most systems of measurement now in wide use by scientists probably had similar beginnings, and, as always, time is the best test of the usefulness of such systems. At present, Fromm's arrangement seems precariously poised on the edge of scientific method, guided by scientific goals but involving more art than science in the application. Perhaps anticipating criticism over the fact that he corrected the scorers in training when their results differed from his, he offered this defense: "The idea that majority agreement or even unanimity of scoring 'reliability' indicates validity of scoring seems to be a misapplication of the democratic ideal to science, confusing the democratic process, which shows the *will* of the majority, with the scientific process, which seeks to discover the *truth*. At best, agreement suggests a probability of correctness, but even an overwhelming majority of scientists may in fact be wrong" (p. 271). The injection of "democracy" into the discussion is, of course, spurious—what is at issue is whether we, the community of scientists, can accept Fromm's and Maccoby's results as valid and reliable measures of theoretically relevant personality variables in this case. Fromm and Maccoby seem to be asking for our faith.

They have selected a research design that puts major emphasis on the holistic description of personality rather than on quantitative measurement of many personality "traits." Their descriptions of character are therefore more global than statistical. Whether different researchers among the same subjects would reach similar results is a concern they explicitly reject as a "misapplication of the democratic ideal."

Research that remains this close to a holistic, humanistic frame will rarely solve operational problems to the satisfaction of most scientists. Fromm and Maccoby, however, did attempt a check on the internal consistency of their coding procedures by comparing codes from their interpretative questionnaire with results of Rorschach and Thematic Apperception Tests done in the same community. The results were mixed: on the one hand, the association between the questionnaire and the other tests was usually statistically significant; on the other hand, the large amounts of disagreement produced by using the various procedures indicated that each was measuring substantially different aspects of "personality."

The attempt by Fromm and Maccoby to relate social character to other sociocultural phenomena is of the greatest potential importance. For example, their results show a number of statistically significant associations between character types and such variables as sex, economic position, and religious behavior, among them: (1) men tend to be classed as "receptive" and "narcissistic," whereas women are most often "hoarding" and "masochistic" (pp. 144–45); (2) the poorest men in the community tend to be classed as "passive-receptive," whereas the most well-to-do are predominantly of the "hoarding" character type (pp. 137–38); (3) men classified as "productive" tend to be those that attend Mass most often (p. 140).

If we could take these findings at face value, then we would have unusually good evidence that differences in individual circumstances such as wealth and division of labor predict differences in character and ideology, lending plausibility to the theoretical framework of the culture-and-personality orientation. The inclusion of all community members permits comparison of subgroups within the community, and this in turn generates more useful statistics for comparisons with other communities.

On balance, however, the findings of Fromm and Maccoby must be treated with reserve. In addition to the operational obscurity of the character codes, the statistical correlations between character and other variables, though significant, are in most cases too low ($0.20 \leqslant r \leqslant 0.30$) to have substantial theoretical significance. The study stands as a challenge to methodological inventiveness rather than as a definitive example of successful research design.

More Rigorous Approaches

Uses of projective materials. If we could simply ask people to tell us their personal characteristics, culture-and-personality researchers could rely on questionnaires for data and concentrate their ingenuity on methods of processing the data. But field experience shows that individuals give misleading information about their personal feelings, even when they are trying to be honest and helpful. Many of the aspects of the personality useful in both clinical practice and cross-cultural research are unconscious, or at least not susceptible to direct verbalization by the informant. Hence culture-and-personality research must rely on a number of "projective" devices for inferring personality states.

The "interpretative questionnaire" used by Fromm and Maccoby is, loosely speaking, such a projective device. Informants are given considerable freedom to express themselves, and the researcher then infers from the responses deep-lying character orientations. But as we have seen in the Fromm and Maccoby example, interpretative questionnaires, and projective devices in general, pose serious operational problems.

The best-known projective device, the Rorschach Inkblot Test, has been used frequently for cross-cultural research (for instances, see Lindzey 1961), but the outcome appears to have been a general loss of faith in the technique by anthropologists (Pelto 1970:112–16; Edgerton 1970:340; Spain 1972:277–79). The main problems are that Rorschach responses are difficult to code and to relate to other specific attributes of the individual, and that interpretation of Rorschach protocols is disputed even within the framework of our culture, let alone others.

Another well-known device, the Thematic Apperception Test (TAT) has, in various modified forms, held greater attraction for anthropologists. The drawings used in the TAT depict recognizable human shapes and situations, but the feelings and activities of the figures in the drawings are deliberately unspecified. Respondents are asked to make up stories about the drawings, and these stories are analyzed to elicit inner states of the respondents. Because the figures in the drawings are clothed and surrounded by artifacts, however, the original TAT drawings are not useful in cultural settings other than the one in which they were drawn; outside that setting, informants focus on minor discrepancies of material culture when the main purpose of the test is to elicit feelings about oneself and interpersonal relations. For this reason, some anthropologists have modified TAT drawings to fit the particular settings in which they have been working. In some cases these modifications have actually been more than mere literal translations of the originals— the content of the scenes has been altered as well according to the specific purposes of the research. Some examples of research using modified TAT drawings follow.

DeVos and Wagatsuma (1961), in their study of Japanese villagers' feelings about family roles, remained close to the original TAT drawings, though they added a few of their own. For the most part, they retained original TAT scenes intact and simply gave the figures and households a Japanese appearance.

Noting that the status of women in the past had tended to be higher in fishing villages than in agricultural villages because of the division of labor (which had given women in fishing villages more direct authority in the household), the authors sought differences in attitudes toward the family in two communities—one a fishing village, the other an agricultural village—both of which were under modern pressure to equalize the status of men and women. Members of the two villages were asked to view the modified TAT drawings and make up stories about them. The nearly 1,200 stories recorded were then analyzed for emotional content concerning family roles. For example, if a story expressed tension in a marriage, this was noted; when the story also specified whether a marriage resulted from parental decisions, or was a "love marriage," a comparison became possible. In the fishing village, stories revealed no differences in marriage tension between arranged and love marriages; but in the farming village love marriages were seen as creating much more tension than arranged marriages. The authors felt that these results reflected the lower status of wives in the agricultural community, where the husband has traditionally had greater loyalty to his parents than to his wife.

In an earlier study, DeVos and Wagatsuma had asked the agricultural villagers directly about marriage and had found that they readily accepted the idea of love marriages. Yet the indirect evidence of their responses to the TAT drawings suggests that love matches, though normatively acceptable, might be avoided in practice because of the tensions they engender. This is just the sort of finding projective devices are useful in establishing. DeVos's and Wagatsuma's demonstration of connections between values and socioeconomic conditions is sounder than that of Fromm and Maccoby primarily because less inference is required to discover a single element like "marital tension" in a story than to discover an individual's whole character from a complex of responses toa questionnaire.

Spindler and Spindler (1965) also used a modified TAT—this one known as the Instrumental Activities Inventory—in their research on acculturation among the Blood Indians of Alberta, Canada. Viewing acculturation as a change in environment to which the Blood would have to adapt by changing their pattern of work, the Spindlers developed a set of drawings of Blood involved in traditional and modern occupations (instrumental activites).

The drawings were less ambiguous than the original TAT ones:

they represented clearly recognizable work scenes and did not have the suggestive interpersonal content of the TAT. The Spindlers' intent in using them was to get people talking about practical aspects of their work and the possibilities they saw for themselves as Indians confronting "whiteman" society. Analysis of the IAI stories, though nonquantitative, revealed a concern among the Blood for autonomy and physical action, as well as a concrete realism, quite different from the instrumental attitudes of the whites with whom they were competing for jobs.

Recently, McElroy (1974) redrew the IAI for a sample of Inuit (Eskimo) children. Subjects were asked to select from a group of drawings those showing the kind of work they would like to do when adults. McElroy was able to treat her results quantitatively because the subjects themselves "coded" the responses simply by choosing a drawing. The study established some statistically significant results: for example, girls were significantly more oriented to what McElroy classed as "modern" occupations than boys, who tended to choose culturally "transitional" kinds of work. (Spindler and Spindler [1965:12] report a related finding among the Blood.) McElroy also included a valuable discussion of the limitations of the IAI technique and made suggestions for its improvement (1974:9–14).

In a far more ambitious study than the three we have just been considering, Edgerton, a member of the Culture and Ecology in East Africa Project (see Goldschmidt 1965), used modified TAT drawings to explore personality differences between cattle pastoralists and hoe agriculturalists in East Africa (Edgerton 1971). Taking an ecological perspective, he and his co-workers proposed that personality differences should exist between members of such contrasting ecological regimes as pastoralism and farming. The difficulty was to design research that would permit the isolation of specific differences resulting from ecology rather than from general cultural-historical factors.

Edgerton's solution was to choose four different cultural groups (Hehe, Kamba, Pokot, and Sebei), within each of which were both farming and pastoral communities. One farming and one pastoral site were chosen from each group, resulting in eight sites altogether. Edgerton reasoned that if pastoralists from distinct cultural groups could be shown to share certain traits with each other that they did not share with their culturally related farming counterparts, then those traits could be said to have arisen from the causal influence of ecological variables (see Goldschmidt's "Introduction" to Edgerton 1971).

In addition to Rorschachs, interviews, photographs, and direct observations, Edgerton used a modified TAT representing interpersonal scenes in the East African context in his research. Separate drawings were made for each of the four cultural groups by a local artist. The drawings were not as close to those in the original TAT as DeVos's and Wagatsuma's were, and they were less specific and concrete than the Spindlers' IAI drawings, on the whole. Regardless, they were successful at all eight sites in eliciting stories from informants, which were then analyzed for "manifest content" by recording the presence or absence of expressions of a large number of specific feelings such as "affection," "direct aggression," and "jealousy of wealth."

Though the TAT and other procedures uncovered some "cultural" responses that were not much affected by the farming/pastoral division, a number of strong differences were found between agricultural and pastoral groups. Quantitative data demonstrated, for example, that pastoralists consistently showed more respect for authority than farmers (Edgerton 1971:176–77), and more open interest in sexuality (pp. 185–88). Drawing on many such findings, as well as on intuitive knowledge based on participant observation, Edgerton developed an ecological argument accounting for pastoral/farmer differences that is remarkable for its balance of scientific rigor, humanist sensitivity, and plain good sense (pp. 271–94).

A type of projective material that has not been subject to much quantitative analysis is the content of dreams. Yet dreams hold promise in cross-cultural research because everyone experiences them, most people are willing to talk about them, and they are autochthonous (i.e., not elicited by stimuli constructed by the researcher). LeVine (1966) used dream analysis to develop a quantitative description of the differences between three cultural groups

(Ibo [Igbo], Yoruba, and Hausa) in Nigeria. He was interested in the relationship between achievement motivation and economic development; his initial analyses of historical and ethnographic data led him to propose that the Ibo should show the most achievement motivation, the Hausa the least, and the Yoruba an amount in between.

Dreams of secondary-school boys were collected and then coded for the presence or absence of achievement imagery. At this level coders reached a good degree of agreement, but it proved impossible to go beyond the nominal level and assess degree of achievement motivation. Nonetheless, LeVine's predictions were confirmed by the presence-absence data: 43 percent of the Ibo dreams contained achievement imagery, whereas only 17 percent of the Hausa dreams did; as expected, the Yoruba were intermediate with 35 percent (LeVine 1966:56).

The applications of projective devices discussed above have been sufficiently modest and cautious that reliability, though always a problem, is not the critical problem it was in the Fromm and Maccoby study. The persistent difficulty with the TAT-type procedures is that each change of the stimulus to suit local culture and research goals introduces uncertainty about the cross-cultural comparability of the results. It is difficult to decide, for example, whether the Japanese farmers' anxieties about love marriages are related to the East African farmers' apparent repression of sexuality in their responses to the drawings. The Rorschach Inkblot Tests are said to be free of cultural bias to a great extent, but the difficulties in their interpretation and the consequent vagueness of the results has restricted their usefulness. A similar vagueness appears to hamper the interpretation of dreams (Strangman 1966:97).

As a rule, any psychological research that infers inner states such as emotions or character dynamics from data collected with projective tests will encounter serious problems of reliability. Evidence is clear that different tests yield different, though not necessarily contradictory, descriptions of the same individual. For example, Maccoby and Foster (1970) used Rorschachs, TATs, and dream interpretations to describe a peasant woman living in Tzintzuntzan, Mexico.

They found that Rorschach protocols were especially likely to reveal "cognitive" traits such as ability to reason, whereas TATs were most revealing of traits related to interpersonal relations (because most TAT cards represent social scenes), and dreams provided clearest evidence of emotions such as loneliness or happiness. Among the researchers we have been considering in this chapter, Edgerton has made perhaps the most systematic use of a variety of projective tests and other eliciting procedures in order to develop a sense of the strong patterns that appeared more than once in the separate bodies of data; his lead is certainly one to follow.

Behavioral observations. A promising direction for new research in the area of culture and personality is in the direct observation and coding of individual behavior, some of the methods for which we discussed in the previous chapter. In this section we review several studies that have put direct observations to good use in analyzing personality differences cross-culturally.

The relation between "behavior" and "personality" is often assumed to be direct, but there is little concrete evidence one way or the other. To explain this with an example, individuals who are scored high on "nurturance" from projective or interview materials are assumed to behave nurturantly, but whether in fact they do has not been demonstrated cross-culturally. Researchers have tended to collect behavioral data on their younger subjects, who do not give useful interviews; older subjects have been interviewed rather than observed. Thus it happens that conventional research design by and large prevents cross-checking the validity of interview measures with behavioral ones. This is unfortunate, because the "socialization environment" is both behavioral and normative; children not only are told what to do, they observe and imitate, feeling their way into proper roles as much as being instructed.

According to our macro-orientation, which might be said to take a psycho-ecological perspective of culture and personality, differences in ecological practices should be reflected in childhood experiences, including behavioral ones. Munroe and Munroe (1974) have provided evidence for this view in the results of their work among the Logoli of Kenya. Taking as their point of departure cross-cultural evidence indicating that extended-family households showed more indulgence to infants than nuclear-family households, the Munroes studied the Logoli, among whom both kinds of households are found. The Munroes initially thought that infants in extended-family households might be shown to be *less* rather than more indulged among the Logoli, since Logoli women are the major food producers for the household, and mothers in extended families almost never take infants with them to work. They visited households at varying times to observe care of infants, noting who the caretaker was at the moment of observation, whether the infant was held, how long it cried before receiving attention, and so on. They found that in extended-family households the mother was indeed less often the caretaker than in nuclear-family households ($r = -.65$); however, they also found that because of the greater number of additional caretakers available in the larger households, infants there were "indulged" *more* often. For example, there was a direct correlation between the amount of time infants were held and size of household ($r = .76$); moreover, there was an inverse correlation between the amount of time that elapsed after an infant cried before it was cared for and family size ($r = -.90$; that is, the larger the household, the shorter the response time). In sum, both "productive labor" and "settlement pattern" were found to influence the behavioral environment of the infant.

An issue to which quantitative behavioral data have been applied is whether sex differences in personality are attributable to genetic determinants or to differences in socialization practices. For example, Ember (1973) found among the Luo of Kenya that some boys were assigned girls' tasks when no other siblings were available for the work; her question was, did their involvement in female tasks alter their behavior in other realms as well? Direct observations of 28 children, made in random order (though not randomly by time of day) were coded by native assistants as "egoistic" (self-serving) or "prosocial" (good for the group); egoistic behavior was further subdivided into "aggression," "dependency," or "dominance." Interviews with children and mothers were used to decide which tasks were identified as "female," and which boys were most involved with female tasks. Ember's data showed that boys who did little female work were highest on egoistic behavior of all kinds, whereas girls were highest on prosocial behavior; boys who did much female work were intermediate, supporting the hypothesis that task involvement is a good predictor of differences in boys' social behavior (see also B. Whiting & Edwards 1974).

The Six Cultures Project. The collection of behavioral data in culture-and-personality research has been strongly influenced by the Six Cultures Project, which originally grew out of dissatisfaction with existing ethnographic materials and the cross-cultural theories of personality development they made possible. It was felt that data in ethnographies had been collected by researchers lacking both training and specific interest in culture and personality; moreover, variations from individual to individual within cultural units were rarely described (see J. Whiting 1966:vii–viii). The main stages of the Six Cultures Project to date have been (1) the formulation, through the common participation of all researchers-in-training in a prefield seminar, of a set of "variables" (self-reliance, nurturance, sociability) that would form the common basis of study in the separate field projects (J. Whiting et al. 1966); (2) fieldwork by separate teams of researchers in Kenya, India, Okinawa, the Philippines, Mexico, and New England; (3) the preparation by each team of a general ethnographic description of its field setting (B. Whiting 1963); and (4) a report on the mothers (Minturn & Lambert 1964); and (5) a report on the children (B. Whiting & Whiting 1975).

By means of the prefield training, a degree of comparability in the kinds of data collected during the fieldwork was guaranteed. Readers of the *Field Guide for a Study of Socialization* (J. Whiting et al. 1966) who were not themselves members of the original seminar, however, will find that the concepts described there are difficult to apply in the field. The *Field Guide* names broad kinds of behavior (nurturance, succorance) and says something about where to look for such behavior (e.g., nurturant behavior might occur "when younger sibling cries or is hurt"). But exactly what to describe was left to individual researchers to work out in the field. Field observations were recorded in prose notes and mailed to universities in the

United States, where trained coders reduced data that were not already quantitative to computer-manipulable form. For example, descriptions of parental care for children were coded along a number of "scales," such as the scale "Amount of Time Mothers Care for Children," which was coded as either 0 (no answer), 1 (never), 3 (sometimes), 5 (about half the time), 7 (usually), or 9 (always).

Now coding in this fashion, far from the field situation and without the intuitive judgments of the fieldworker, pays a price in loss of information. For example, in *Children of Six Cultures* we learn that behavior coded as "Assaults" is very different from behavior coded as "Assaults Sociably." Multidimensional analysis of behavioral data suggests that "Assaults" behavior is associated with other behaviors, such as "Reprimands," that are called "authoritarian-aggressive" by the authors; by contrast, "Assaults Sociably" behavior is classed with "Acts Sociably" as "sociable-intimate" at the opposite end of the dimension from "authoritarian-aggressive." But when we look for the procedure whereby these two categories were distinguished, we find that the main criterion was apparently whether or not the prose description of the assault stated that it was accompanied by laughter (B. Whiting & Whiting 1975:66–69; 193–94). Thus whereas the text distinguishes between "sociable" and "nonsociable" assaults, the real distinction appears to have been between "assaults with laughter" and "assaults without laughter." From this example we can see why fieldworkers interested in duplicating this study elsewhere will be unable to know—owing to the lack of precise operationalization of concepts—whether their coding decisions at this level of precision (i.e., the level of actual measurement) will correspond to those made in the original study.

Losses of information in coding, and the possibility of miscoding in cross-cultural studies, are probably necessary costs of cross-cultural comparability. The judgment that must be made is whether the costs have been justified by the benefits—and in the Six Cultures study they have, by results that are as sound and useful as any that appear in the anthropological literature. As an example, we may look at some of the observations on children. The data on children are more interesting than those on mothers because of the differing research strategies used: data on mothers came from extensive interviews, and though the data are phrased in behavioral terms, they merely report a mother's evaluation of her own probable behavior in hypothetical situations; but data on children were based on direct observations of activity over five-minute periods and really do represent behavior patterns.

Whiting and Whiting found that societies where children showed high frequencies of behaviors classed as "sociable-intimate" tended to have high frequencies of nuclear-family residence (79 percent–96 percent); on the other hand, societies where children tended toward "authoritarian-aggressive" behavior had low frequencies of nuclear households (33 percent–46 percent; 1975:114–15). Analysis of the quantitative data, as well as a very helpful mix of nonquantitative ethnographic background, suggested to the Whitings the following associations (1975:127–28):

Sociable-Intimate	*Authoritarian-Aggressive*
nuclear families	extended families
loose residence rules	rigid residence rules
husband-wife sleep together	husband-wife sleep apart
low overt husband-wife aggression	high husband-wife aggression
father-child relations close	father-child relations distant

These results, and others like them, are interesting and suggestive and will no doubt contribute to the shape of culture-and-personality research for many years to come. Their quality is, relatively speaking, very high indeed, the Whitings having been careful to make their judgments flow directly from ethnographic detail and the quantitative results of data analysis. The Whitings have taken the opposite approach to that of Fromm and Maccoby. We recall that, for the latter, personality was fundamentally a "system" concept: an individual was said to possess a "social character" that could be described as the integrated product of a small number of holistically complex dimensions. The Whitings, by contrast, have chosen to look at a large number of separate variables, each operationally simpler and clearer than the character types of Fromm and Maccoby, but none automatically linked to the others in a systemic sense. The "systemness" of the variables is then permitted to emerge from their correlations with each other. The difference in results is seen in the lesser scope and drama of the Whitings's findings, compensated for by their greater precision, rigor, and replicability.

The Whitings have been criticized for remaining too close to their quantitative, "objective" approach and thus sacrificing a deeper understanding: "Would we not also gain something from a comparative analysis of the six cultures undertaken by someone thoroughly familiar with the data—someone imaginative, speculative, willing to make inferences that could be documented with data?" (Honigmann 1976:217). Honigmann's criticism misses the mark, though, by not facing the implication of the phrase "documented with data": speculative and inferential conclusions are just those that cannot be documented with data. From a strictly empiricist stance, even the Whitings's report is full of speculation and inference, much of which would be considered unjustified by a laboratory-oriented scientist. Nonetheless, Honigmann's point is an important one. Culture-and-personality research must strike a balance between quantitative findings and intuitive conclusions without becoming overcommitted to one or the other. It is perhaps a recognition of this that has led recently to a revived interest among methodologically oriented researchers in open-ended, lengthy interviews as a source of data (Edgerton 1970:345; LeVine 1973:215–25). LeVine has even suggested that psychoanalytically trained fieldworkers should collaborate with native social scientists, wherever possible, to interpret the latent meanings of verbal and nonverbal behavior. The value of interviews in which informants are encouraged to talk openly about what is on·their minds lies in developing the fieldworker's intuition. The dilemma facing the interviewer committed to an approximation of scientific rigor (in that sense of the "hard" sciences used in Chapter 1),however, is that the more structured the interview, the more likely it will produce results subject to quantitative analysis, whereas the less structured the interview, the more likely it will follow paths unanticipated by the researcher and productive of serendipitous insights.

In this chapter we have reviewed several studies done from an explicit ecological perspective. Data, for the most part quantitative, have revealed relationships between "personality" characteristics and variables such as wealth, farming versus herding or fishing, settlement patterns, and task assignment, all of which fall well within the ecological definition of the cultural core. These cases establish culture-and-personality research as a vital and effective part of cultural anthropology, unusually responsive to the need for more operational research designs. Three of the problems encountered deserve special recognition.

First, these studies have taken a quantitative approach to the problem of *sharing* of personality characteristics, in contrast to earlier approaches that tended to describe whole communities or regions in terms of single personality orientations. Now it is recognized that differences in individual life experiences, which can often be described in ecological terms as stemming from the division of labor, the nature of work, and social relations of production, lead to predictable differences in personality within single communities or regions.

Second, we have identified a major inconsistency in research practice between studies of children, which concentrate on directly observed behavior, and studies of adults, which rely heavily on interviews. There is no a priori reason why adult behavior cannot also be coded; and, though it is true that children cannot answer all the questions adults can, the degree to which children can respond to interviews has not really been tested cross-culturally. If we are not to remain bound by the unverified assumption that people behave in the ways they say they do when responding to interview questions, then a main priority for future research in culture and personality must be to combine behavioral and normative approaches in describing individual personalities.

Finally, we have seen that culture-and-personality research embodies in a particular form the general incompatibility between humanist and scientific perspectives. Those devices that aim to reveal latent, holistic "character," such as the Rorschach, interpretative questionnaires, and even dream analysis, are vague and must be intuitively understood. Those devices that aim at the manifest and objective, such as the several variations on the TAT, are more reliable measures, but describe traits of personality rather than whole persons. If it is to have the breadth to include both kinds of information, culture-and-personality research requires designs that include a battery of procedures from the operationally explicit to the intuitively rich.

CHAPTER SEVEN

The Maximization Orientation

FEW IDEAS IN Western thought have deeper roots or wider currency than that individual behavior may be understood as an effort to identify one's own self-interest, and then to act in accordance with it. In anthropology, the interest in "rational choice" has centered in the subfield known as Formal Economics, though it appears loosely and implicitly in such formulations as Barth's "transactions" (Barth 1966) and Foster's "dyadic contract" (Foster 1961). It is also implicit in arguments made frequently by ecological anthropologists that a given socioeconomic system is adjusted so that something of value, such as nutritional well-being or the population size of a region, is "maximized" or "optimized" (Douglas White 1973).

Studies under the maximization orientation focus on decision processes occurring within the individual. This essential individualism is generalized by social scientists in the form:

$$A_i = V_i \times P_i$$

where A_i is the expected reward of alternative i, V_i is the measure of value of outcome i, and P_i is the probability of success of i. The "expected reward" to the individual of a given alternative is thus the product of the value of its outcome times the probability of its success, and maximization theorists assume that, given a variety of alternatives, an individual will choose the one likely to yield the largest reward.

As Homans has shown, this formulation is sufficiently general to apply to explanations in psychology, history, economics, and anthropology (1967:43), but the very generality of this abstract form of maximization theory renders it trivial unless operationalized.

> To say that an individual strives to maximize his satisfactions is to state little more than a truism. Unless satisfactions are expressed in some more concrete form, such as money, they are ill-defined and of course may shift from time to time for the same person and also be different for various individuals. All that is really said is that our behavior is goal-minded and that the various immediate goals are themselves measurable with respect to one another and can be scaled. It certainly does not help us to predict human behavior, since the only way we know what is desired is to watch the choices people make. So, we are faced with a dilemma. If we state that people act so as to maximize something broad enough ("satisfactions") to subsume all our more specific goals, we say very little. If we state that people act so as to maximize one particular goal—power, money, income, or whatever we choose—then usually we are incorrect. But the idea of maximization cannot be abandoned since any discussion of purposive or goal-oriented behavior, or any analysis of choice, does imply a maximization theory and we may as well make explicit a common notion in the social sciences, and for that matter in all of our everyday thinking. (Burling 1962:817.)

Measurement and Maximization

Referring to our basic formula, $A_i = V_i \times P_i$, we can readily identify the information needed in a maximization analysis. Usually the frame of reference is narrowed by making some assumptions about which goals are shaping individual decisions; for example, we could assume our subjects are motivated to maintain a nutritional diet. Then we may take three basic steps: first, we should identify each alternative action (A_i) open to an individual (e.g., gardening, hunting, marketing, etc.); second, we should measure the value or "utility" (V_i) of the outcomes of each action (e.g., the value to the individual of the meat, produce, etc. resulting from his actions); and third, we should estimate the subjective probability (P_i) that action A_i will result in the outcomes measured by V_i (e.g., if hunting is action (m), then what do our subjects believe is the probability (P_m) that game of value V_m will in fact result?).

From an ecological perspective, the starting place for measuring "value" is those processes of clear biological relevance to the individual. Input-output description (Chapter 4) is therefore a necessary antecedent to maximization analysis. Maximization is a psychological orientation, however, referring primarily to actors' states of mind. Even though in practice many maximization arguments assume that the "objective" value of an alternative—as measured by food value, money, or some other standard—is the one being used by the actors in making their decisions, such assumptions set the cognitive decision process entirely aside in a sort of "black box" that is never opened.

If it is accepted that some form of maximization or decision process is involved in human behavior in every cultural setting, then attention is directed to the question, "What is being maximized?" Economists in practice generally choose cash profit as the measure of value, but for anthropologists, who need a cross-culturally general standard of value, the use of cash profit has led to serious problems of operationalization (Cook 1973:797). In this chapter we review several studies that have used quantitative data to analyze observed human situations from a maximization orientation. All the studies treat specific, culturally contrasting ways of making a living, and all rely to some degree on cash measures of value. The limits of cash as a measure, and the need for truly cognitive studies of decision-making, will become clear as the examples are presented. The chapter closes with discussion of a mathematical model, based on the maximization orientation, that successfully predicts many features of a complex marketing system.

Maximization Relying Principally on Cash Measures

For an anthropologist with an economic orientation, the obvious solution to the problem of measuring utility is to use cash values. In this section we shall examine two studies that used cash to describe the outcomes of the strategies available to individuals in given situations.

Zinacantan. For our first example, we resume the discussion of Zinacanteco farmers begun in Chapter 4 (Frank Cancian 1972). We

TABLE 7.1

Expected Net Returns to Zinacanteco Farmers
Under Normal Conditions, in Pesos

Amount of corn seeded	Distance from Zinacantan			
	zone 1	zone 2	zone 6	zone 9
1 *almud*	428	571	691	714
2 *almudes*	637	834	1,268	1,385
4 *almudes*	638	988	1,950	2,217
6 *almudes*	608	1,154	2,647	3,015

SOURCE: Frank Cancian 1972: 101.
NOTE: The higher the zone number, the greater the distance from Zinacantan.

recall that through quantitative measurement of input (costs of land, seed, transportation, and labor other than the farmer's own, since the latter was considered "unmeasurable" in cash terms), a table of net return (value) of alternative economic strategies was generated (Table 4.1, reproduced here as Table 7.1). A major goal of Cancian's analysis was to discover whether or not observed Zinacanteco farmers' strategies conformed to the "rational" pattern predicted from the data in the table.

We may view Table 7.1 as an estimate, using cash values, of the "utility function" employed by Zinacanteco corn farmers in deciding where and how much to plant each year. Cancian showed that a Zinacanteco wishing to support his family by farming needed to achieve a minimal family income of about 900 pesos per year on average (1972: 103). From the data in his table, he predicted that no farmer who planted only one *almud*, or who planted only in zone 1, would achieve the minimum required income by that strategy. This prediction was borne out in practice: the only farmers Cancian found planting one *almud* of corn were those who pursued a "mixed economic activity" strategy combining farming with wage labor or commercial activities; similarly, no farmers planted in zone 1, except for occasional short-term investments (1972: 103–4). Two other predictions based on the table were not borne out, however: the first was that Zinacanteco farmers would plant most in the farthest zone; the second, that they would plant as many *almudes* as possible. Investigation showed that in both instances just the opposite was the case. Cancian found that 94 farmers planted in zone 2, 43 in zone 6, and 29 in zone 9; moreover, 80 planted 2 *almudes*, 44 planted 4 *almudes*, and only 30 planted 6 *almudes* (1972:98–99).

In asking why more Zinacantecos did not farm in zone 9, Cancian discovered factors whose effects he had not taken into account in constructing his original hypotheses. The distant lands had only recently become available for farming, and farmers considering a switch to them faced the prospect of initial costs that might prove prohibitive; moreover, at the outset there was considerable uncertainty about the potential benefits of bringing the new lands into production. We can see the problem: Cancian's hypotheses were framed on the basis of data gathered at a single point in time well after the introduction of the new lands; but it takes people time to assess the relative value of changes in existing patterns of production, and for the Zinacantecos a sufficient period of time had not yet elapsed to bring them into line with Cancian's value projections.

Support for this notion is supplied by the diachronic data on land use Cancian provides (see Table 7.2). We can see that between 1957 and 1966 the corn farmers in Cancian's sample were changing their pattern of land use *in the direction* predicted by the cash maximization model. The increased availability of all-weather roads and of governmental price-stabilization as the period wore on had an important effect on this development, too.

In asking why the Zinacantecos did not plant more *almudes*, Cancian found that in the matter of choosing a scale of operations, too,

TABLE 7.2
*Percentages of Zinacanteco Farmers Planting in
Different Zones, 1957–66*

Year	Zone						
	2	4	5	6	7	8	9
1957	44%	28%	15%	10%	1%	–	1%
1960	34	26	19	16	5	–	1
1963	23	28	19	15	2	6%	6
1966	13	22	21	12	4	12	15

SOURCE: Frank Cancian 1972: 122.

farmers had to take into account a number of factors. For example, larger scale entailed greater risk, required more capital investment, was more profitable the greater the managerial skill of the farmer, and was somehow related to "something that must be labeled self-image" (p. 106). Clearly, the farmer's total personal situation entered into the decision of what scale to choose.* Cancian concluded his analysis with an attempt to explain why some individuals chose to gamble on higher earnings in the face of uncertainty, whereas others did not. To this end he constructed an explicit theory of the role of economic status in risk-taking, from which predictions of the probable risk facing an innovator could be derived. When compared with the actual statuses of innovating individuals, these predictions were strongly borne out.

The net effect of the data Cancian presents is to provide strong support for the argument that the model of cash maximization presented in Table 7.1 *can* successfully predict farmers' decisions, provided the recent changes which give that model its current shape are taken into account.

But by this point Cancian's argument has moved a long way from its simple cash maximization beginnings. The final form is much more realistic, but the quantitative precision of the earlier form has been lost. The usefulness of the cash maximization model is undeniable: "As I see it, the data in the body of this book clearly support the position of those who see subsistence agriculture as dominated by economic forces and describable in terms of economic theory. The study's emphasis on the uncertainty characteristic of a change situation suggests limits on the applicability of economic theory; but wherever information is adequate, and sometimes before information is adequate, Zinacantecos respond to economic incentives" (1972:192). On the other hand, the facts show that the majority of Zinacantecos still did not conform to the predictions of the cash maximization model at the time of the study. Cancian stresses the role of uncertainty during change, but also shows the relevance of

---

*The problem of how to estimate these sorts of utility considerations in quantitative terms is not addressed by Cancian, and indeed is not addressed in most anthropological studies of maximization.

personal abilities, self-image, and economic rank as aspects of decision-making. Thus while confirming the value of cash maximization analysis in predicting aspects of Zinacanteco corn farming, Cancian simultaneously reveals the limitations of such analysis. This suggests the need to extend the measurement of "utility" beyond the calculations of cash profits.

The same point applies to many anthropological studies of economic behavior. Cook, for example, offered extensive quantitative time-series data showing that Zapotec villages in Mexico produced maize-grinding *metates* for market in response to seasonal changes in the market prices of *metates* (1970:780–83). But by far the greater part of his analysis was given over to the nonquantitative listing of other variables also influencing *metate* production, which included competing needs for labor in agriculture, the requirements of the ritual cycle, and the effects of weather.

Cape Coast markets. An interesting measurement problem arises when there is reason to believe that cash maximization is important to the people making decisions, but when people's strategies cannot be directly expressed in cash terms. Gladwin and Gladwin (1972) faced this problem among Fante fish-sellers of Cape Coast, Ghana. They asked market women to describe how they made their market decisions. In some cases, the descriptions were easily quantified— sheer numerical quantities of fish, for example, were one important consideration. But other factors resisted easy quantification. For example, fish-sellers used a large number of terms for describing market supply and demand, such as "the fish came in plenty" (supply large) or "the market was sweet" (demand large). Since the Gladwins were interested in constructing a decision model that would predict actual behavior, they needed some way to translate these qualitative expressions into quantitative values.

From their preliminary work, the Gladwins had discovered some basic facts about Cape Coast markets. Those markets close to the shore presented fish-sellers with the advantages of low overhead and low risk, but with the disadvantages of relatively heavy competition, low sales volume, and small profit potential. Markets in the hinterland, several hours away by truck, presented opportunities for high sales volume and large profits, though risk and overhead costs involved in going there were relatively great. In the absence of purely quantitative data such as those with which Cancian constructed his model of Zinacanteco farmers' marketing strategies, the Gladwins adopted the following technique for assigning quantitative values to the qualitative terms fish-sellers used in describing market conditions: they followed fish-sellers to market and asked them to describe the characteristics of the market on a given day; when the consensus among fish-sellers was that the market was "sweet," the Gladwins took careful note of the typical cash values fish brought on that day. In this way the Gladwins were able to substitute purely quantitative data into the maximization equation over time.

The matter of probability of success (e.g., that the market will be "sweet" on any given day) was more difficult, however. Though fish-sellers talked freely about past and present states of markets, they modestly refrained from speculating about the future. This forced the Gladwins to estimate probabilities based on their own market observations. These and similar results were then worked into a complex decision model predicting fish-sellers' behavior, but the model failed to predict the observed market behavior of the fish-sellers. The Gladwins, rather than question the adequacy of their model, discussed certain biases in their observational data that they believed might account for the discrepancy.

But here I think we must exercise caution. Anthropologists who use maximization theory are sometimes too ready to expect decision models based on cash profit to predict actual behavior. The examples thus far demonstrate that cash maximization models based even on careful fieldwork do not predict behavioral outcomes with a high degree of accuracy. There are always exceptions, and usually the exceptions predominate. Recognition of this fact should not alarm proponents of the maximization orientation, since all this means is what anthropologists have long acknowledged—that individuals rarely maximize *only* cash returns. Security, prestige, and other values may carry overwhelming weight in particular contexts. Economists, after presenting their theoretical arguments in abstract mathematical terms, can set out a correspondence rule stating that "in this particular case, we will let cash be our measure of utility"; but as we have seen, this simple solution does not take the anthropologist very far.

Alternatives to Cash

Indifference analysis. It is perhaps inevitable that anthropologists working under the maximization orientation will have to accept lower levels of measurement than those permitted to economists by their use of cash values. Simon, in fact, has argued that individual decision-makers operate with fairly crude measures of utility, and probably seek an "adequate" level of some valued good rather than the maximum of it. Under such circumstances ordinal and even nominal scales of measurement may serve very well (Simon 1957:245–52).

Edel (1969) has suggested that the technique of "indifference analysis" may be useful to anthropologists. The basic idea of indifference analysis is to locate the combinations of desired goods between which an individual is indifferent; such combinations can then be regarded as equivalent in terms of "psychic income." For example, if I do not care whether I get a combination of six bushels of wheat and one pair of shoes, or two bushels of wheat and three pairs of shoes, then both combinations have equivalent value to me. But if I regard either combination as less desirable than four bushels of wheat and three pairs of shoes, then this latter combination may be ranked as "higher" in utility.* Since any decision is likely to be the product of the weighing together of a *combination* of valued goods, such as money and prestige and leisure, "a complete map of an individual's preferences would require many dimensions. . . . The utility function . . . need not include only tangible goods. Leisure, time spent in ritual, the well-being of other people, prestige, or power over others all may enter the utility function. Although

---

*Actually, it is conceivable that indifference analysis could achieve numerical measures of utility (see Luce & Raiffa 1957:19–23, 371–84); but, as Edel points out, utility is most often taken as an ordinal scale.

economists do not normally treat such cases (save for that in which leisure is treated as a wanted good), conceptually there is no reason why they should not be included" (Edel 1969:423).

Conceptually (i.e., theoretically) there is no difficulty, to be sure, but practically the measurement difficulties are enormous. First, individual wants must be identified; second, the outcomes of particular decisions must be analyzed into their want-fulfilling components; and, finally, individuals must judge which outcomes will leave them feeling equivalently well-off. Characteristically, after having been told there is no reason not to do this, we are told nothing about how to go about doing it. In particular, it is likely in many situations that the last determination—individual judgments of equivalence—will be impossible to make, whether through interviews or through observations.

Mfantse fishing crews. As an example of a more practical approach to maximization using an alternative to simple cash measures, we may taken Quinn's (1971) study of Mfantse fishing-crew composition.

Recognizing the limitations of cash profit as an index of utility, Quinn attempted to identify the "bundle" of considerations Mfantse fishermen used in deciding whether to stay with or leave particular fishing-boat crews. In addition to cash earnings, she included various measures of "attraction" to fishing boats, such as cash invested in equipment, claims to inherit equipment, kinship relations, feelings of friendship, and skill. She then correlated these variables with a large number of decisions to leave or to stay. Her findings showed that cash earnings of the crew were apparently not a relevant consideration in such decisions, but that investments in or claims on equipment, ability to participate in decisions, and presence of kinsmen were all of major importance.

Quinn's research design has much to recommend it. She focused on a fundamental problem in the lives of Mfantse fishermen, and succeeded in establishing a solid decision model in the partial absence of cash values for utility. Informants were asked to describe the considerations they used in making their decisions. This resulted, as it often does, in a list of "decision criteria" in no particular order of importance. But, having extensive data on fishermen's actual decisions to stay with particular crews rather than leave and join others, Quinn asked in each case which decision criteria were involved. The decision criteria could then be ordered according to their importance as measured by how often they figured in observed outcomes.

Maximization and Markets

Maximization reasoning applies to individuals, but, as the above examples illustrate, maximization *analysis* generally applies to groups of individuals ("Zinacanteco corn farmers," "Mfantse fishermen"). Economic theory is particularly concerned with predicting the flows of goods and services in *markets*, where it is assumed that each individual is maximizing utility (read *profit*). Again, as in the examples we have already considered, there is some doubt whether marketing models based on the maximization of profit will predict observed outcomes of human decisions in nonindustrial settings.

Smith's research on markets in Guatemala (1972; 1975) is of special interest because it applies to the whole marketing region of Western Guatemala, a geographical area much more extensive than the ones most anthropologists study. Smith's study is an unusually successful example of maximization analysis for several reasons: first, she developed a mathematical model that predicted observable features of a marketing system; second, her comprehensive quantitative data provided a genuine test of the predictions of the model; and third, her analysis led finally beyond monetary costs, providing an additional illustration of the limits to the monetary definition of utility.

Smith's mathematical model was based on "location theory," which is concerned with how individual "economic units" such as households, villages, and markets locate themselves in geographical space to their own "best advantage" (see G. Skinner 1964; Plattner 1975; Lösch 1967:5). The primary assumption is that the geographical space is an "isotropic landscape—one on which population and purchasing power are uniformly distributed and on which economic resources, including transport facilities, are located without bias" (Smith 1972:4). In such an idealized setting, transportation costs would be a simple function of distance, and no inequalities in resource distribution would distort the placement of economic units. Assuming that individuals and groups are trying to maximize profits, and that demand is constant over the landscape, a number of definite propositions can be developed from this simple starting point.

The first proposition is that market centers will be uniformly distributed across a landscape, rather than randomly or in a cluster; markets will come to lie at the centers of hexagonal marketing regions. Can such a proposition be tested? In his highly original and influential study, Skinner (1964) offered graphic evidence of the application of location theory to Chinese markets. He began with a map of a particular region in Szechwan, visually rearranged the markets to approximate a uniform geometric space, and then transformed that "first approximation" into a uniform landscape with hexagonal marketing regions (see Figure 7.1). The problem with this "eyeball" technique comes in justifying the leap from map to geometric space (Garner 1967:310). Smith also uses Skinner's visual abstraction technique to good effect (Smith 1975:13–16), but of greater interest are her quantitative measures in support of the abstraction.

First Smith computed the measure Rn, from "nearest neighbor" analysis (Clark & Evans 1954). Rn, a measure of spacing specifically concerned with "the manner and degree to which the distribution of individuals in a population on a given area departs from that of a random distribution" (Clark & Evans 1954:446), can vary from a value of 0 for a completely clustered distribution to a value of 2.15 for one that is completely uniform (all points equidistant from each other); random distributions have a value of $Rn = 1.0$. The value of Rn for markets in western Guatemala was 1.31. Although this value is closer to randomness than to uniformity, many studies from other parts of the world indicate that it is rare to find a value of Rn larger than this, owing to the influence of such natural and cultural barriers to perfect uniformity as mountains, rivers, and political boundaries (Smith 1972:8).

Second, since it followed from the model that the marketing area of each market town should border on the market areas of exactly six other towns, Smith examined the locations of the 127 townships in her sample and found them to have a mean number of contacting sides of 5.93 (1972:6–7).

Third, from location theory it can also be deduced, though somewhat indirectly, that there exists a hierarchy of functions such that higher-order markets perform the same functions as lower-order markets *plus* some new functions (Smith 1972:137–52). Here Smith's data consisted of direct observations of the kinds of goods, numbers of sellers, and traveling distances covered by sellers for a large number of markets. Analysis of the traveling patterns of sellers resulted in her distinguishing ten "local market regions" that were self-sufficient with regard to each other, but tied individually to higher-order market centers. Within a local system, markets could be ranked according to the kinds of commodities each offered for sale. In fact, markets could be scaled relative to the "commodity bundles" they offered. For example, at the lowest-order markets one found such basic goods as "mixed produce" and "dry food staples"; only when one reached the intermediate and higher-order markets were such goods as shoes and trucks available; and only at the highest-order markets could one find enamelware or cheese, in addition to all the goods found in lower-order markets.

Although Smith's data supported the notion of a hierarchy of function of markets, they appeared to show that markets did not fall into discrete levels but rather formed a continuum between the lowest- and highest-order markets. Smith pursued this question, including not only the number of commodity bundles available, but also the total range of variation in goods, the number of sellers present in the market, and the number of different places of origin of sellers in the market. Combining these measures according to explicit procedures (1972:194–202), Smith arrived at the conclusion that discrete levels could be discerned within local market systems. Table 7.3 presents an abbreviated example of the kinds of differences Smith found between levels.

Smith's data provide very convincing evidence of the usefulness

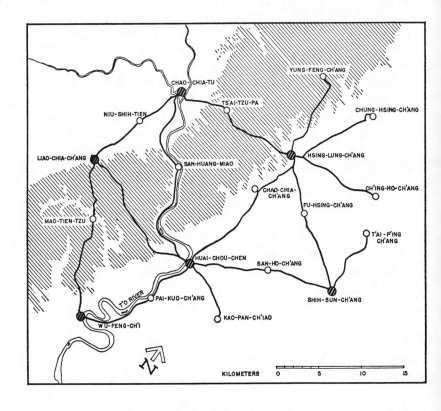

Fig. 7.1. Visual abstraction from map to geometric space. *Above*: Markets in Szechwan. *Opposite, top*: First approximation. *Opposite, bottom*: Hexagonal marketing areas. Source: G. Skinner 1964:22–23.

Key to diagrams on opposite page:

——————— LIMITS OF STANDARD MARKETING AREAS	○ STANDARD MARKET TOWNS
– – – – – LIMITS OF INTERMEDIATE MARKETING AREAS	◍ HIGHER-LEVEL CENTRAL PLACES
——————— ROADS CONNECTING STANDARD MARKETS TO INTERMEDIATE MARKETS	⦚⦚⦚⦚ MOUNTAINS ABOVE 500 METERS

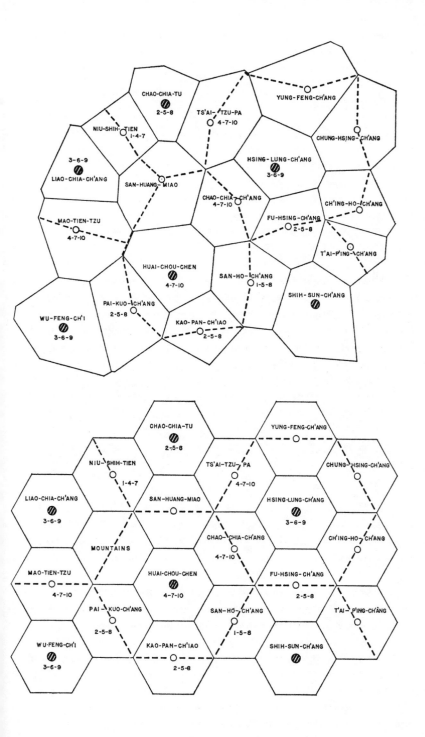

TABLE 7.3
Marketplace Levels in the Totonicapán Local Market System

Measure	Level 3 (lowest)	Level 2 (intermediate)	Level 1 (highest)
Ave. no. of available commodities	23	27	29
Ave. no. of sellers	438	1,243	2,022
Ave. no. of varieties of goods	62	95	130
Ave. no. of origins of sellers	11	23	66
No. of marketplaces	3	2	1

SOURCE: Smith 1972:202.

of location theory in analyzing nonindustrial market systems. Her work is also noteworthy for showing the value to anthropology of creating mathematical models and testing them with quantitative data, something model-builders in the past seldom did. As we might expect, though, many particulars of her theory were not supported by the data (Smith 1972:292–307). Furthermore, consideration of many noneconomic factors is required to account for diversity within and between the local market subsystems. As Smith concludes: "In Guatemala, . . . variations in market areas and populations occur that are not entirely explicable in terms of [the model]. Marketplace evolution appears to be a complex process that also involves ethnic group interactions, peasant access to economic and political power, and traditional forms of peasant social organization" (1972:372). Both for its mathematical and quantitative sophistication, and for the broad ethnographic context within which the analysis is set, Smith's work can serve as a standard to be studied and followed.

The special attraction of maximization analysis is that the theory combines logical-deductive form with intuitively sensible content. It is incontrovertible that when individuals act, they attempt to maximize something of importance to them.

In each of the examples in this chapter the problem has been to make the theory "work" by predicting or accounting for the observed outcomes of individual decisions. In these studies, as in most done by anthropologists, we encounter real limits to the use of monetary value in predicting individual behavior. Cash profit or efficiency is certainly one factor in the decisions people make—but it is one among many. Field research must include efforts to uncover how informants view their own decision processes. The individual's perception of value will then be seen to extend beyond cash to general considerations of compatibility, trust, and prestige.

Quantifying such "nonpecuniary" variables is difficult, but not impossible, as Quinn's work has shown. Certainly, at some point nonquantitative arguments are necessary to round out the holistic view of the decision process; this was true in each case reviewed above. But the recognition that nonquantitative "decision analyses" are weak and uninformative by themselves should lead to efforts to increase the predictability of maximization models by extending the scope of quantitative arguments at the expense of the "other" (qualitative) factors.

CHAPTER EIGHT

The Cognitive/Structural Orientation

IN THIS CHAPTER central issues in cultural anthropology that have been deferred in the earlier chapters finally come to the surface. We will be concerned with the description and analysis of "structure," by which is generally meant those orderly mental phenomena, such as rules, designs, or "meaning systems," characteristic of the members of a community and thought to organize their perceptions and behavior. Structure in this loose sense is the object of nearly every analysis by cultural anthropologists, but our focus here will be on those structural studies that show explicit concern for operational definitions and quantitative demonstrations. The majority of such studies fall within the subdiscipline known as "cognitive anthropology" (see Tylor 1969).

The concerns of modern structural and cognitive anthropologists merge historically with the study of norms and values. In the past, however, anthropological studies of norms and values tended to be intuitive and ad hoc, based on procedures that were rarely explicit. Through immersion in the culture and knowledge of myths and folklore, the anthropologist was said to develop an integrated, systemic notion of the basic values to which individuals responded in behaving. Dorothy Lee stated her method of studying values in the following terms:

To make this inquiry, I have worked minutely with each culture, over a period of years. I have paid attention even to apparently irrelevant detail, until some item struck a resonant note. I have then gone back and forth in my reading, seeing new relevance, noticing the obscure or seemingly trite or obvious. I have done this until nothing remained queer any more, and little seemed inexplicable. At this point I made tentative predictions as to what I should find in the linguistic structure, and in the mythology. If these predictions were confirmed, I went back to the descriptive account, strengthened in my conclusions and with my vision sharpened, and then I went to the language with the search for further confirmation. This process occupied much time; but even apart from the time-consuming work, I found that the process of understanding a radically different codification of reality was one of long duration, one of waiting until the acquaintance ripened and the bewildering and contradictory became clear and simple.

Eventually, I plunged into the experience of another culture, until I found myself liking what the members of the other society liked, frightened by what gave them fear, grieved by their sorrows, delighted in the situations which filled them with satisfaction and joy; and until their categories seemed natural and right, and my own rigid and misleading. In fact, I sometimes lost myself in the way of life of the society I was studying until my children complained that, after all, they were not Trobrianders or Tikopia! What I had to say seemed so obvious to me that, at this point, I could bring myself to write at all only by reminding myself that I was writing for people who were ignorant of this particular culture. (D. Lee 1959:3–4.)

At some point, no doubt, anthropologists must bring such intuitive involvement to bear in analyzing meaning systems. The problem with Lee's method is that it cannot specify in any precise way the degree of realism achieved. We can only accept or reject her analysis on the basis of whether it makes sense to us; and when dealing with cross-cultural meanings, this is the least dependable of criteria. Unfortunately, this failure to face the problem of ethnocentrism detracts from the believability of many structural analyses (Kultgen 1975:384).

The research techniques discussed in earlier chapters, with few exceptions, implicitly assume that the anthropologist knows in advance what should be observed and measured; whether the native "culture-bearers" would see their world in the same way as the anthropologist, or would be able to understand the anthropologist's description, has not been regarded as an issue until this chapter. But no matter how accurate we consider our techniques to be in describing events as they happen, they are open to the charge of ethnocentrism in that they are our invention merely applied in other cultural settings.

Ethnoscience, which aims at an explicit methodology for studying how community members express their knowledge and understanding of the world, confronts the problem of ethnocentrism head-on. In a sense, it attempts to equip us to listen on the frequencies community members themselves use to communicate their perceptual understandings: "Whenever we wish to know what people are doing and why, or what they are likely to do, we must know what phenomena they see, for these are the phenomena to which they respond. And we must know what they believe to be the relations among these phenomena and what they perceive as the possible courses of action for dealing with them" (Goodenough 1970:104). The difficulty here is that this excludes from the outset such attitudes or knowledge as informants may not be able to express verbally—for example, the feeling on hearing a piece of music, or the meaning of a facial expression. Despite its limitations, however, ethnoscience offers a starting point for a rigorous and systematic investigation of "norms" and "values."

Its procedures may be summarized as follows: (1) collection of a corpus of terms through use of eliciting frames (Black & Metzger 1965; Metzger & Williams 1966); (2) reduction of the corpus to a set of stable, mutually contrasting terms; (3) investigation of the semantic organization of the reduced set of terms, using the principles by which native speakers contrast terms and group them into larger categories; and, (4) development of a set of native "rules of correspondence" by which informants relate their "native concepts" to the world of practical experience. Together, these procedures approach the goal of ethnoscientific research as stated by Goodenough (1964), a description "of whatever it is one has to know or believe in order to operate in a manner acceptable to [a society's] members."

As an example of these procedures in practice we may take Metzger's and Williams's (1966) analysis of "Tzeltal firewood." With the help of bilingual informants in a community of Maya Indians in Chiapas, Mexico, the authors were able to develop simple question frames about how the Tzeltal view their world. These frames yielded information with a minimum of ambiguity and a high degree of reliability between informants. A basic starting point in any culture is to develop a frame for class inclusion, such as, "What are the names of kinds of _____?" Examples of such questions in Tzeltal are:

> Q. *b'itik sb'il te sb'al me?tik hk'ašeltik ta spisil balamilal e.* (How are they named, the things of mother earth in all the world?)
> A. *?ay b'ayel ta hten.* (There are many of the kind.)
> Q. *b'inti sb'il te sb'ab'i hten.* (What is the name of a first kind?)
> A. *?ay kirsánoetik.* (There are people.)
> Q. *b'inti sb'il te šča?tenel.* (What is the name of a second kind?)
> A. *?ay čanb'alametik.* (There are animals.)

Continuous and exhaustive application of the *b'inti sb'il* frame resulted in a taxonomy of Tzeltal natural categories (Figure 8.1).

Other frames were then used to learn how informants relate categories to behavior. A "use" frame ("How do they serve us, _____?") elicited such uses for trees as house-building, tool handles, and firewood. A "value" frame ("Which is a good kind of _____ in the world?") then uncovered criteria concerning, e.g., which kinds of wood should or should not be used for firewood ("burns strongly," "dries slowly").

Because the question frames are explicit, such research can be replicated and the reliability of the results closely examined. Nonetheless, Metzger's and Williams's study, and other, similar ones, have raised a number of important questions. First, in what sense do these analyses represent actual patterns of thought in the community (i.e., have *psychological validity*)? Second, what is the evidence that community members in general, as opposed to a few well-trained informants, *share* these patterns? Third, what relationship is there, if any, between the cognitive analyses and the actual day-to-day *behavior* of community members? And, fourth, how are such analyses to be compared *cross-culturally*, if the very instru-

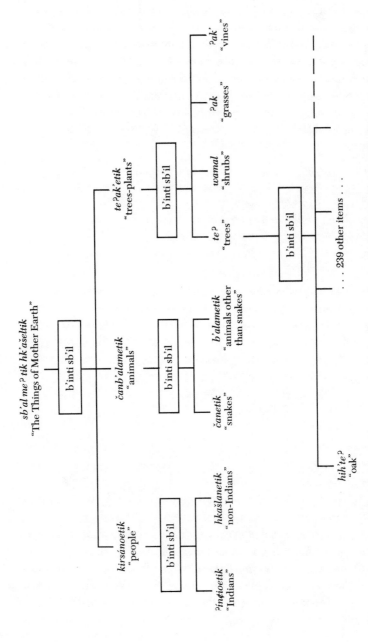

Fig. 8.1. Tzeltal categories for "The Things of Mother Earth." Adapted from Metzger & Williams 1966: 392–93.

ments of research (e.g., frames) must be fashioned anew in each community? We may take these problems one at a time.

Psychological Validity

Ethnoscientific analyses usually aim for the orderly results exemplified by Metzger's and Williams's taxonomy of Tzeltal categories. As Burling has pointed out, however, there are usually several formal structures that can be constructed for any set of contrasting terms (Burling 1964). The problem is to decide on the best structure. For example, we may take the case of English kin terms (Romney & D'Andrade 1964). Even if we restrict the discussion, for the sake of simplicity, to a primary listing (by informants) of male kin terms, we can propose at least two different schemes to segregate the terms from one another (Figure 8.2). The two paradigms in Figure 8.2 represent substantially different semantic spaces. For example, in paradigm 1 grandfather and grandson are placed far apart, whereas in paradigm 2 they are adjacent. Are both correct, or is one closer than the other to approximating the meaning the terms have for a set of informants? If we cannot answer this question, then it is difficult to see what usefulness either analysis has.

Some have "solved" the problem in the simplest fashion—by denying that it has a solution. In this view, the mind is a "black box" that cannot be observed. A model of cognitive process should be judged on its elegance, or its mechanical prediction of behavior. "Since anthropologists cannot get inside the informant's head, psychological reality is an empty concept. Mind-like mechanical verbal behavior seems best suited for the validation of assumptions" (Werner 1972:272). Werner shifts the focus away from "psychological reality," but we are left wondering how to know when a given case of mechanical verbal behavior is "mind-like."

> Let us consider the implications of rejecting an interest in native cognition as an aim of semantic analysis via componential, or any other, method. Such a refusal renders trivial the claim that the analysis is semantic at all. If all that can be said of the product of these operations is that they predict a certain kind of verbal behavior, there is certainly no need to call the results semantic. If the analyst claims, in effect, that the meaning of the terms is merely their meaning to him and that he has no

PARADIGM 1: Lineal Construct

Generation	Lineal C_1	Co-lineal C_2	Ablineal C_3
+2	grandfather		
+1	father	uncle	
0	ego	brother	cousin
−1	son	nephew	
−2	grandson		

PARADIGM 2: Reciprocal Construct

Generation	Direct	Collateral
+2	grandfather	
−2	grandson	
+1	father	uncle
−1	son	nephew
0	brother	cousin

Fig. 8.2. Alternative paradigms for American-English male kinship terms. Source: Romney & D'Andrade 1964:147–53.

way of demonstrating what they mean to anyone else, and in particular to their native users, the sense of semantic employed is minuscule. And if he matches terms with categories in a "universal" frame, all that he can show is that the objects referred to by certain terms have certain social, biological, or other objective characteristics: i.e., that they are male, older or younger than the speaker, related to him by blood or by marriage, and so on. While all this is by no means useless information to a student of the society, it is gratuitous to call it semantic, in any anthropological sense, since the only cognitive process considered is that of the analyst himself (Wallace 1965:229–30).

The productive response to the problem is to devise testing procedures whereby the competing predictions of different paradigms can be compared for degree of fit with some body of data. In the case of English kin terms, the two paradigms in Figure 8.2 differ in one way in their implications for the "distance" or "closeness" with which relatives will be viewed by ego. To examine the perceived distance of relatives from one another, Romney and D'Andrade employed the *triads test* (1964: 160–67). Informants were requested to select, for every combination of three terms (e.g., father, son, uncle), which *two* were most alike or which *one* was most different (e.g., father-son *versus* uncle). Using 116 informants (public high school students), they tabulated the average number of times each pair was classified as similar. Only eight pairs out of 28 occurred with a frequency greater that expected by chance; these statistically significant pairs are shown for each of the two competing paradigms in Figure 8.3. The better paradigm is the one in which terms linked

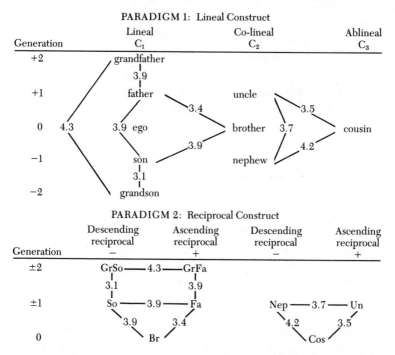

Fig. 8.3. Similarity judgments of American-English kinship terms. Source: Romney & D'Andrade 1964: 165.

with high frequency are in adjacent positions. In the first paradigm, several of the most frequently linked pairs are separated from each other by more than one component (e.g., father and brother are in different generations *and* different "lines"), whereas in the second paradigm all the frequently linked pairs are separated on only one dimension. In fact, a very economical representation of the triads test data is achieved by revising the second paradigm slightly so that "reciprocals" (grandfather-grandson, father-son, and uncle-nephew) are set side-by-side and all the frequently linked pairs are adjacent.

Sanday (1968) has replicated the Romney and D'Andrade study with a small sample of informants, similarly having informants list terms for relatives. But Sanday used an "information-processing" approach, paying careful attention to the order in which terms were listed by informants. Her assumption was that the decision to list a particular relative was related to the previous relative listed by one of a set of "operators," such as "child" or "sibling." Thus, if the term "brother" followed the term "sister," the sibling operator was assumed to have been used. Her results showed some support for the psychological validity of *both* paradigms in Figures 8.2 and 8.3, but the study involved too few subjects to be conclusive (quantitative data have been insufficient or lacking altogether in other information-processing analyses as well; see Quinn 1974:251). If data problems can be solved—and we must expect even greater problems working in languages other than English—the information-processing approach could find wide applications.

At this point it should be clear that any description of "native cognition" depends heavily on the methods employed in making it. Cognition is not a monolithic "thing" waiting to be discovered, but rather a loosely conceived domain that any particular research technique describes only in part. Cognitive researchers frequently note that different measures of a given cognitive function, such as "similarity judgments" (see Szalay & D'Andrade 1972:54–55), rarely correlate perfectly, indicating that they measure different aspects of the function. Researchers can be expected to choose methods that come closest to their theoretical assumptions concerning cognition (see Cancian 1975:37–40).

As a whole, ethnoscience is characterized by a bias toward order. Metzger and Williams, for example, tried many different question frames before finding those that reduced ambiguity to a minimum (1966:390–91). Thus it is not surprising that their results were taxonomically neat. It does not follow, however, that cognitive process is as orderly as this. Ambiguity, in fact, may be an important part of the actual workings of individual cognitive processes. Kensinger (1975), through many years of study among the Cashinahua of the Peruvian Amazon, gradually became aware of considerable ambiguity in the Cashinahua definitions of their own kinship universe. Informants disagreed with one another about the appropriate behavior between specific relatives, and they changed their views as circumstances changed. Kensinger found it necessary to keep in mind that his informants were working simultaneously on three different levels: the *ideal* (rules), the *pragmatic* (if I understand him, rules for breaking the rules), and the *real* (what happens on the ground):

> An ethnography which focuses on the cultural ideals will in all likelihood picture the society as a neat, orderly, tightly structured system, something like the pictures of homes in *Better Homes and Gardens* magazine. The pragmatic view will give us a picture which, while neat, orderly, and clean, shows the wear and tear of prolonged use. A realistic picture, however, is more likely to show how that same home looks during and after the daily round of family activity. Much behavior is only understandable if the cultural ideals are clearly kept in mind, just as the good housewife apologizes for her house not being in Better-Homes-and-Gardens condition, or [for its being] in a shambles, when somebody unexpectedly drops in for coffee. Clearly, all three views are needed (Kensinger 1975:23).

An exceptionally frank and well-done study showing the influence of different research procedures on the description of cognition in cultural research has been reported by Cole and associates (1971) among the Kpelle of Liberia. Using eliciting frames, the authors generated a long list of Kpelle "things," which was then shortened for experimental purposes. Two examples will illustrate their methods. First, they asked informants to "free-associate" to the terms (e.g., "What do you think of when I say 'shirt'?"). Items on the list

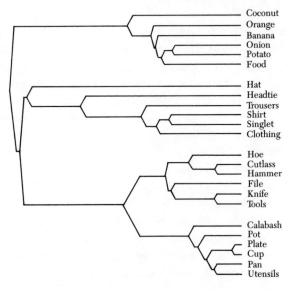

Fig. 8.4. Kpelle "things" clustered by free association. The closer to the righthand side of the figure the lines join, the more closely associated are the items. Source: Cole et al. 1971:74.

that were associated with other items on the list were clustered, resulting in Figure 8.4.

Second, in a separate experiment, the real objects named on the list were placed in front of informants, who were asked to group the objects into a limited number of piles. Again, the objects were clustered, this time as shown in Figure 8.5. Comparing Figures 8.4 and 8.5, we can see that, at the level of gross categories ("food," "clothing," "tools," and "utensils") both figures present similar "cognitive maps." But within categories objects have been rearranged. For example, in Figure 8.4 onion and potato are very close, but in Figure 8.5 they are far apart. Furthermore, the authors reported that the degree of ambiguity or orderliness in informant responses varied from one research technique to another (Cole et al. 1971:67–68). In particular, when the technique emphasized order among terms, the results fell into the familiar taxonomic pattern. But other techniques, such as *informally* asking men to list "things" and then to group them into subgroups, led to an order based on use and function, rather than formal semantic order. "Our interpretation of these data is that semantic classes can serve as a means of organizing verbal behavior, but the extent to which this happens in naturally occurring contexts is very much open to question. It is quite possible that in our desire to find "the" classification of Kpelle nouns, we overlooked situations where quite different kinds of classification would dominate" (Cole et al. 1971:90).

In sum, the anti-ethnocentric stance of cultural anthropology requires that we be open to the native viewpoint. This means not only listening to them speak to *us*, but developing procedures for learning how they communicate about the world with one another. As methods for doing this have improved, however, it has become clear that each different method describes a different aspect of the loose category "cognition." Ethnoscientists have been perhaps overly dependent on techniques that eliminate disorder and ambiguity. This implies the need to expand the scope of cognitive analysis. Multiple techniques, such as those Cole and his associates used among the Kpelle, can help fill this need. In the following two sections, where the problems of sharing among informants and of the behavioral correlates of cognition are treated, further ways of expanding cognitive research are described.

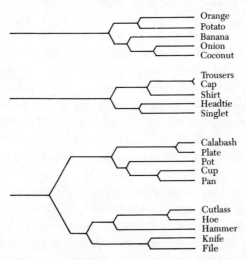

Fig. 8.5. Kpelle "things" clustered by placing objects on chairs. For explanation, see legend to Fig. 8.4. Source: Cole et al. 1971:82.

Sharing

By definition, culture is shared. Anthropologists recognize, of course, that individual beliefs and actions do not exactly replicate cultural *standards* as they are set by the community; but it is the standard expectations and behavior *patterns* that are of the first importance (Goodenough 1970:101). Selby (1976:5) has even ruled nonshared aspects out of the picture altogether, writing that "the quirks and behavioral idiosyncrasies of individual human beings are of surpassing uninterest."

This presents us with the practical problem of determining which aspects of cognition are shared within a group, and which are not. Whereas in the past descriptions of whole areas of cognition were derived from one or a few informants and presented in absolutistic formal analyses, the trend has recently turned toward statistical analyses of quantitative data drawn from samples of community members. This in turn has led to the recognition that the concepts people use in talking about the world are not as perfectly bounded and discrete as the contrast sets and paradigms of cognitive analysis have assumed; instead, concepts are found to have *core* meanings, that are widely shared and *peripheral* meanings that vary to some degree among informants (Berlin et al. 1974:56–57; Sankoff 1971: 403). Individual idiosyncrasies must be identified before they can be eliminated from an analysis, and this means that the degree of cognitive sharing must be demonstrated and not merely asserted.

In this section we will look at the methods and results of several cognitive studies that have sampled a range of informants. Our first example concerns the extent of agreement among informants in their use of a range of kin terms. This is an especially important case because so many formal semantic analyses in cultural anthropology have dealt with systems of kin terminology. Using rigorous elicitation procedures among the Akamba of Kenya, Fjellman (1971) obtained a set of consanguineal kin terms from each of twenty informants. He was interested in finding the rules for assigning genealogical relatives to kin-term categories. Although he recognized that the ideal data for this task would derive from "a *statistically* satisfactory random sample of actual usage in which the full range of culturally relevant situations was *naturally* represented," he had to settle for a more practical goal—namely, to predict usage as observed within the interview situation (1971:7).

The problem Fjellman encountered was that substantial differences existed among the twenty informants in how they applied terms to particular biological kin. For example, the term *nau* was always used to refer to biological father; but six informants extended the term also to father's brother, whereas the others used a different term, *nwendw'au*. Whether or not the father term is extended to father's brother is a basic feature of a kin terminological system, and informant disagreement on the matter has not been discussed much in the literature.

Even more disturbing was the fact that this kind of disagreement was not rare. A case analogous to father and father's brother was that of mother and mother's sister. The term *mwaitū* always applied to mother, but was often extended to mother's sister and other members of mother's patrilineage (MBD, MBSD, MBSSD, MFZ). On the other hand, mother's sister is sometimes called *mwendya* instead, and in those cases the term *mwendya* is also extended (to MBD, MBSD, MBSSD). Is mother's sister *mwaitū* or *mwendya*?

> I have no adequate explanation for what is going on. I can merely add this case as evidence for my general caveat that most published componential analyses may well be using ideal types as their sets of data. With one or a few informants it is easy to argue that inconsistent usage is the result of mistakes. If data are collected from a larger group of individuals, these same mistakes may crop up often enough to suggest that they are actually culturally relevant patterns of optional labeling. These patterns may be complementary, or, as in the case of *mwaitu* and *mwendya*, contradictory. Both kinds of patterns, but especially the latter, argue also against facile associations of kin terminology and social behavior (Fjellman 1971:87–88).

Disagreements among informants should be expected by cultural researchers, and will often be intrinsic to the way the system works, as Harris (1970) has argued for racial identity in Brazil. Eliciting racial terms by means of a series of stylized illustrations (shown in Figure 8.6) reflecting racial differences along a number of dimen-

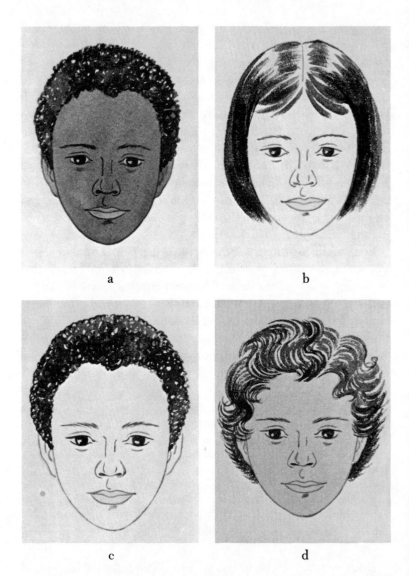

Fig. 8.6. Drawings for eliciting Brazilian racial terms: a) *preta*, b) *branca*, c) *sarará*, d) *morena*. Source: Harris 1970:4.

sions (skin color, hair form, and lip and nose shapes), Harris discovered that 100 informants responding to 72 different drawings produced an astonishing 492 different racial terms. The median individual used only nine different terms for the entire set of illustrations, but no single illustration received fewer than twenty different terms. In the application of specific terms to specific illustrations, therefore, there was substantial ambiguity within the sample of informants. Harris believes that such ambiguity is a common characteristic of those domains where confusion, for one reason or another, is useful.

> The ambiguous output of the Brazilian racial calculus casts doubt on the assumption that the codes or rules associated with the abstract distinctions and actual identification of many classes of phenomena constitute intersubjectively uniform sets. Equally plausible is the assumption that actual classificatory performance is the expression of indeterminate and variable "competence." . . . This assumption is especially attractive if the prime social function of the rules is not the maintenance of orderly distinctions but the maintenance or even maximization of noise and ambiguity. Brazilian racial categories appear to constitute such a domain (Harris 1970:12).

Sampling informant responses does not show merely that disagreement takes place, however. It also helps sort out the noise from the pattern in the cognitive system. Sanjek (1971), for example, has shown that even such a disorderly array as the Brazilian racial terms can yield an impressive degree of order. Using Harris's illustrations, Sanjek interviewed 60 members of a small community in Northeast Brazil. Informant responses to the drawings resulted in a corpus of 116 distinct racial terms for that community alone; as in Harris's larger study, separate informants used the same term differently, and the same illustrations received different racial labels. However, despite many discrepancies, analysis showed that informant responses were closely related to cognitive dimensions of "skin color" and "hair form."

In order to present his data in useful tables, Sanjek reduced the number of terms in two ways. First, employing a measure of the *salience* of a term (the number of informants who listed the term at least once), Sanjek reduced the corpus to the eleven most fre-

TABLE 8.1

Number of Responses Using the Brazilian Racial Term
"Branca" Elicited by Various Illustrations

Illustration showed skin color	Illustration showed hair form		
	Straight	Wavy	Kinky
Light	153	135	26
Medium	44	51	15
Dark	0	0	0

SOURCE: Sanjek 1971:1132.

quently listed terms and their modifiers, which accounted for 74 percent of all occurrences. Second, by using results from a separate questionnaire on racial categories given to 40 informants, Sanjek was able to establish equivalences among certain terms that could reduce the number of separate terms to be dealt with even further.

Table 8.1 presents data on the frequency with which the term *branca* ("white") was applied to illustrations according to the skin color and hair form represented in them. The table gives a clear sense of the variation in use of the term, while leaving no doubt that the term is applied to those of lighter skin color and straighter hair.

Similar tables were constructed for the other salient racial terms. The results are presented graphically in Figure 8.7. There it can be clearly seen that the terms *branca* and *preta* ("white" and "black") divide the space diagonally into an upper-left (white) half and a lower-right (black) half. Likewise, the terms *sarará* and *cabo verde* (no English equivalents) divide the space diagonally into upper-right and lower-left halves. These four terms leave an ambiguous middle ground conveniently filled by the term *morena*. These quantitative results are summarized in a "componential paradigm" in the lower right of the figure.

The discriminations made by Sanjek's informants almost certainly are based on an ability to make fine distinctions along continua that the stylized illustrations measure using three-point scales (straight-wavy-kinky, light-medium-dark). The administration of the test to a large number of informants gives a much more continuous sense of the distribution of the terms in the semantic space defined by hair

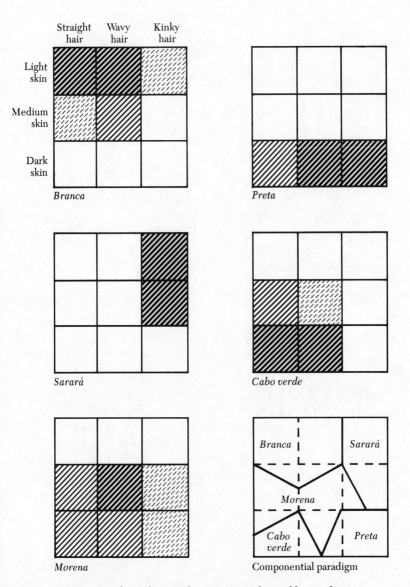

Fig. 8.7. Components of Brazilian racial terms. Heavy diagonal lines indicate more than twice expected frequency; light diagonals between once and twice expected frequency; dashed diagonals between half and full expected frequency; blank less than half expected frequency. Adapted from Sanjek 1971:1132–35.

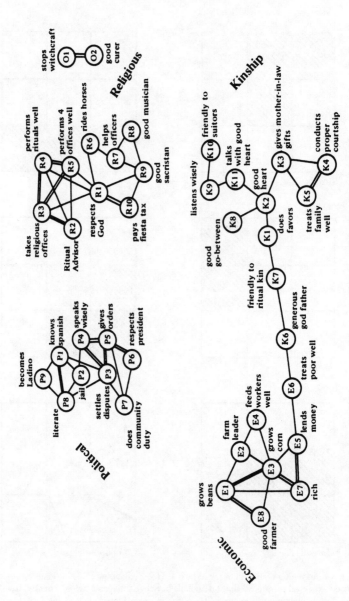

Fig. 8.8. Zinacanteco "good norms." Source: Francesca Cancian 1975:58.

form and skin color. Sanjek's final model, therefore, represents continuous interpretations of the space, as opposed to the rigid, typological paradigms commonly presented where quantitative data are not available.

As a final example of the way in which quantitative data have been used to characterize the shared patterns of cognition within a community, we take Francesca Cancian's (1975) study of norms in Zinacantan, Mexico. By "norms" she means shared conceptions of appropriate or expected behavior and the accompanying sanctions for bringing behavior into line with those conceptions. Working with 30 informants, she asked them to form subgroups of similar statements out of a selected sample of 100 normative statements. Examples of normative statements are "Juan is good because he has taken four religious offices," and "Juan is bad because he steals horses." Any two statements could receive a similarity score anywhere from 0 to 30, depending on how many informants grouped them together as "similar." Figure 8.8 is a graphic example of Zinacanteco "good norms," where lines between concepts represent high frequencies of similarity judgments. For example, the set of "Kinship" statements ("K" numbers) and that of "Economic" statements ("E" numbers) are linked by a chain of similarity judgments from E5 (lends money) to E6 (treats poor well) to K6 (generous godfather) to K7 (friendly to ritual kin) and thence to K1 (does favors). Strong relations of similarity between norms are represented in the figure by double lines; thus we see that in the Political domain statements P3 (settles disputes), P4 (speaks wisely), and P5 (gives orders) form a tight cluster of norms. Figure 8.8 is a simple and pleasing means of representing an informative array of data, and one that could not have been constructed with any reliability without the quantitative data generated by Cancian's research design.

The results described in this section demonstrate that cognitive descriptions can benefit from sampling many informants. Single informants will probably respond to cognitive research in ways similar to the community pattern, but some responses will always be idiosyncratic; the only way to discover which is core and which is periphery is to sample. This does not mean abandoning the search for patterns of cognition; on the contrary, it will lead to a more realistic sense of what kinds of patterning can be expected to occur.

Cognition and Behavior

In keeping with the ecological perspective of this book, analyses of semantic organization and rule sets should be taken not as ends in themselves but as part of the process of understanding how members of particular communities meet their basic needs (compare Frake 1962:53–54). Many anthropologists have wondered whether the charts and diagrams of cognitive anthropologists were not trivial examples of formalism for its own sake (see Berreman 1966:351; Vayda & Rappaport 1968:491; Harris 1968:570–72). But it is well to keep in mind that terms for firewood, kinship, or race, for example, no matter how unimportant they may sometimes appear to us, are of great importance to the people who use them. We as anthropologists cannot afford to ignore this. What gives many analyses the appearance of triviality is that their authors have made little or no effort to connect the cognitive analysis to the conduct of daily life among the people.

The general failure to distinguish normative data from behavioral data (in order to compare them) has resulted in an intolerable situation: when we read ethnographic accounts of life in other communities, we are rarely in a position to decide whether the descriptions refer to observed behavior, normative statements of informants, or the author's intuitive mix of the two. There would be no problem if behavior and norms coincided always and everywhere, but the disconcerting truth is that "we know very little about what norms are and how they relate to social action" (Francesca Cancian 1975:1). When Cancian attempted to relate her analysis of Zinacanteco norms to the activities of community members in a variety of contexts (e.g., where they farmed, whether or not their children attended school), she found no relationship; and that, in her opinion, has been the general rule in the social sciences: "The main finding of more than four decades of research on attitudes and behavior is that there is no clear relation between them" (Francesca Cancian 1975:110). This result may come about not so much because norms and behavior are unrelated as because so little careful research on the matter has been published, but this remains to be seen. Certainly, no more debilitating problem than this one exists in current anthropological practice.

Kronenfeld's (1973) study of kin terms and behavioral expectations among the Fanti people of Ghana approached the problem from a cognitive perspective. His research question was straightforward: does a knowledge of kin *categories* permit us to make reliable predictions of behavioral expectations among kinsmen? The extant literature on kinship suggested strongly that it should. Kronenfeld took a large number of "behaviors," such as "inheriting from," "living with," "spanking," and so on, and asked informants to judge the appropriateness of the behavior between particular known relatives. He found that very few predictions about expected behavior could be made simply by knowing people's kinship relations.

Further analysis revealed, however, that underlying both sets of data were a common set of dimensions, including generation and genealogical closeness, from which features of the data could be predicted. The validity of these two dimensions was enhanced when they appeared as the two main factors in a multivariate analysis of the "behavioral expectations" data. The proposition that kin terms *directly* designate "behaviorally relevant" classes of persons is thus not borne out in this study.

Kronenfeld's research demonstrates the need to reexamine old assumptions about kinship and behavior. But his "behavioral" data are, methodologically speaking, really cognitive data, because they reflect informants' judgments rather than their actually observed behavior. The underlying dimensions of genealogical closeness and generation are important in predicting behavioral *expectations*; but whether these expectations are in turn related to observable behavior between kinsmen remains to be seen.

Following fieldwork among sharecroppers on a plantation in northeastern Brazil, I compared a cognitive paradigm based on ethnoscientific eliciting procedures with behavioral data (Johnson 1974). In describing agricultural land, the sharecroppers had used a core set of terms organized according to two dimensions of contrast: "fertility," and "humidity" (see Figure 8.9, top). Informants had also described correspondence rules for which crops should be planted

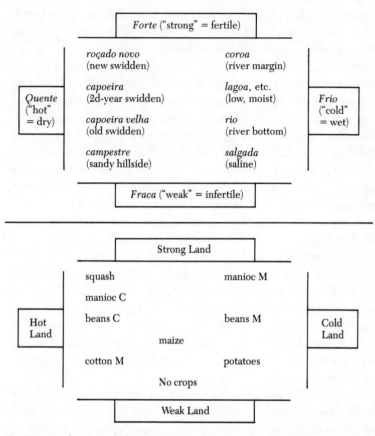

Fig. 8.9. Land types and planting rules on a Brazilian plantation. *Top*: Land types. *Bottom*: Corresponding crops. M beans are 3-month beans (*de moita*); C beans are 5-month beans (*de corda*). M manioc is the *Manipeba* variety; C is the *Carregadeira* variety. M cotton is the *Mocó* type. Source: A. Johnson 1974:90.

in which kinds of land (Figure 8.9, bottom). From direct observations and interviews with the 44 male househeads on the plantation, I had obtained a description of actual planting practices that could be compared with the cognitive paradigm and the correspondence rules associated with it.

The words "no crops" in Figure 8.9 mean that the weakest lands —sandy hillsides and saline land—should not be planted; the data showed that no one did plant in those types of land. In this case, there were no observed discrepancies between the rules of correspondence and the observed planting practices. For other types of land, however, I found a number of discrepancies. In order to judge the degree of conformity between correspondence rules and behavior, I began with the null hypothesis that there was no relation between the two. Under the null hypothesis, crop frequencies in particular types of land would simply be proportional to the amount of each type of land that was available. Four of the types of land—"new swidden," "second-year swidden," "river margin," and "low wetlands"—together accounted for over 90 percent of all the sharecroppers' produce. Figure 8.10a shows that of the total land area represented by these four types of land, 54 percent was in new

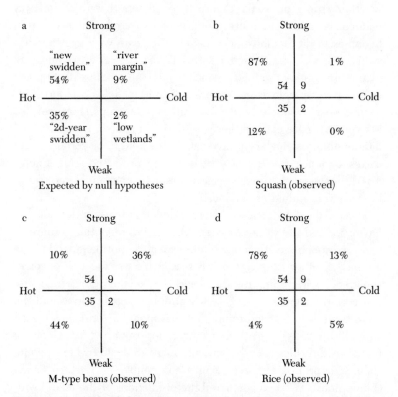

Fig. 8.10. Expected and observed proportions of crops by land type, northeastern Brazil, M-type beans are the 3-month variety (*de moita*).

swidden, 35 percent in second-year swidden, 9 percent in river margin, and 2 percent in low wetlands. Under the null hypothesis, the expected crop proportions should be the same: 54 percent of crops should be grown in new swidden, 35 percent in second-year swidden, etc. Deviations of crop proportions in the direction predicted by the correspondence rules in Figure 8.9 were taken as evidence that the rule "works." For example, the correspondence rule for squash specifies the hottest, strongest soils available; that the rule works is confirmed by the crop proportions in Figure 8.10b.

I found that many other crops were planted in close agreement with the correspondence rules, but that this was not always the case. For example, M-type beans were said to "prefer" cold land, whether strong or weak. Figure 8.10c shows that this crop was planted in cold land more often than expected under the null hypothesis, but that fully 54 percent of the beans were grown in hot swidden land. One reason for this is that beans are commonly planted in single-crop fields, which is not compatible with the best use of river-margin lands, where mixed-crop fields are the rule. Second-year swidden is planted with single crops, however, so M-type beans are planted there (as is, often manioc). Incidentally, I did not obtain enough cognitive data in the field to be certain of the correspondence rule for rice; it could be predicted from Figure 8.10d, however, that rice is regarded as a "strong land" crop, suitable for either humid or dry soils.

These data show a close correspondence between rules and behavior in land use in northeastern Brazil. Whether this is more or less correspondence than one might expect cannot be judged in the absence of other studies, but it is reasonable to expect close correspondence where important ecological matters are concerned, because of the significance of such matters in people's lives and the opportunities to test and refine the correspondence rules with each agricultural cycle. Geoghegan (1970), for example, developed a model of the rules used by one informant to decide where people should "appropriately" reside in a community of Eastern Samal (Philippines). He then compared the predictions of the model with the actual residence locations of 285 people and found a high level of correspondence between the two. Whether cognition and behavior in other domains will show such close correspondence as in these two examples, however, is something that will not be known until many further studies over a wide range have been completed.

Cross-Cultural Comparison

Cognitive research is close to the heart of cultural anthropology because it deals so directly with ethnocentrism. As we have seen, the central contradiction of cultural anthropology is that despite our desire to be free of bias, the entire enterprise of cross-cultural research is fundamentally ethnocentric, emerging at a particular point in history under definite economic, social, and ideological conditions. We charge ourselves with the responsibility of rendering fair and unbiased descriptions of other cultural realities; and yet, not only are the standards of description (sampling, reliability, validity) products of our own culture, but so is the very notion of fieldwork, and the institutional framework that supports it.

Is it possible to describe another culture in a way that will make it meaningful to us without in the process distorting what it means to its own people? In any pure sense, the answer is "no." Nonetheless, the problems and procedures discussed in this chapter can help to approximate the ideal. We can reasonably hope to permit native culture-bearers to have more influence on our descriptions. For example, asking informants to list the "things" of their world, and to group them according to similarity, is a kind of compromise between the incompatible poles of faithfulness to single cultures and comparability across cultures. Undoubtedly our theoretical predilections will shape the outcome, but nondirective questions at least give the informants a certain freedom to respond, and careful ethnoscientists always develop ways of allowing informants to review and correct the emerging description. At the same time, the questions are similar enough across cultures that comparison becomes possible (Berlin & Kay 1969:5–14), albeit with increasingly greater ambiguity at higher levels of abstraction (see Goodenough 1972:98–130).

The cognitive tradition in cultural anthropology can profitably be preserved and built upon. The pressure for a more scientific anthropology, as seen in previous chapters, tends toward concepts and methods of analysis that would appear fantastic or incomprehensible to members of culturally distinct communities—concepts such as "network" or "character," for example. It may be that our informants have analogous terms for related concepts, but our professional subculture seems often to deemphasize native perspectives in favor of the ones familiar to us. One of anthropology's main contributions to social science and the rest of Western knowledge is a critique of Western social thought capable of taking us out of the cultural present in which we live by giving voice to the representatives of other cultural realities.

CHAPTER NINE

Computer Analysis of Cultural Systems

CULTURAL ANTHROPOLOGISTS need have little trouble collecting large amounts of quantitative data. There are plenty of variables, of immediate relevance for theory and practice, that require no more than the physical presence of the ethnographer and a willingness to count. If the data are collected in an orderly manner, and particularly if explicit coding procedures are used, then the initial description of the variables is easily done with a desk-top calculator or, for very large numbers of observations, with a computer using standard programs.

Integrating such low-level information into systemic descriptions or explanation, however, is not easy, nor is it even obvious how to set about doing so. This is a problem for which few well-tested solutions now exist. New techniques of unquestionable promise have recently become available, but they require some trial-and-error exploration to be made useful for particular research problems. Even then, researchers who hope for complete solutions probably will have to settle for partial success.

In this chapter, two approaches to processing quantified data into systems of many variables are discussed. The first, computer simulation, is not especially sophisticated in a mathematical or statistical sense, but employs the vast bookkeeping abilities of modern computers to enable us to assemble a large number of variables measured separately during field research into a coherent, intuitively satisfying system that is at once complex and realistic, yet relatively formal. The second approach is multivariate analysis, which is the name given to statistical techniques used to describe interrelations between more than two variables. Although one can use a large number of variables in the analysis, one usually hopes that patterns among a smaller number of variables or underlying dimensions will be found to predict variations in the numerous variables with which analysis began.

Here I will discuss examples of these techniques in order to give a sense of how they might be useful to cultural anthropologists. Computer simulation is not difficult, but it cannot really be taught: each researcher will devise a system that is to some degree unique, for he will have had to write a unique computer program for that system. From the proliferation of multivariate techniques suited to different purposes, I can examine here only a few of particular promise to anthropologists. Both approaches are near the leading edge of a developing cultural anthropology, and the specific directions they will take cannot yet be foreseen.

Computer Simulation

A computer simulation is a computer program that defines the variables of a system, the range of values those variables may take on, and their interrelations in enough detail for the system to be set in motion to generate some *output*. The main function of a computer simulation is to explore the properties and implications of a system that is too complex for logical or mathematical analysis: "Today if [someone] says he understands how a complex system works, it is fair to insist that he demonstrate this by programming a computer to imitate its behavior. . . . If he cannot do this, his understanding is certainly incomplete and perhaps illusory" (Grodins 1965:143). As we saw in Chapter 2, however, systems are always analytic constructs; therefore, we should say not that the computer imitates the system, but that the computer simulation *is* the system, or rather one particular form of the system. A computer simulation generally has an ad hoc or "homemade" quality that makes it less rigorous than a mathematical model; nonetheless, it is still more rigorous than the loose constructions anthropologists usually refer to as "models" (see Barth 1966; Banton 1965).

Throughout the 1960's articles appeared in the major social-science journals heralding the advent of computer simulation. Shubik (1960:917) saw in it the potential "for the growth of a new scientific institutional economics," and Abelson (1968:275) called it "a striking innovation in social scientific practice." Early authors (who generally had not done much simulation themselves) agreed remarkably about the advantages of the method. Simulations could include large numbers of variables, in contrast to the small numbers that could be dealt with in mathematical equations, and so were capable of greater realism. The expression of a systemic concept in computer language forced careful specification of variables, parameters, and interconnections, introducing greater rigor than prose texts were capable of. Construction of a computer simulation often led to unexpected insights or discoveries about the system (serendipity). The output of the simulation could be compared with empirical observations for verification. And the properties of the system itself could be modified and changes in the output observed, a form of experimentation that made possible the prediction of changes in the phenomena being studied.

Experimental simulations. Generally speaking, the more dramatically successful computer simulations are those that reach the level of experimentation, permitting predictions of system output as a result of changes in system variables (Watt 1964; Poole et al. 1964; Kunstadter et al. 1963; Gilbert & Hammel 1966). Computer simulations such as these, however, require comprehensive and detailed knowledge of the system. The simulation reported by Watt, for example, predicts future changes in a regional water system; the predictions are plausible, however, only because there was ample information on such factors as rainfall, runoff, reservoir capacities, pipelines, and growth in demand, and on how those factors affected one another, to serve as the basis for the simulation.

In the 1970's, except in similar cases of well-developed theory and empirical knowledge, the momentum of computer simulation appears to have been lost. Most of the systems that social scientists would like to simulate are not particularly well understood. I suspect that the vast majority of attempted computer simulations have collapsed somewhere in the preparation of the first subroutine, where it became obvious that few of the variables to be included were quantified or even quantifiable as defined, and that few of the relationships between them could be specified at the level of accuracy made necessary by the computer.

Exploratory simulations. Though there is a bias in favor of computer simulations that reach the experimental stage—for these are the only ones considered interesting enough for publication in scholarly journals—even simulations of less success tell us so much about any system we are dealing with that they can be useful in theory building, in helping make unanalyzed processes explicit, in suggesting new ways of thinking, and in preparing for further field research. To exemplify these potential benefits, we may take a topic that is understood well enough to be readily simulated, but that entails interesting problems: the simulation of population processes.

Our example concerns whether members of traditional communities are able to follow their marriage rules, given that such communities are small and that a person available for marriage may not always find a potential spouse of the proper category (Kunstadter et al. 1963; see also Gilbert & Hammel 1966). The problem may be phrased as two specific questions. First, if there is a strong (prescriptive) marriage rule, what is the maximum proportion of correct marriages that could possibly result, given demographic realities? Second, if marriages were completely at random (avoiding incest, however) what proportion by chance would conform to the marriage rule?

The approach taken by Kunstadter and his associates was to write a computer program simulating well-known population processes such as birth, reproduction, and death. The result was a "system," a sheer symbolic abstraction made up of a list of "persons" who had attributes and who related to each other in accordance with the rules of the system. Since the system was created in a computer language—that is, with full and explicit statement of all variables and the rules for relating them—there was very little ambiguity in it, in contrast to the systems anthropologists usually describe.

A computer simulation has the advantage of the bookkeeping capabilities of the computer, so that large amounts of information can be stored with perfect memory and manipulated without error. According to Gilbert and Hammel (1966:71) a computer may be regarded as "a clerk with several virtues, but [a clerk] no better than its instructions."

> To appreciate the way in which this clerk operates, one should realize that a computer is, in principle, nothing more than a desk calculator and a note pad. In using a desk calculator, an operator selects items from the note pad or other storage location (such as his own memory) and transfers them into the calculator. He then performs certain manipulations of the data so entered by punching particular buttons in a certain sequence, reads the results, and transfers these back to the note pad. A *computer* combines the desk calculator and the note pad (storage) in one system so that storage, retrieval, and manipulation of items are mechanized. The *program* for the computer mechanizes the operator in directing the computer which items to select from storage, which operations to perform on them, and which results to place back in storage (Gilbert & Hammel 1966:71).

With the computer, a realistic, multivariate system is possible without loss of precision. In the Kunstadter example, the following were among the variables included: crude birth rate; crude death rate; age-specific mortality rates; age-specific marital fertility; sex ratio at birth; and age at marriage. In the simulated population, which changed in units of one year, each single person had a chance of marrying, according to age and the availability of appropriate spouses; each married woman had a chance of giving birth; and everyone had a chance of dying, again according to age. Probabilities for these events were fed into the computer as parameters (which could be varied to simulate different processes); such probabilistic, or stochastic, simulations are sometimes referred to as "Monte Carlo models." They are more realistic than mechanical-deterministic models, and allow us to represent processes (such as death) about which probabilities are known, but for which it is impossible to predict the outcome in a mechanical way for each person.

For a computer simulation to operate, it is necessary to be exact about processes that are easily left vague in ordinary descriptions. In the present example, the authors were required to raise and answer the following questions about their "population":

Question	Resulting assumption of the model
1. Will some individuals remain unmarried?	1. All women should marry.
2. What happens when a spouse dies?	2. Widows and widowers may remarry.
3. Is polygamy allowed?	3. No.
4. Who is a preferred spouse?	4. For a male, the matrilateral cross-cousin.
5. What if no preferred spouse is present?	5. Mates are selected at random from the pool of opposite-sex individuals who do not fall under incest prohibitions.
6. Are children born out of wedlock?	6. No; only married women over age thirteen bear children.

Some of these questions, but rarely all of them, are answered precisely in textual descriptions of real-world populations. Yet the computer simulation demands a high degree of precision on these issues. To take a single example, the authors stated in their introduction that if no matrilateral cross-cousin were available, "a mate would be selected at random from unmarried individuals with whom marriage was not restricted by the incest taboo" (Kunstadter et al. 1963:512). In the computer program, this statement had to be made more precise: any man and woman whose father, father's father, or father's father's father were in any combination the same person, fell under the incest prohibition. Since the computer takes our instructions literally, it helps develop a literal sense of the implications of the system in our minds. For example, children of the same mother whose fathers are unrelated could have married in this system—whether or not such an occurrence is likely in actual small populations. Those who work with computer simulations find that the level of detail forced on the model-builder by the requirements of the program raise many similar issues that easily might have been overlooked in the midst of so many variables and possibilities for interrelating them. In this respect, a computer simulation develops rigor in a way similar to mathematical treatment of a problem as in the example of the Natchez Paradox (Chapter 3).

If a computer simulation is brought to this point, many advantages will have been realized already. The model-builder will have explored in detail a system that was previously vague and inchoate. Weaknesses in the data (there always are some) will have become apparent, and implicit assumptions will have had to be made explicit. The simulation, however, will be of little interest to colleagues at this stage. The benefits of the exercise will be reflected in the greater clarity of the textural descriptions made after the simulation has been done.

As mentioned earlier, it is the experimentation stage that makes computer simulation most interesting to others. In the Kunstadter example, the program was run under various parameters. The following findings illustrate the unique value of such a computer experiment:

First, under a matrilateral cross-cousin marriage rule in a population of roughly 200 people, and after many trials to permit random fluctuations to balance out, over 90 percent of the results showed that between 15 and 40 percent of marriages conformed to the rule. The average was 28 percent. Hence it appears extremely unlikely that in small communities such a prescriptive marriage rule could ever be close to 100 percent effective unless more than half of the population were to remain unmarried.

Second, lowering the age at marriage increased the rate of cross-cousin marriage because the increase in family size resulted in more cousins. This experimental finding suggests the need for more field research on actual ages at marriage in relation to preferential marriage rules.

Third, when the preference rule was removed from the simulation so that all marriages took place at random (with incest prohibitions maintained, however) then only 1 to 2 percent of marriages involved matrilateral cross-cousins. It seems, therefore, that in small communities where preferential marriages make up 10 to 20 percent of all marriages, the marriage rule is definitely operating. These percentages, which appear very small in light of prescriptive marriage rules, thus appear large when we consider what is likely by chance and what is possible given the demographic realities.

This example illustrates a number of the advantages of including computer simulation in the analysis of cultural systems: (1) the identification of data gaps needing further research; (2) the development of a detailed sense of the complexity of the processes being investigated; (3) the achievement of greater formalism in the statement of the system; (4) the development of a kind of dynamism possible only where the myriad "bookkeeping" details can be handled by the computer rather than by the researcher; and (5) the attainment of the ability to study properties of the system by controlling some variables while varying others.

Programs can be written in computer languages that are easy to learn, such as FORTRAN, or PL1, and the speed of modern computers makes frequent runs of the program possible. The results of a simulation are probably not going to be publishable, at least at the start, and this is a consideration for young scholars who face career evaluations based in part on their publications. But the rewards in terms of understanding the system one is studying are substantial and worth and effort. If we all took the time to try to simulate by computer the systems we describe in our articles and books, we at least would be more humble in what we say, and at best would make a lot more sense as we say it.

Multivariate Analysis

Any use of statistical procedures for describing the interrelationships between more than two variables can be called "multivariate analysis." As we have seen, bivariate analyses, adapted to laboratory research settings, often appear simplistic when used to analyze complex sociocultural data. Multivariate techniques offer a way of involving more variables in the analysis. Still, in many cases the goal of the analysis will be to reduce the complexity of many observed variables to a small number of variables (often "unobserved" as "factors" or "dimensions") that appear to explain a large proportion of the variability in the directly observed variables.

Linear techniques. Multivariate techniques based on computation of correlation or regression measures are often called *linear* techniques because of the assumption that the relationship between the variables can be best described by a straight line ($y = ax + b$) with some scatter around it. The range of application of linear techniques is limited, since in many cases the linearity of a relationship is impossible to verify, or may even appear implausible.* Furthermore, the measurement of variables is assumed to be numerical. If these conditions (and certain others) are met and a correlation coefficient, r, is computed, then the quantity r^2 (the "variance") may be thought of as estimating the amount of variation in y that may be explained by variations in x. In multivariate analysis this reasoning is generalized for many variables.

For example, suppose we have reason to believe that some dependent variable y is substantially influenced by two independent variables, x_1 and x_2. We may suspect that a son's prestige is determined both by the father's prestige and by the son's wealth. Positive correlations between y and x_1 and y and x_2 might then be taken as evidence in favor of our hypothesis. But here an error may enter, since it is very likely that the two "independent" variables are themselves correlated. Such an error would occur if the correlation between son's prestige and father's prestige were spurious, a mere artifact of the real correlation between father's prestige and son's wealth, and between son's wealth and son's prestige. We need some method for eliminating the effect of a correlation between the two independent variables on their separate correlations with the dependent variable.

A method for dealing with this problem is *partial regression* analysis. Hadden and DeWalt (1974), for example, have reanalyzed correlation data concerning the prediction of "deferred goal gratification behavior" among rural Ugandans from knowledge of three independent variables: age, degree of modernization, and occupa-

---

* For example, variables in the analysis of modern sociocultural change might well curve upward exponentially rather than linearly.

TABLE 9.1

Correlations Between Independent Variables and Deferred Goal Gratification Behavior

Independent variables	Predicted correlation	Observed correlation	Partial regression coefficient
Age	negative	−.206	−.155
Modernization	positive	.164	.260
Occupational status	positive	−.033	−.275

SOURCE: Hadden & DeWalt 1974:107–8.

tional status (Pollnac & Robbins 1972). The first column of Table 9.1 presents the direction of correlations predicted by Pollnac and Robbins. On the basis of actual correlations (next column), they decided that only age had a strong enough influence to be regarded as significant. But after Hadden and DeWalt uncovered the mutual influences of the independent variables by partial regression (third column), degree of modernization appeared to have a much stronger effect on deferred gratification than age; and occupational status, which before had appeared unrelated, emerged as an unexpectedly strong *negative* factor, contrary to original expectations.

The interrelations among these variables may be analyzed still further if reasonable assumptions about causal priority among the "independent" variables can be made. For example, if age can be assumed to be causally prior to occupation, it becomes possible to segregate the *direct* effect of age on deferred gratification from the *indirect* effect of age *by way of* occupation. Hadden and DeWalt present a lucid overview of this technique, known as *path analysis*, with suggestions for potential uses in cultural anthropology.

A closely related problem is to locate, from a large set of potential "independent variables," those few whose effects on the dependent variables appear to be strongest. Kronenfeld (1973), in his analysis of the behavioral expectations of the Fanti toward particular categories of kinsmen (see Chapter 8), used *multiple regression* analysis to select from among a number of independent variables.

With multiple regression techniques it is possible to state how much of the variance of a dependent variable is accounted for by a

combination of independent variables. Among the Fanti, Kronenfeld identified a number of independent variables, such as which
kintypes were regarded by informants as superior to which others
("emic superiority"), which kintypes appeared to be superior to
which others by such criteria as generation, relative age, or skew-
ness of terminology ("etic superiority"), which kintypes were classed
as "cross" or "parallel," and so on. One set of dependent variables
concerned which types of kin could appropriately initiate or receive
verbal abuse, physical punishment, and so on. Multiple regression
analysis revealed that a combination of "etic superiority" and "genealogical closeness" variables predicted punishment variables very
effectively (accounting for about 88 percent of the variance). Many
other independent variables, such as "sex" or "lineage," accounted
for very small amounts of the variance. In this case the mutual
effects of the independent variables, which in some cases were
certainly correlated themselves, were not being investigated. Nonetheless, it may be noted that when other dependent variables relating to behavioral expectations of kin were studied, it was also found
that independent variables reflecting superiority and genealogical
closeness were consistently the strongest predictors of kin-behavior
expectations, thus reducing the large number of independent variables to a very few "important" ones (Kronenfeld 1973:1586–87).

As a final example of linear multivariate techniques, we may take
discriminant analysis, a technique for discovering the precise nature
of differences between subgroups of a population, as measured by a
number of variables. In his study of agricultural strategies among
the Awa of Highland New Guinea, for example, Boyd (1976) sus-
pected that households containing at least one married, productive
adult male (patrifocal) followed different agricultural strategies from
households containing none (matrifocal). Since patrifocal households
were larger, had more consumers per producer, and raised more
pigs (which could also be regarded as consumers) than matrifocal
households, their garden activities should have reflected these differences.

The procedure of discriminant analysis is to search for those variables, among all for which measures exist, that discriminate be-

tween the groups most sharply—that is, the variables on which the variance *between* subgroup means is greatest relative to the variance *within* subgroups.* For example, Boyd's analysis showed, among other things, that matrifocal households raised more staple root crops per consumer (including pigs) than did patrifocal households, and that patrifocal households (which had more pigs) planted sweet potato gardens (for pig food) much more often than did matrifocal households. It was these variables that effectively discriminated patrifocal from matrifocal households, whereas others that might have done so in fact did not.

One of the most useful aspects of discriminant analysis is that it is possible, once subgroups have been selected for analysis, and once those variables that discriminate them most effectively have been located, to reexamine individual cases to see if they behave according to the classification. Among the Awa, Boyd found that several of the households he had classified as "patrifocal" exhibited agricultural behavior much closer to the matrifocal pattern, and vice versa. Such "exceptional" cases, when further analyzed, suggested new variables influencing agricultural strategies. For example, the one polygynous household in Boyd's sample was classified initially as patrifocal, but was found to be agriculturally more like a matrifocal household owing to the influence of the second wife on the overall agricultural strategies of the household; in another example, households containing adult males who had been away for wage labor showed matrifocal tendencies resulting from the men's lower agricultural work inputs relative to the women's in their households; and, finally, in one of the matrifocal families, in which the only producer was an infirm widow, food production per consumer was low enough to put the house within the range of the typical patrifocal household. The simple distinction with which Boyd began (whether a married adult male was present in the household or not) is now further analyzable into a number of variables concerning the divi-

*A variety of discriminate analysis, "canonical discriminant factor analysis," will search for "unobserved" variables, or factors, that discriminate between subgroups even more effectively than any of the "observed variables" given in the analysis; see Van de Geer 1971:184–86, 270.

sion of labor by sex, the age and physical well-being of the household workers, and the participation of those workers in outside income-producing labor.

In this section we have shown a few of the potential uses of linear multivariate techniques in cultural anthropology. Partial regression and path analysis allow us to devise refined causal arguments involving many variables; multiple regression provides the opportunity to select combinations of independent variables that together account for the variance in a dependent variable; and discriminant analysis makes possible precise exploration of differences between groups we already think are different, with more sensitive classifications as the result.

Multidimensional scaling. Recently, interest among social scientists in techniques for discovering order in multivariate data has turned to a set of procedures known as multidimensional scaling techniques. The goal of multidimensional scaling is to find a small number of unobserved variables (dimensions) that account for a large proportion of the variance in a set of observed variables. In this respect they are like *factor analysis*, a linear multivariate of great power (see Driver & Schuessler 1957), but one that has been little used so far in the analysis of data from individual cultures. Multidimensional techniques have the advantages over linear techniques of making no assumptions of linearity, of requiring the measurement of variables at only the rank (ordinal) level, and of emphasizing low dimensional representations of the data that can be readily *visualized* in graphic displays, and whose results can thus be more easily grasped and thought about than those of factor analyses (Shepard 1972:2–3, 10). The following two examples illustrate how readily visualized and interpreted multidimensional scales are.

D'Andrade and Egan (1974) used a variety of multidimensional scaling known as "smallest space analysis" (SSA) in their study of the association between colors and emotions among U.S. college students and Tzeltal-speakers from Aguacatenango, Mexico. Noting that Western Europeans and North Americans found it natural to describe colors in emotional terms, D'Andrade and Egan devised an eliciting procedure whereby informants chose from among an array of 157 Munsell color chips differing in hue, brightness, and saturation the color that best corresponded to each of nine emotion terms (e.g., happy, worried, angry, very good). After dealing with the difficult problem of finding translation equivalents of the English emotion terms in Tzeltal (readers may judge how adequately; see pp. 50–51), D'Andrade and Egan administered the test to 26 English speakers and 26 Tzeltal speakers; all informants found the task possible, and none gave "wild, erratic, or inconsistent answers" (p. 57).

The test results were the frequencies with which each chip was associated with each emotion term in the two languages. The problem was to decide whether the associations between colors and emotions were similar in the two cultures (which would support the interpretation that color-emotion associations are innate), or were different (which would support the interpretation that color-emotion associations are culturally determined). The method of smallest space analysis (Lingoes 1965:1972) is to search for a small number of dimensions defining a space within which the most similar objects in the analysis will be placed most closely together. In the present example, the objects were the eighteen emotion terms (nine terms × two languages). Since SSA works with measures of similarity, a matrix of correlation coefficients (Pearson's r) was calculated for each pair of emotion terms, using the frequencies with which color chips were chosen as the observations; in fact, any measures of "proximity" (correlation, association, distance) could have been used here (Shepard 1972b:24–26). D'Andrade and Egan found that two of the resulting dimensions were adequate to represent the similarities and differences between emotion terms; in general, the researcher selects the number of dimensions (ideally small) in accordance with how well they represent the data ("goodness of fit").

The results of smallest space analysis (Figure 9.1) indicated that American-English-speakers and Tzeltal-speakers relate emotion terms to colors in remarkably similar ways. For example, speakers of both languages tended to see the degree of saturation of a color as related to emotions along a "positive-negative" dimension (the horizontal dimension in Figure 9.1); in general, the more saturated a color chip, the more positive the emotion terms with which it was

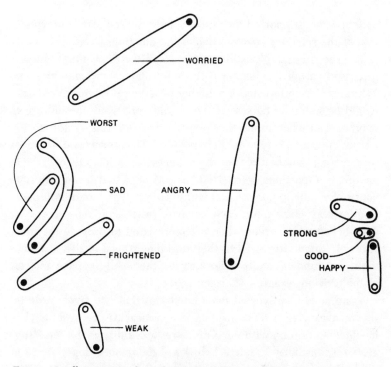

Fig. 9.1. Smallest space analysis of Tzeltal and English color terms. Solid dots are the Tzeltal words, open dots the English words. Source: D'Andrade & Egan 1974:60.

associated. The other dimension which emerged from the computer analysis is represented by the vertical axis in Figure 9.1. The authors left this dimension unnamed; this often happens in multidimensional analyses, where the dimensions uncovered achieve a mathematical standard of "best fit" with the data, but do not necessarily correspond to any familiar contrasts that we can meaningfully label. Hence, although only one of the dimensions has a clear meaning, the two together result in a useful display, in which any particular emotion term, whether used by a Tzeltal-speaker or an American-English-speaker, appears in roughly the same part of the space; in no case did the Tzeltal subjects use colors and emotions so differently from the American subjects that their two terms for the same emotion appeared on opposite sides of the space. These results strongly supported the "innate" over the "cultural" interpretation of the relations between colors and emotions.

The second example is from the work of the Six Cultures project discussed earlier in Chapter 6 (B. Whiting & Whiting 1975). The Whitings were interested in whether observed behavior of children would be found to be systematically different from one culture to another. In this example, the "objects" were kinds of children's behavior, such as "assaults" or "offers help." To control for differences in the total number of observed behaviors from one culture to another, proportions were used instead of actual frequencies; to control for individual variation within cultures, the median proportion for each culture (on each behavior) was taken. The scores for each behavior class were then intercorrelated to provide the measures of "proximity" used in the multidimensional analysis, a technique not fundamentally different from the smallest space analysis of the previous example (Kruskal 1964).

Again, analysis revealed two dimensions that effectively ordered the behavior classes. Dimension A, the vertical axis, represents a behavioral continuum with nurturance-responsibility at the top ("suggests responsibility," "offers help") and dominance-dependence at the bottom ("seeks dominance," "seeks help"). Dimension B moves from authoritarian-aggressive behavior at the left ("assaults," "reprimands") to sociable-intimate behavior at the right ("assaults sociably," "acts sociably"). As in the colors of emotions example, outcomes that appear close together in the two-dimensional space are those likely to be found together in the cultures studied.

With these results it becomes possible to ask whether children in different cultures have behavior patterns that fall in different regions of the two-dimensional space. The Whitings argued that this was indeed the case. Dimension A, for example, appeared negatively correlated with "cultural complexity"; the less complex the Whitings judged a culture to be, the more nurturant-responsible was the behavior of the children in that culture. Similarly, Dimension B was related to household structure; children in cultures with predominantly nuclear-family households tended toward sociable-intimate behavior, whereas a predominance of extended-family

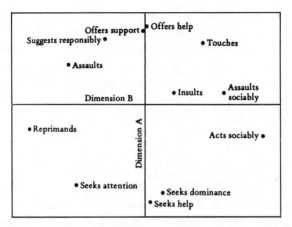

Fig. 9.2. Multidimensional scaling of cultural medians for twelve types of social behavior. Source: B. Whiting & Whiting 1975:69.

households was associated with authoritarian-aggressive behavior in children.

In short, the Whitings' use of multidimensional scaling succeeded on two counts: first, by demonstrating the existence of patterns in children's behavior cross-culturally, as seen in Figure 9.2; and second, by relating those patterns of behavior to other variables of acknowledged cross-cultural significance, such as "cultural complexity" and "household structure."

A caution on the use of multivariate techniques. The results of multivariate analysis discussed in this section all refer to issues of genuine interest in cultural anthropology; which attributes of kinsmen condition behavioral expectations; how differences in household composition affect interpersonal relations; whether complex psychological processes are innate or culturally determined. Any suspicion that sophisticated data-processing techniques can only be applied to trivial issues should now be dispelled.

Perhaps, nonetheless, it would be best to end on a note of caution. With the development of "canned" computer programs, data-processing capabilities are now available to the untutored that just a few years ago were available only to the most skilled (and industrious) of statistical analysts. This growth has been too fast, and has not been accompanied by a proper concern for user training at the undergraduate and graduate levels. In particular, we must not forget that the assumptions of linearity and interval measurement underlying the "linear" techniques are fundamental to the mathematical nature of those techniques. Yet it is easy for the student to ignore this fact, feeling that others commonly do so, and hoping that if the findings are interesting, uncertainty about whether these assumptions have been met will evaporate because the methods "worked." In most cases it is probably true that violation of the assumptions will not grossly affect the results, but over a large number of cases such violations are certain to increase the frequency of type I error (rejecting the null hypothesis when in fact it is true). In a more general sense, there is a sort of opportunism in making use of results that are "interesting" or "suggestive" when their procedural bona fides is in doubt that is contrary to the best intentions of scientific methods. This is a compelling argument for preferring multidimensional scaling techniques over the more demanding linear methods.

We cannot uncritically adopt statistical techniques and then act as though they are somehow external to the goals of the research, mere tools that will leave final results untouched. As Van de Geer put it, statistical models "tend to merge with scientific concepts as such."

> In personality research, for instance, factors obtained from factor analysis tend to become proper scientific concepts, and it is difficult (some methodologists might even say impossible, I among them) to separate the empirical evidence for those concepts from the mathematical assumptions in the model. In an advanced science one cannot tell what portion of a concept is empirical and what portion assumed. At first sight, models look like just tools, just techniques, just hired servants to do housecleaning jobs. However, before long, the relation develops into something more than a relation between maidservant and master: the master marries the girl (Van de Geer 1971:173).

At that point we will have to wonder, Who is in charge, the researcher or the technique?

Nonetheless, multivariate techniques are useful if properly applied. Data should be collected whenever possible in a sufficiently quantitative form to permit use of the more powerful techniques. When multivariate analyses are then related to systemic conceptions of a broader ethnographic sort (as in B. Whiting & Whiting 1975), their full relevance for cultural anthropology becomes evident.

CHAPTER TEN

Conclusion

ANTHROPOLOGY BEGINS by acknowledging the existence of diverse cultural realities, among which our own, subsuming the science of anthropology, is just one. Cultural constructions of reality are not normally perceived as "mere constructions"; on the contrary, they appear natural and common sensical to those who share them. The means by which anthropologists develop self-awareness about cultural reality is through immersion in another cultural setting. Participant observation puts us in direct touch with alternative constructions of reality, forcing us to modify those habitual behaviors and understandings that no longer meet our goals in a satisfactory way. The lessons of ethnographic experience heighten our sensitivity to the limits of our culture's ways of constructing reality from the vast range of possibilities.

Participant observation develops intuition and contributes to a holistic sense of community life. In time an awareness of the patterning or unity of disparate beliefs and activities grows that helps to crystallize the contrast between our own cultural experience and that of natives in the communities we study. This humanistic, integrated awareness, however, is not alone sufficient to overcome ethnocentrism; in fact, it may be quite ethnocentric. An effective counter to ethocentrism depends on strengthening the theories that allow us to predict the conditions under which given cultural features occur. Strong theory is only possible if standards exist for comparing data from a variety of cultural settings, for comparisons cannot be made simply on the basis of individualized ethnographic descriptions of particular societies. Only operational definitions and representative samples can guarantee the reliability of cross-cultural comparisons.

Scientific theories are not separate from data collection. Theoretical propositions are tested against data, which means they are restricted in a practical sense to the kinds of data we know how to collect. Theoretical reasoning in a vacuum, leaving operational details vague, can be a bad habit to get into, just because it is so easy to make plausible, scientific-sounding statements in the abstract that turn out in actual field research to refer to nothing measurable.

Operational definitions and explicit sampling procedures do not entirely eliminate bias, as we have seen; theoretical variables such as "relationship" or "cognition" have different meanings according to the specific research procedure being used to describe them, and preference for one procedure over another can amount to bias. Operationalism, however, does lead us to separate the testable from the nontestable aspects of theoretical thought, and helps expose bias to public view.

Somehow, a balance between the strengths of science and humanism must be found. The modern notion of "system" leads in that direction. A system is a construct of the analyst, representing a "best effort" to become precise about the variables used in particular descriptions and about the influences of the variables on one another. It is a step away from the powerful but limited bivariate causal approach of the laboratory sciences, toward holism and recognition of the need to comprehend complex natural situations. The unfortunate tendency is for such systemic analyses to move so far from a causal framework that they dissolve in the ineffectual tangle of weak functionalism.

This is a danger in every cultural research project. Reality is not as neatly bounded as the systems we "discover" through reasoning and research. Merely describing "what is there" is no solution because "what is there" is infinitely greater than what we see, given our cultural preconceptions. We have no choice but to be aware of the purposes that direct us to select, from the huge number of potential observations, those we actually make. This is the change that has taken place as cultural descriptions have moved from the old-style comprehensive ethnography to the new-style problem-oriented ethnography. Haphazard or intuitive eclecticism is being replaced by explicit identification of core and peripheral variables.

For fieldworkers, this means that some matters require more attention than others. Any field project will have a set of core variables that should be measured at the highest feasible level of quantification, and across a representative sample of community members. The result should be a careful, systemically interrelated "data skeleton" of reliable findings. Around this core a more humanistically complete description can be built, without limiting the cross-cultural comparability of the core description. Perfect harmony between science and humanism may not be possible in anthropology, but we should be able to achieve a fairly good mix.

In this book, the centrifugal pressures of the systems approach have been countered by the perspective of cultural ecology, beginning with the idea that a set of "basic needs" can be identified that must be met in all cultural systems. Initially, basic needs are defined in biological terms, because the science of human biology has the capability of identifying with considerable reliability processes that, if interrupted or improperly provisioned, lead to malfunction and death of the organism. But the theory of basic needs can properly be expanded to include sociological, emotional, and even aesthetic needs. Whichever orientation or combination of orientations is selected in research, the core concept of needs becomes the basis on which variables are selected and ordered.

Many of the shortcomings of current anthropological practice can be overcome, and often all that is required is a change of attitude, or a small amount of additional training. The quality of field data can generally be improved—without investing additional time or money in a research project—if the researcher is aware of a few basic problems, among which the following are especially serious.

The first is the fear of being wrong. One can always avoid untrue statements simply by speaking in generalities and qualifiers. As Burling pointed out (see Chapter 7), we can make maximization analysis tautologically true simply by failing to specify what is being maximized. Once we specify the measure of utility, e.g., money, we are bound to be at least partially wrong. It is helpful to keep in mind that anthropology is a cooperative enterprise; being found wrong can be regarded not as an embarrassment to the individual but as an advance for the whole field. Being wrong is better than being trite or confused.

Another problem is the tendency to think in typological terms, and to dispute typological issues. This is one reason why the orientations identified in earlier chapters are preferable to such subfield designations of anthropology as "economic," "social," and "political." Arguments about the proper subject matter of those subfields are often acrimonious, whereas in fact no subfield has clear boundaries; each evidently employs a mix of strategies and priorities, judging from the real practice of individual "economic anthropologists," "social anthropologists," and so on. With the *orientations* it is acknowledged from the outset that they have core priorities and procedures, but no clear boundaries; furthermore, each is compatible with each of the others, not contradictory. Together, they provide a repertoire of understandings and techniques that are the building blocks of effective research design.

Typological thinking has also led to descriptions that have none of the fluidity and ambiguity of daily life. Structures become hard and determinate, unlike the people who are supposed to share them. Quantitative description, by contrast, always controverts the mechanical structuralist view. No two brothers treat each other exactly the same, no two informants share perfectly isomorphic pictures of the world, and all patterns that do emerge have fuzzy edges and tend to overlap. In place of typologies we want a sense of continuous shading between categories, of peaks and valleys and flows rather than points and lines in abstract space.

Typologies are effective summaries when global overviews, based on scattered data, are desired. The "normative bias" of ethnographic reports is a natural outcome of the pressure to produce holistic descriptions of human societies—certainly the most complex of natural phenomena—based on only a year or two of field research. But a compromise is possible. Early in the fieldwork, before intensive structural interviewing with informants is possible, it is still feasible to visit households, work sites, and public places to observe individuals as they go about their business. Behavioral observations are quantifiable, and when randomly sampled, permit the statistical descriptions against which normative structures can be compared. Until behavioral observations have an equal role alongside normative data in anthropological research, it is unlikely that many cross-cultural predictions of concrete usefulness will emerge.

Finally, less effort and fewer printed pages should be devoted to arguments over issues that cannot be resolved with data. Open discussion of priorities and purposes is helpful insofar as it broadens and clarifies our ideas of what we are doing. It is wasteful when it does not also lead to formulation of testable propositions and subsequent research. Debate on many issues in cultural anthropology, such as the relative "efficiency" of differing production systems, or the "rationality of decision-making" in traditional communities, is *premature* in that the central terms at issue (here, efficiency and rationality) are used by different writers with different meanings that are rarely spelled out. The debates surrounding such issues could well be suspended in an effort to reach agreement on what kinds of new data would resolve them: if it turns out that they cannot be resolved with data, then we would know something important and might prefer to get on with other matters. Identifying those issues on which discussion is premature, and uncovering the urgent issues hidden within them, will lead to research designs that are more satisfying to develop, more effective to carry out in the field, and more likely to produce useful results.

Reference Matter

Bibliography

Abelson, Robert. 1968. Social simulation. In Gardner Lindzey and Eliot Aronson, eds., Psychology. Menlo Park, Calif.: Addison-Wesley.

Alland, Alexander. 1975. Adaptation. *Annual Rev. of Anthrop.* 4:59–73.

Arkin, Herbert, and Raymond R. Colton. 1962. Tables for statisticians. New York: Barnes and Noble.

Baker, Paul T., and William T. Sanders. 1972. Demographic studies in anthropology. *Annual Rev. of Anthrop.* 1:151–78.

Banton, M. 1965. The relevance of models for social anthropology. ASA Monograph 1. London: Tavistock.

Barnes, J. A. 1972. Social networks. *Addison-Wesley Modular Publications in Anthrop.* 26.

Barth, Fredrik. 1959. Segmentary opposition and the theory of games. *J. Roy. Anthrop. Inst.* (London) 89.

———— 1966. Models of social organization. Occasional Paper 23. Roy. Anthrop. Inst. of Great Britain and Ireland.

Belshaw, Cyril. 1965. Traditional exchange and modern markets. Englewood Cliffs, N.J.: Prentice-Hall.

Ben-David, Joseph. 1973. Squeezing the subjectivity out of knowledge. Review of Robert K. Merton, The Sociology of Science. *New York Times Book Review*, Nov. 11, 1973.

Berlin, Brent, and Paul Kay. 1969. Basic color terms. Berkeley: Univ. of California Press.

Berlin, Brent, Dennis E. Breedlove, and Peter H. Raven. 1974. Principles of Tzeltal plant classification. New York: Academic Press.

Berreman, Gerald. 1966. Anemic and emetic analyses in social anthropology. *Amer. Anthrop.* 68:346–54.

Bertalanffy, Ludwig van. 1968. Modern system theory. New York: Braziller.

Black, Mary, and Duane Metzger. 1965. Ethnographic description and the study of law. *Amer. Anthrop.* 67:141–65.

Blackburn, Thomas R. 1971. Sensuous-intellectual complementarity in science. *Science* 172:1003–7.

Blalock, Hubert M., Jr. 1972. Social statistics. New York: McGraw-Hill.

Blau, Peter. 1967. Power and exchange in social life. New York: Wiley.

Bogue, Donald J. 1970. A model interview for fertility research and family planning evaluation. Chicago: Univ. of Chicago Press.

Bohm, David. 1957. Causality and chance in modern physics. New York: Harper.

——— 1965. The special theory of relativity. New York: Benjamin.

Boserup, Ester. 1965. The conditions of agricultural growth. Chicago: Aldine.

Bott, Elizabeth. 1971. Family and social network: Roles, norms, and external relationships in ordinary urban families. London: Tavistock.

Boulding, Kenneth E. 1968. General systems theory: The skeleton of science. In Walter Buckley, ed., Modern systems research for the behavioral scientist. Chicago: Aldine.

Bourguignon, Erika. 1973. Psychological anthropology. In John J. Honigman, ed., Handbook of social and cultural anthropology. Chicago: Rand McNally.

Boyd, David. 1976. Crops, kiaps, and currency: Flexible behavioral strategies among the Ilakia Awa of Papua New Guinea. Ph.D. dissertation, Univ. of California, Los Angeles.

Braidwood, Robert J. 1967. Prehistoric men. Glenview, Ill.: Scott Foresman.

Buchler, Ira, and Hugo Nutini. 1969. Game theory in the behavioral sciences. Pittsburgh, Pa.: Univ. of Pittsburgh Press.

Buchler, Ira R., and Henry A. Selby. 1968. Kinship and social organization: An introduction to theory and method. New York: Macmillan.

Burling, Robbins. 1962. Maximization theories and the study of economic anthropology. *Amer. Anthrop.* 64:802–21.

——— 1964. Cognition and componential analysis: God's truth or hocus-pocus? *Amer. Anthrop.* 66:20–28.

Burton, Michael. 1973. Mathematical anthropology. *Annual Rev. of Anthrop.* 2:189–99.

Cancian, Francesca M. 1975. What are norms? New York: Cambridge Univ. Press.

Cancian, Frank. 1965. Economics and prestige in a Maya community. Stanford, Calif.: Stanford Univ. Press.

———— 1966. Maximization as norm, strategy, and theory. *Amer. Anthrop.* 68:465–70.

———— 1972. Change and uncertainty in a peasant economy: The Maya corn farmers of Zinacantan. Stanford, Calif.: Stanford Univ. Press.

Carneiro, Robert. 1970. A theory of the origin of the state. *Science* 169:733–38.

Cassirer, Ernst. 1961. The logic of the humanities. New Haven, Conn.: Yale Univ. Press.

Chapple, E. D., and C. M. Arensberg. 1940. Measuring human relations: An introduction to the study of the interaction of individuals. *Genetic Psychology Monographs* 22:3–147.

Chayanov, A. V. 1966. The theory of peasant economy. Homewood, Ill.: Irwin.

Chen, Kwan-Hwa, and Gerald F. Murray. 1976. Truths and untruths in village Haiti: An experiment in Third World survey research. In J. Marshall and S. Polgar, eds., Culture, natality, and family planning. Carolina Population Center. Chapel Hill: Univ. of North Carolina.

Childe, V. Gordon. 1951. Man makes himself. New York: Mentor.

Clark, Philip J., and Francis C. Evans. 1954. Distance to nearest neighbor as a measure of spatial relationships in populations. *Ecology* 35:445–53.

Cohen, Ronald, and Raoul Naroll. 1973. Method in cultural anthropology. In Raoul Naroll and Ronald Cohen, eds., A handbook of method in cultural anthropology. New York: Columbia Univ. Press.

Cole, Michael, and John Gay. 1972. Culture and memory. *Amer. Anthrop.* 74:1066–84.

Cole, Michael, John Gay, Joseph A. Glick, and Donald W. Sharp. 1971. The cultural context of learning and thinking. New York: Basic Books.

Colson, Anthony C., and Karen F. Selby. 1974. Medical anthropology. *Annual Rev. of Anthrop.* 3:245–62.

Cook, Scott. 1970. Price and output variability in a peasant-artisan stoneworking industry in Oaxaca, Mexico: An analytical essay in economic anthropology. *Amer. Anthrop.* 72:776–801.

———— 1973. Economic anthropology: Problems in theory, method, and analysis. In J. Honigmann, ed., Handbook of social and cultural anthropology. Chicago: Rand McNally.

Coombs, Clyde H. 1964. A theory of data. New York: Wiley.

Cronbach, Lee J., and P. E. Meehl. 1956. Construct validity in psychological tests. In Herbert Feigl and Michael Scriven, eds., The foundations of science and the concepts of psychology and psychoanalysis. Minnesota Studies in the Philosophy of Science 1. Minneapolis: Univ. of Minnesota Press.

Dalton, George. 1969. Theoretical issues in economic anthropology. *Current Anthrop.* 10:62–102.

D'Andrade, Roy G. 1973. Cultural constructions of reality. In Laura Nader and Thomas Maretzki, eds., Cultural illness and health. Washington, D.C.: Amer. Anthrop. Assn., Anthrop. Studies 9.

——— 1974. Memory and the assessment of behavior. In H. Blalock, ed., Measurement in the social sciences. Chicago: Aldine.

D'Andrade, Roy G., and M. Egan. 1974. The colors of emotion. *Amer. Ethnologist* 1:49–63.

Davenport, William. 1960. Jamaican fishing: A game theory analysis. Yale Univ. Publications in Anthrop. 59.

DeHavenon, Anna Lou, and Marvin Harris. 1976. Hierarchical behavior in domestic groups: A videotape analysis. Manuscript, Columbia University.

Deutsch, Morton, and Robert M. Krauss. 1965. Theories in social psychology. New York: Basic Books.

DeVos, George, and Hiroshi Wagatsuma. 1961. Value attitudes toward role behavior of women in two Japanese villages. *Amer. Anthrop.* 63:1204–30.

Draper, Patricia. 1975. Cultural pressure on sex differences. *Amer. Ethnologist* 2:602–16.

Driver, Harold E. 1962. The contribution of A. L. Kroeber to culture area theory and practice. *Int'l J. of Amer. Linguistics*, Memoir 18. Bloomington: Indiana Univ. Publications in Anthrop. and Linguistics.

Driver, Harold E., and James L. Coffin. 1975. Classification and development of North American Indian cultures: A statistical analysis of the Driver-Massey sample. Transactions of the Amer. Philosophical Society 65, Part 3.

Driver, Harold E., and Alfred E. Kroeber. 1932. Quantitative expression of cultural relationships. *Univ. of California Publications in Amer. Archeology and Ethnology* 31:211–56.

Driver, H. E., and K. F. Schuessler. 1957. Factor analysis of ethnographic data. *Amer. Anthrop.* 59:655–63.

Edel, Matthew. 1969. Economic analysis in an anthropological setting: Some methodological considerations. *Amer. Anthrop.* 71:421–33.

Edgerton, Robert B. 1970. Method in psychological anthropology. In Raoul Naroll and Ronald Cohen, eds., A handbook of method in cultural anthropology. New York: Columbia Univ. Press.

——— 1971. The individual in cultural adaptation. Berkeley: Univ. of California Press.

Eggan, Fred. 1955. Methods and results. In Fred Eggan, ed., Social anthropology of North American tribes. Chicago: Univ. of Chicago Press.

———— 1961. Social anthropology and the method of controlled comparison. In Frank W. Moore, ed., Readings in cross-cultural methodology. New Haven, Conn.: HRAF Press.

Ember, Carol R. 1973. Feminine task assignment and the social behavior of boys. *Ethos* 1:424–39.

Epstein, A. L. 1961. The network and urban social organization. *Rhodes-Livingstone Inst. J.* 29:28–62.

Erasmus, Charles J. 1955. Work patterns in a Mayo village. *Amer. Anthrop.* 57:322–33.

Feigl, Herbert. 1956. Some major issues and developments in the philosophy of science of logical empiricism. In Herbert Feigl and Michael Scriven, eds., The foundations of science and the concepts of psychology and psychoanalysis. Minnesota Studies in the Philosophy of Science 1. Minneapolis: Univ. of Minnesota Press.

Firth, Raymond. 1946. Malay fishermen. 2d ed. New York: Norton.

———— 1975. An appraisal of modern social anthropology. *Annual Rev. of Anthrop.* 4:1–25.

Fjellman, Stephen. 1971. The organization of diversity: A study of Akamba kinship terminology. Ph.D. dissertation, Stanford University.

Forcese, Dennis P., and Stephen Richer. 1973. Social research methods. Englewood Cliffs, N.J.: Prentice-Hall.

Fortes, M. 1953. The structure of unilineal descent groups. *Amer. Anthrop.* 55:17–41.

Foster, George M. 1961. The dyadic contract: A model for the social structure of a Mexican peasant village. *Amer. Anthrop.* 63:1173–92.

———— 1963. The dyadic contract in Tzintzuntzan. II, Patron-client relationships. *Amer. Anthrop.* 65:1280–94.

———— 1967. Tzintzuntzan: Mexican peasants in a changing world. Boston: Little, Brown.

Frake, Charles O. 1962. Cultural ecology and ethnography. *Amer. Anthrop.* 63:113–32.

Freud, Sigmund. 1961. Civilization and its discontents. New York: Norton.

Fromm, Erich. 1941. Escape from freedom. New York: Avon Books.

Fromm, Erich, and Michael Maccoby. 1970. Social character in a Mexican village: A sociopsychoanalytic study. Englewood Cliffs, N.J.: Prentice-Hall.

Garner, B. J. 1967. Models of urban geography and settlement location. In Richard J. Chorley and Peter Haggett, eds., Models in geography. London: Methuen.

Geertz, Clifford. 1963. Agricultural involution. Berkeley: Univ. of California Press.

Geoghegan, William. 1970. Residential decision-making among the Eastern Samal. Manuscript, Univ. of California, Berkeley.

Gilbert, John P., and E. A. Hammel. 1966. Computer simulation and analysis of problems in kinship and social structure. *Amer. Anthrop.* 68:71–93.

Gilliland, Martha W. 1975. Energy analysis and public policy. *Science* 189:1051–56.

———— 1976. Reply to comments. *Science* 192:12.

Gladwin, Hugh, and Christina Gladwin. 1971. Estimating market conditions and profit expectations of fish sellers at Cape Coast, Ghana. In George Dalton, ed., Studies in economic anthropology. Washington, D.C.: Amer. Anthrop. Assn.

Goldschmidt, Walter. 1965. Theory and strategy in the study of cultural adaptability. *Amer. Anthrop.* 67:402–8.

———— 1971. Introduction. In Robert B. Edgerton, The individual in cultural adaptation. Berkeley: Univ. of California Press.

Goodenough, Ward. 1964. Cultural anthropology and linguistics. In Dell Hymes, ed., Language in culture and society. New York: Harper and Row.

———— 1970. Description and comparison in cultural anthropology. Chicago: Aldine.

Gould, Peter R. 1969. Man against his environment: A game theoretic framework. In Andrew P. Vayda, ed., Environment and cultural behavior. Garden City, N.Y.: Natural History Press.

Gouldner, Alvin W., and Richard A. Peterson. 1962. Notes on technology and the moral order. New York: Bobbs-Merrill.

Greenberg, Daniel. 1967. The politics of pure science. New York: New American Library.

Grodins, Fred S. 1965. Computer simulation of cybernetic systems. In Ralph W. Stacy and Bruce D. Waxman, eds., Computers in biomedical research. New York: Academic Press.

Gross, Daniel R. 1975. Protein capture and cultural development in the Amazon basin. *Amer. Anthrop.* 77:526–49.

Gross, Daniel R., and Barbara A. Underwood. 1971. Technological change and caloric costs: Sisal agriculture in northeastern Brazil. *Amer. Anthrop.* 73:725–40.

Hadden, K., and B. DeWalt. 1974. Path analysis: Some anthropological examples. *Ethnology* 13:105–28.

Harary, Frank, Robert Z. Norman, and Dorwin Cartwright. 1965. Structural models: An introduction to the theory of directed graphs. New York: Wiley.

Harrington, Charles, and John W. M. Whiting. 1972. Socialization process and personality. In Francis L. K. Hsu, ed., Psychological anthropology. New ed. Cambridge, Mass.: Schenkman.

Harris, Marvin. 1964. The nature of cultural things. New York: Random House.

———— 1968. The rise of anthropological theory. New York: Crowell.

———— 1970. Referential ambiguity in the calculus of Brazilian racial identity. *Southwestern J. of Anthrop.* 26:1–14.

———— 1975. People, culture, nature. New York: Crowell.

Haskins, C. 1974. Scientists talk of the need for conservation and an ethic of biotic diversity to slow species extinction. *Science* 184:646–47.

Hassan, Fekri A. 1974. Population growth and cultural evolution. *Reviews in Anthrop.* 1:205–12.

Heider, Karl G. 1972. Environment, subsistence, and society. *Annual Rev. of Anthrop.* 1:207–26.

Henry, Jules. 1951. The economics of Pilaga food distribution. *Amer. Anthrop.* 53:187–219.

Hobhouse, L. T., G. C. Wheeler, and M. Ginsberg. 1915. The material culture and social institutions of the simpler peoples: An essay in correlation. London: Routledge and Kegan Paul.

Holton, Gerald. 1973. Thematic origins of scientific thought. Cambridge, Mass.: Harvard Univ. Press.

Homans, George. 1958. Social behavior as exchange. *Amer. J. of Sociology* 63:597–606.

———— 1967. The nature of social science. New York: Harcourt, Brace and World.

Honigmann, John J. 1976. Anthropology of childhood. *Reviews in Anthrop.* 3:213–18.

Huettner, David A. 1976. Net energy analysis: An economic assessment. *Science* 192:101–4.

Hymes, Dell. 1965. The use of computers in anthropology. The Hague: Mouton.

Jelliffe, D. B. 1966. The assessment of the nutritional status of the community. Geneva: World Health Organization.

Johnson, Allen. 1974. Ethnoecology and planting practices in a swidden agricultural system. *Amer. Ethnologist* 1:87–101.

———— 1975. Time allocation in a Machiguenga community. *Ethnology* 14:301–10.

———— 1977. The energy costs of technology in a changing environment: A Machiguenga case. In Heather Lechtman and Robert Merrill, eds., Material Culture. Proceedings of the 1975 American Ethnological Society. St. Paul, Minn.: West Publishing Co.

Johnson, Allen, and George C. Bond. 1974. Kinship, friendship, and exchange in two communities: A comparative analysis of norms and behavior. *J. of Anthrop. Research* 30:55–68.

Johnson, Orna R. 1977. Domestic organization and interpersonal relations among the Machiguenga Indians of the Peruvian Amazon. Ph.D. dissertation, Columbia University.

Johnson, Orna R., and Allen Johnson. 1975. Male/female relations and the organization of work in a Machiguenga community. *Amer. Ethnologist* 2:634–48.

Kardiner, Abram. 1939. The individual and his society. New York: Columbia Univ. Press.

——— 1945. The psychological frontiers of society. New York: Columbia Univ. Press.

Kay, Paul. 1971. Explorations in mathematical anthropology. Cambridge, Mass.: M.I.T. Press.

Keesing, Roger M. 1974. Theories of culture. *Annual Rev. of Anthrop.* 3:73–97.

Kemeny, John G., J. Laurie Snell, and Gerald L. Thompson. 1966. Introduction to finite mathematics. 2d ed. Englewood Cliffs, N.J.: Prentice-Hall.

Kensinger, Kenneth M. 1975. Studying the Cashinahua. In Jane P. Dwyer, ed., The Cashinahua of eastern Peru. The Haffenreffer Museum of Anthropology, Brown University.

Kish, Leslie. 1965. Survey sampling. New York: Wiley.

Kozelka. Robert. 1969. A Bayesian approach to Jamaican fishing. In Ira Buchler and Hugo Nutini, eds., Game theory in the behavioral sciences. Pittsburgh, Pa.: Univ. of Pittsburgh Press.

Kroeber, Alfred E. 1952. The nature of culture. Chicago: Univ. of Chicago Press.

Kronenfeld, David. 1973. Fanti kinship: The structure of terminology and behavior. *Amer. Anthrop.* 75:1577–95.

Kruskal, J. B. 1964. Multidimensional scaling by optimizing goodness of fit to a nonmetric hypothesis. *Psychometrika* 29:1–27.

Kuhn, Thomas. 1970. The structure of scientific revolutions. 2d ed. Chicago: Univ. of Chicago Press.

Kultgen, John. 1975. Phenomenology and structuralism. *Annual Rev. of Anthrop.* 4:371–87.

Kunstadter, P., R. Buhler, F. Stephan, and C. Westoff. 1963. Demographic variability and preferential marriage patterns. *Amer. J. of Physical Anthrop.* 2:511–19.

Langham, Max R., W. W. McPherson, Henry M. Peskin, Robert F. Mueller, and David E. Reichle. 1976. Comments on Gilliland 1975. *Science* 192:8–12.

Lee, Dorothy. 1959. Freedom and culture. Englewood Cliffs, N.J.: Prentice-Hall.

Lee, Richard. 1968. What hunters do for a living, or, how to make out on scarce resources. In Richard Lee and Irven DeVore, eds., Man the hunter. Chicago: Aldine.

Leontieff, Wassily. 1966. Input-output economics. New York: Oxford Univ. Press.

LeVine, Robert A. 1966. Dreams and deeds. Chicago: Univ. of Chicago Press.

——— 1973. Culture, behavior, and personality. Chicago: Aldine.

Lewis, Oscar. 1951. Life in a Mexican village: Tepoztlan restudied. Urbana: Univ. of Illinois Press.

Lindzey G. 1961. Projective techniques and cross-cultural research. New York: Appleton-Century-Crofts.

Lingoes, J. 1965. An IBM 7090 program for Guttman-Lingoes smallest space analysis-1. *Behavioral Sciences* 10:183–84.

——— 1972. A general survey of the Guttman-Lingoes nonmetric program series. In R. Shepard, A. Romney, and S. Nerlove, eds., Multidimensional scaling. Vol. 1, Theory. New York: Seminar Press.

Linton, Ralph. 1939. Preface. In Abram Kardiner, The individual and his society. New York: Columbia Univ. Press.

——— 1945. Preface. In Abram Kardiner, The psychological frontiers of society. New York: Columbia Univ. Press.

Lösch, August. 1967. The economics of location. New York: Wiley.

Luce, R. D., and H. Raiffa. 1957. Games and decisions. New York: Wiley.

Maccoby, Michael, and George M. Foster. 1970. Methods of studying Mexican peasant personality: Rorschach, TAT and dreams. *Anthrop. Quarterly* 43:225–42.

McCollough, Celeste, and Loche Van Atta. 1963. Statistical concepts: A program for self-instruction. New York: McGraw-Hill.

McElroy, Ann. 1974. The assessment of role identity: Problems of administering the Instrumental Activities Inventory to Inuit children. Paper presented at the 73d Annual Meeting of the American Anthropological Association, Mexico City.

McEwen, William J. 1963. Forms and problems of validation in social anthropology. *Current Anthrop.* 4:155–83.

Malinowski, Bronislaw. 1927. Sex and repression in savage society. Cleveland, Ohio: World.

——— 1939. The group and the individual in functional analysis. *Amer. J. of Sociology* 44:938–64.

——— 1945. The dynamics of culture change. New Haven, Conn.: Yale Univ. Press.

Mead, Margaret. 1954. Theoretical setting. In Margaret Mead and Martha Wolfenstein, eds., Childhood in contemporary cultures. Chicago: Univ. of Chicago Press.

—— 1966. New lives for old. New York: Dell.

—— 1976. Towards a human science. *Science* 191:903–9.

Meehan, Eugene J. 1968. Explanation in social science: A system paradigm. Homewood, Ill: Dorsey.

Metzger, Duane, and Gerald Williams. 1966. Some procedures and results in the study of native categories: Tzeltal "firewood." *Amer. Anthrop.* 68:389–407.

Minturn, Leigh, and William W. Lambert. 1964. Mothers of six cultures: Antecedents of child rearing. New York: Wiley.

Mitchell, J. Clyde. 1967. On quantification in social anthropology. In A. L. Epstein, ed., The craft of social anthropology. London: Tavistock.

—— 1974. Social networks. *Annual Rev. of Anthrop.* 3:279–99.

Montgomery, Edward. 1972. Stratification and nutrition in a population in southern India. Ph.D. dissertation, Columbia University.

Montgomery, Edward, and Allen Johnson. 1976. Machiguenga energy expenditure. *Ecology of Food and Nutrition* 6:97–105.

Montgomery, Edward, John W. Bennett, and Thayer Scudder. 1973. The impact of human activities on the physical and social environments: New directions in anthropological anthropology. *Annual Rev. of Anthrop.* 2:27–61.

Moore, Omar Khayyam. 1969. Divination: A new perspective. In Andrew P. Vayda, ed., Environment and cultural behavior. Garden City, N.Y.: Natural History Press.

Munroe, Ruth H., and Robert L. Munroe. 1974. Household density and infant care in East African society. In Robert A. LeVine, ed., Culture and personality. Chicago: Aldine.

Murdock, George Peter. 1940. The cross-cultural survey. *Amer. Sociological Rev.* 5:361–70. (Reprinted in Frank Moore, ed., Readings in cross-cultural methodology. New Haven, Conn.: HRAF Press.)

—— 1949. Social structure. New York: Macmillan.

—— 1967a. Ethnographic atlas: A summary. *Ethnology* 6:109–236.

—— 1967b. Ethnographic atlas. Pittsburgh, Pa.: Univ. of Pittsburgh Press.

—— 1972. Anthropology's mythology. The Huxley memorial lecture, 1971. Proceedings of the Royal Anthrop. Inst. of Great Britain and Ireland for 1971.

Murphy, Jane M. 1976. Psychiatric labeling in cross-cultural perspective. *Science* 191:1019–28.

Murphy, Robert F. 1970. Basin ethnography and ecological theory. In Earl H. Swanson Jr., ed., Languages and cultures of western North America. Pocatello: Idaho State Univ. Press.

—— 1971. Dialects of social life. New York: Basic Books.

Nadel, S. F. 1951. The foundations of social anthropology. Glencoe, Ill.: The Free Press.

Nag, Moni, ed. 1974. Population and social organization. The Hague: Mouton.

Nagel, Ernest. 1961. The structure of science. New York: Harcourt, Brace and World.

Naroll, Raoul. 1970. What have we learned from cross-cultural surveys? *Amer. Anthrop.* 72:1227–88.

―――― 1973. Galton's problem. In Raoul Naroll and Ronald Cohen, eds., A handbook of method in cultural anthropology. New York: Columbia Univ. Press.

Nash, Manning. 1967. "Reply" to reviews of primitive and peasant economic systems. *Current Anthrop.* 8:249–50.

Nelson, Richard K. 1969. Hunters of the northern ice. Chicago: Univ. of Chicago Press.

Netting, Robert. 1968. Hill farmers of Nigeria. Seattle: Univ. of Washington Press.

―――― 1974. Agrarian ecology. *Annual Rev. of Anthrop.* 3:21–56.

Odum, Howard T. 1971. Environment, power, and society. New York: Wiley.

Otterbein, Keith F. 1970. The developmental cycle of the Andros household: A diachronic analysis. *Amer. Anthrop.* 72:1412–19.

Parzen, Emanuel. 1960. Modern probability theory and its applications. New York: Wiley.

Pelto, Pertti J. 1970. Anthropological research: The structure of inquiry. New York: Harper and Row.

Pelto, Pertti, and Gretel Pelto. 1975. Intra-cultural diversity: Some theoretical issues. *Amer. Ethnologist* 2:1–18.

Plattner, Stuart. 1975. Rural market networks. *Scientific Amer.* 232:66–79.

Pollnac, R. B., and M. C. Robbins. 1972. Gratification patterns and modernization in rural Buganda. *Human Organization* 31:63–72.

Poole, I. R., P. Abelson, and S. Popkin. 1964. Candidates, issues, and strategies: A computer simulation of the 1960 presidential election. Cambridge, Mass.: M.I.T. Press.

Popper, Karl. 1968. The logic of scientific discovery. New York: Harper and Row.

Quinn, Naomi. 1971. Mfantse fishing crew composition: A decision-making analysis. Ph.D. dissertation, Stanford University.

―――― 1974. Getting inside our informants' heads. *Reviews in Anthrop.* 1:244–52.

Rapoport, Anatol. 1968. Foreword. In Walter Buckley, ed., Modern systems research for the behavioral scientist. Chicago: Aldine.

Rappaport, Roy A. 1971. Nature, culture, and ecological anthropology. In Harry L. Shapiro, Man, culture and society. New York: Oxford Univ. Press.

Read, Dwight, and Catherine E. Read. 1970. A critique of Davenport's game theory analysis. *Amer. Anthrop.* 72:351–55.

Redfield, Robert. 1953. The primitive world and its transformations. Ithaca, N.Y.: Cornell Univ. Press.

Richardson, Harry W. 1972. Input-output and regional economics. New York: Wiley.

Romney, A. K. 1971. Measuring endogamy. In Paul Kay, ed., Explorations in mathematical anthropology. Cambridge, Mass.: M.I.T. Press.

Romney, A. K., and Roy G. D'Andrade. 1964. Cognitive aspects of English kin terms. *Amer. Anthrop.* 66:146–70.

Rosenthal, Robert, and Ralph L. Rosnow. 1975. The volunteer subject. New York: Wiley.

Sahlins, Marshall. 1965. On the sociology of primitive exchange. In M. Banton, ed., Models in social anthropology. London: Tavistock.

———— 1972. Stone age economics. Chicago: Aldine.

Sanday, Peggy. 1968. The "psychological reality" of American-English kinship terms: An information-processing approach. *Amer. Anthrop.* 70:508–23.

Sanjek, Roger. 1971. Brazilian racial terms: Some aspects of meaning and learning. *Amer. Anthrop.* 73:1126–43.

———— 1972. Ghanaian networks: An analysis of interethnic relations in urban situations. Ph.D. dissertation, Columbia University.

Sankoff, Gillian. 1971. Quantitative analysis of sharing and variability in a cognitive model. *Ethnology* 10:389–408.

Saucier, Jean-François. 1974. The patron-client relationship in traditional and contemporary Rwanda. Ph.D. dissertation, Columbia University.

Selby, Henry. 1976. Norms and behavior. *Reviews in Anthrop.* 3:1–8.

Shepard, R. N. 1972a. Introduction. In R. Shepard, A. Romney, and S. Nerlove, eds., Multidimensional scaling. Vol. 1, Theory. New York: Seminar Press.

———— 1972b. A taxonomy of some principal types of data and of multidimensional methods for their analysis. In R. Shepard, A. Romney, and S. Nerlove, eds., Multidimensional Scaling. Vol. 1, Theory. New York: Seminar Press.

Shubik, Martin. 1960. Simulation of industry and the firm. *Amer. Economic Rev.* 50:908–19.

Siegel, Sidney. 1956. Nonparametric statistics for the behavioral sciences. New York: McGraw-Hill.

Simon, Herbert A. 1957. Models of man: Social and rational. New York: Wiley.

Sioli, Harald. 1973. Recent human activities in the Brazilian Amazon region and their ecological effects. In Betty Meggers, Edward S. Ayensu, and W. Donald Duckworth, eds., Tropical forest ecosystems in Africa and South America. Washington, D.C.: Smithsonian Institution Press.

Siskind, Janet. 1973. Tropical forest hunters and the economy of sex. In D. Gross, ed., Peoples and cultures of native South America. New York: Doubleday.

Skinner, B. F. 1956. Critique of psychoanalytic concepts and theories. In Herbert Feigl and Michael Scriven, eds., The foundations of science and the concepts of psychology and psychoanalysis. Minnesota Studies in the Philosophy of Science 1. Minneapolis: Univ. of Minnesota Press.

Skinner, G. William. 1964. Marketing and social structure in rural China, part I. *J. of Asian Studies* 24:3–43.

Smith, Carol A. 1972. The domestic marketing system in western Guatemala: An economic, locational, and cultural analysis. Ph.D. dissertation, Stanford University.

—— 1974. Economics of marketing systems: Models from economic geography. *Annual Rev. of Anthrop.* 3:167–201.

—— 1975. Production in western Guatemala: A test of Von Thünen and Boserup. In Stuart Plattner, ed., Formal methods in economic anthropology. Washington, D.C.: American Anthropological Association.

Snow, C. P. 1959. The two cultures and the scientific revolution. New York: Cambridge Univ. Press.

Spain, David H. 1972. On the use of projective tests for research in psychological anthropology. In Francis L. K. Hsu, ed., Psychological anthropology. Cambridge, Mass.: Schenkman.

Spindler, George, and Louise Spindler. 1965. The instrumental activities inventory: A technique for the study of the psychology of acculturation. *Southwestern J. of Anthrop.* 21:1–23.

Spooner, Brian, ed. 1972. Population growth: Anthropological implications. Cambridge, Mass.: M.I.T. Press.

Stent, Gunther S. 1975. Limits to the scientific understanding of man. *Science* 187:1052–57.

Stever, H. Guyford. 1975. Whither the NSF?—the higher derivatives. *Science* 189:264–67.

Steward, Julian H. 1955. Theory of culture change. Urbana: Univ. of Illinois Press.

Strangman, Eugene. 1966. The use of dream reports for the cross-cultural measurement of N achievement. In Robert A. LeVine, Dreams and deeds. Chicago: Univ. of Chicago Press.

Street, John. 1969. An evaluation of the concepts of carrying capacity. *The Professional Geographer* 21:104–7.

Szalai, Alexander, ed. 1972. The use of time: Daily activities of urban and suburban populations in twelve countries. The Hague: Mouton.

Szalay, Lorand B., and Roy G. D'Andrade. 1972. Scaling versus content analysis: Interpreting word association data from Americans and Koreans. *Southwestern J. of Anthrop.* 28:50–68.

Textor, Robert. 1967. Cross-cultural summary. New Haven, Conn.: HRAF Press.

Thomas, David Hurst. 1976. Figuring anthropology. New York: Holt, Rinehart, Winston.

Thomas, Lewis. 1973. Natural science. *Science* 179 (Editorial, Mar. 30, 1973).

Thomas, R. B. 1973. Human adaptation to a high Andean energy flow system. Occasional Papers in Anthropology, No. 7. University Park: Pennsylvania State Univ. Dept. of Anthropology.

Tönnies, F. 1955. Community and association. London: Routledge and Kegan Paul.

Toulmin, Stephen. 1972. Human understanding. Princeton, N.J.: Princeton Univ. Press.

Tylor, Edward B. 1889. On a method of investigating the development of institutions. (Reprinted in Frank Moore, ed., Readings in cross-cultural methodology. New Haven, Conn.: HRAF Press.)

Tylor, S., ed. 1969. Cognitive anthropology. New York: Holt, Rinehart, Winston.

Van de Geer, J. 1971. Introduction to multivariate analysis for the social sciences. San Francisco: W. H. Freeman.

Vayda, Andrew P., and Bonnie McCay. 1975. New directions in ecology and ecological anthropology. *Annual Rev. of Anthrop.* 4:293–306.

Vayda, Andrew P., and Roy A. Rappaport. 1968. Ecology, cultural and non-cultural. In James A. Clifton, ed., Introduction to cultural anthropology. Boston: Houghton Mifflin.

Vickers, William T. 1975. Meat is meat: The Siona-Secoya and the hunting prowess-sexual reward hypothesis. *Latinamericanist* 11 (1). Gainesville: Univ. of Florida Center for Latin American Studies.

Vogt, Evon Z. 1969. Zinacantan: A Maya community in the highlands of Chiapas. Cambridge, Mass.: Harvard Univ. Press.

Wagner, Roy. 1975. The invention of culture. Englewood Cliffs, N.J.: Prentice-Hall.

Wallace, Anthony F. C. 1965. The problem of the psychological validity of componential analyses. *Amer. Anthrop.* 67 (5, part 2):229–48.

Watt, K. E. F. 1964. Computers and the evaluation of resource management strategies. *Amer. Scientist* 52:408–18.

Weiner, J. S., and J. A. Lourie. 1969. Human biology: A guide to field methods. Oxford: Blackwell Scientific Publications.

Werner, Oswald. 1972. Ethnoscience 1972. *Annual Rev. of Anthrop.* 1:271–308.

White, Benjamin. 1976. Production and reproduction in a Javanese village. Ph.D. dissertation, Columbia University. (Printed by the Agricultural Development Council, P.O. Box 62, Bogor, Indonesia.)

White, Douglas. 1973. Mathematical anthropology. In J. Honigmann, ed., Handbook of social and cultural anthropology. Chicago: Rand McNally.

White, D. R., G. P. Murdock, and R. Scaglion. 1971. Natchez class and rank reconsidered. *Ethnology* 10:369–88.

White, Leslie. 1949. Energy and the evolution of culture. The science of culture. New York: Grove Press.

Whitehead, Alfred North. 1925. Science and the modern world. New York: The Free Press.

Whiting, Beatrice, ed. 1963. Six Cultures, studies of child rearing. New York: Wiley.

Whiting, Beatrice, and Carolyn P. Edwards. 1974. A cross-cultural analysis of sex differences in the behavior of children aged three through eleven. In Robert A. LeVine, ed., Culture and personality. Chicago: Aldine.

Whiting, Beatrice, and John W. M. Whiting. 1975. Children of six cultures: A psycho-cultural analysis. Cambridge, Mass.: Harvard Univ. Press.

Whiting, John W. M. 1966. Preface. In John W. M. Whiting et al., Field guide for a study of socialization. New York: Wiley.

———— 1973. A model for psycho-cultural research. Distinguished lecture. Annual Report of the American Anthropological Association.

Whiting, John W. M., et al. 1966. Field guide for a study of socialization. New York: Wiley.

Whitten, Norman, and Alvin Wolfe. 1973. Network analysis. In John J. Honigmann, ed., Handbook of social and cultural anthropology. Chicago: Rand McNally.

Wilson, David Sloan. 1975. Review of Michael E. Gilpin, Group selection in predator-prey communities. *Science* 189:870.

Wolf, Eric. 1957. Closed corporate communities in Mesoamerica and central Java. *Southwestern J. of Anthrop.* 13:1–18.

Wolf, Eric, and Edward Hansen. 1972. The human condition in Latin America. New York: Oxford Univ. Press.

Index